Money with a Volume

G000099825

Microfinance and Poverty Reduction

Money with a Mission
Volume 1

Microfinance and
Poverty Reduction

James Copestake, Martin Greeley, Susan Johnson,
Naila Kabeer and Anton Simanowitz

ITDG
PUBLISHING

Published by ITDG Publishing
Schumacher Centre for Technology and Development
Bourton Hall, Bourton-on-Dunsmore, Warwickshire CV23 9QZ, UK
www.itdgpublishing.org.uk

© Institute of Development Studies 2005

First published 2005

ISBN 1 85339 614 1

All rights reserved. No part of this publication may be reprinted
or reproduced or utilized in any form or by any electronic, mechanical,
or other means, now known or hereafter invented, including photocopying
and recording, or in any information storage or retrieval system,
without the written permission of the publishers.

A catalogue record for this book is available from the British Library.

The contributors have asserted their rights under the Copyright Designs and
Patents Act 1988 to be identified as authors of their respective contributions.

ITDG Publishing is the publishing arm of the Intermediate Technology
Development Group Ltd. Our mission is to build skills and capacity
of people in developing countries through the dissemination of
information in all forms, enabling them to improve the quality
of their lives and that of future generations.

Typeset by RefineCatch Limited, Bungay, Suffolk
Printed in India by Replika Press

Contents

Acknowledgements

This book is the work of a large group of people undertaken over a period of five years. Our shared goal was nothing less than to rethink and reshape the way we thought about microfinance, and to do so in an open, collaborative way that would have a practical effect on the way microfinance is managed and could contribute to global poverty reduction. This involved forming a global network (*Imp-Act*) to facilitate the exchange of ideas and coordinate research carried out by more than thirty microfinance organizations across four continents. The network included not only staff of these organisations, but a large number of consultants and collaborators, members of supporting and umbrella organizations, and staff in three UK universities.

Particular thanks for getting this book to print are due to Clare Tawney for diligent and flexible sub-editing, to Jennefer Sebstad for providing detailed comments on the entire draft, and to the staff of ITDG Publications. We would also like to acknowledge and thank the following people for their contributions to the work of the *Imp-Act* programme on which the book is based. No such list can ever be definitive and our thanks go to others we have missed, as well as to the many users and non-users of financial services who responded positively to requests for information.

Irina Aliaga Romero (FINRURAL, Bolivia), Elena Alexeeva (FORA, Russia), Aniceta R. Alip (CARD, Philippines), Jaime Aristotle B. Alip (CARD, Philippines), María Alvarado Vásquez (PROMUC, Peru), Ted Baumann (Community Microfinance Network, South Africa), Brian Beard (Opportunity International, USA), Demecia Benique Mamani (PROMUJER-Peru, Peru), Jorge Bernedo Alvarado (Consultant, Peru), Georgina Blanco-Mancilla (Translator), Alyson Brody (Secretariat), Antoinette B. Bolaños (Asian Institute of Management, Philippines), Deborah Caro (Cultural Practice, LLC, USA), Miriam Cherogony (K-Rep Development Agency, Kenya), Augustine Cheruiyot (K-Rep Development Agency, Kenya), Ronald Chua (Asian Institute of Management, Philippines), Monique Cohen (Microfinance Opportunities, USA), Marie Jo Cortijo (Consultant), Patrick Crompton (FINCA International, USA), Anup Dash (CYSD, India), Peter Dawson (University of Bath, UK), Stephen Devereux (IDS, UK), Chris Dunford (Freedom From Hunger, USA), Ever Egusquiza Canta

(Copeme, Peru), Godwin Ehigiamusoe (LAPO, Nigeria), Mark Ellison (University of Bath, UK), Laura Foose (ACT, USA), Grzegorz Galusek (MFC, Poland), Carter Garber (IDEAS, USA), Mateo Garcia Cabello (Translator), John Gaventa (IDS, UK), Stanley Garuba (LAPO, Nigeria), Laura Elena Garza Bueno (Colegio de Postgraduados, Mexico), Frank de Giovanni (Ford Foundation, USA), Maja Gizdic (PRIZMA, Bosnia-Herzegovinia), Jennifer Grant (Translator), Shantana R. Halder (BRAC, Bangladesh), Syed Hashemi (CGAP, USA), John Hatch (FINCA International, USA), Dirk van Hook (Cerudeb, Uganda), Alfredo Hubard (CAME, Mexico), Uwa Izekor (LAPO, Nigeria), Biljana Jahic (BosVita, Bosnia-Herzegovinia), Susan Johnson (University of Bath, UK), Lalaine M. Joyas (Microfinance Council of the Philippines), Dana de Kanter (SEEP, USA), Ana Klincic (DEMOS, Croatia), Sean Kline (Freedom From Hunger, USA), Katherine E. Knotts (Secretariat), Olga Kostukova (FORA, Russia), M. Udaia Kumar (SHARE, India), Jean-Paul Lacoste (Ford Foundation, Chile), Marie Jennifer de Leon (Microfinance Council of the Philippines), José Andrés Loayza Pacheco (PROMUC, Peru), Reynaldo Marconi Ojeda (FINRURAL, Bolivia), Kalipe Mashaba (SEF, South Africa), Imran Matin (BRAC, Bangladesh), Michal Matul (MFC, Poland), Julian May (University Natal, South Africa), Zanele Mbeki (WDB, South Africa), Jamie McDade (CERUDEB), Allister McGregor (University of Bath, UK), Delores McLaughlin (PLAN International, USA), Gustavo Medeiros Urioste (FINRURAL, Bolivia), Rekha Mehra (Ford Foundation, India), Anibal Montoya Rodriguez (COVELO, Honduras), Juan Pedro Mora Sono (Consultant, Peru), Paul Mosley (University of Sheffield, UK), George Muruka (K-Rep Development Agency, Kenya), Leonard Mutesasira (*MicroSave*, Uganda), David Myhre (Ford Foundation, Mexico), Regina Nakayenga (FOCCAS, Uganda), Richard Nalela (CERUDEB, Uganda), D. Narendranath (PRADAN, India), Miguel Navarro (ODEF, Honduras), Lizbeth Navas-Aleman (Translator), Max Nino-Zarazua (Translator), Ben Nkuna (SEF, South Africa), Candace Nelson (Editor), Jamee Newland (Secretariat), Helzi Noponen (Consultant, India), Daniela Olejarova (Integra, Romania), Kathryn O'Neill (Editor), Lydia Opoku (Sinapi Aba Trust, Ghana), Ana Ortiz Monasterio (Translator), Katarzyna Pawlak (MFC, Poland), Anna Portisch (Secretariat), Pedro Pablo Ramirez Moreno (Colegio de Postgraduados, Mexico), Isabel Ramos (CAME, Mexico), Camelia Reyes Emba (CAME, Mexico), June Rock (University of Sheffield, UK), Kate Roper (SEF, South Africa), Catherine van de Ruit (University of Natal, South Africa), Suzy Salib-Bauer (Opportunity International, USA), Raul Sanchez (Katalyis, Honduras), Rodney Schuster (UMU, Uganda), Alla Serova (FORA, Russia), Namrata Sharma (CMF, Nepal), Shalik Ram Sharma (CMF, Nepal), Roshan Shrestha (CMF, Nepal), Frances Sinha (EDA, India), Sonthi Somayajulu (SHARE, India), Julius Ssegirinya (CERUDEB, Uganda), Moses Ssimwogerere (UMU, Uganda), Sonya Sultan (BRAC, Bangladesh), Ruomei Sun (FPC, China), Nelson Tasenga (FOCCAS, Uganda), Chizoba Unaeze (SEF, South Africa), Iris Villalobos Barahona (Katalysis, Honduras), Alice Walter (Consultant, France), Andrew Watson (Ford Foundation, China), John de Wit (SEF, South Africa), Gary Woller (SEEP, USA), Graham Wright

(*MicroSave*, Kenya), Katie Wright-Revolledo (University of Bath, UK), Hugo Yanque Martinez (PROMUC, Peru), Emma Zapata (Colegio de Postgraduados, Mexico).

Finally, we would like to extend a sincere note of appreciation to the Ford Foundation Development Finance Affinity Group for initiating, funding and actively contributing to the *Imp-Act* programme as it developed. Their good faith, patience and flexibility set a model for us all. It was a lively, challenging, often messy and sometimes fraught experience – one that none of us will forget or would have missed.

Figures

Tables

CHAPTER ONE

Introduction

James Copestake and Anton Simanowitz, with Katherine Knotts

Why money with a mission?

Microfinance has become a familiar term across the world. Presidents refer to it in their speeches, donors feature it in their development reports, and a growing number of private fund managers are investing in it. Type it into the internet search engine, *Google* and you will get more than half a million hits. The UN should even have declared 2005 to be 'the year of microfinance'; though unfortunately they ignored savings, insurance and other services by declaring it the 'year of microcredit' instead.

The new-found global status of microfinance does not mean it has reached maturity as an industry, nor does it mean that it has a secure future. Indeed, if microfinance is viewed solely as a self-conscious departure from other forms of finance then the term could possibly become obsolete quite quickly. Where profitable, microfinance faces the prospect of being absorbed into 'mainstream' financial institutions; where unprofitable, it risks losing the subsidies on which it depends, ceasing to exist. However, microfinance can also be defined in relation to its customers (rather than in relation to other forms of finance) as the supply of savings, credit, insurance and other financial services in a way that is appropriate to the problems and aspirations of relatively poor clients.[1] Defined this way, it will remain important so long as poverty persists and for as long as poorer people have inferior access to financial services.[2]

For much of their lives, specialist providers of microfinance (referred to in this book as microfinance institutions or MFIs) have been preoccupied with demonstrating that they can be sustainable and operate on a sufficient scale to make a significant impact on development. Cost control, innovation, client responsiveness, commercialization, scaling-up and competitiveness have all been an important part of this quest. It quickly became clear that the drive to be sustainable required MFIs to measure, monitor and manage their financial performance carefully in terms of profit/loss and subsidy dependence. At the same time few, if any, MFIs were interested in profit for its own sake, still less in pursuing a narrow goal of profit maximization. In short, profitability is a means to growth (to expand portfolio, to innovate, to attract investors); growth is necessary for sustainability.

This then raises the question of what other goals MFIs have. If profit (by which we include avoiding losses or excessive subsidy dependence) is only a means to an end, then how far and in what ways are they being successful in adding value to society? If MFIs are not just interested in money, what is their wider mission and how do they do more than just pay 'lip-service' to it? For example, most MFIs are self-consciously trying to reach customers that are badly served, if at all, by both regulated financial organizations and by the informal financial services of friends, moneylenders and pawnbrokers. But how far are they succeeding and how can they do better? These are the central questions in this book; 'money' in the title is shorthand for MFIs' financial performance, and 'mission' refers to what we call their wider 'social performance' (as discussed below).

Profitability, when viewed as a means to sustainability and expansion of services is not necessarily in conflict with the mission of poverty reduction (Otero, 1999). Indeed, it is a precondition for sustainable poverty reduction. However, there are numerous strategic trade-offs to be made between the two along the way (Morduch, 1999; Morduch, 1998; Mosley and Hulme, 1998). For example, many MFIs have emphasized the importance of profitability to growth in order to expand access or breadth of outreach. Meanwhile, others have opted for slower growth while putting greater emphasis on poverty reduction through reaching poorer customers, or depth of outreach, as well as providing better value for money to clients, or quality of outreach. Slow growth may prove unsustainable because an MFI fails to achieve a minimum scale of activity, but over-ambitious growth may turn out to be self-defeating if customers are badly served and the reputation of the MFI suffers. The challenge facing MFIs, and a central concern of this book, is how to strike the best possible balance.

This book is one of the final outputs of a five-year action-research programme called *Imp-Act* (Improving the Impact of Microfinance on Poverty). In commissioning this programme, the Ford Foundation had in mind three concerns and one conviction.[3] The first concern was with a lack of transparency about the social costs and benefits of microfinance, revealed in part by a certain amount of naïve and often self-serving optimism about what it could achieve on its own.[4] The second was that the social mission of microfinance might be lost in the drive to commercialize. The third concern was that mainstream donor approaches to evaluation and impact assessment of microfinance did not attach much value to practitioners' own views and priorities, or indeed reveal much respect for them. Finally, the conviction was that specialist MFIs needed to build and retain a capacity for internal learning and innovation, taking into account both social and financial goals.

These ideas spawned the *Imp-Act* programme. Its design and implementation was also based on the belief that innovation would result from allowing MFIs a greater opportunity to develop and manage their own projects and systems for generating information about impact. The next section elaborates on the central issues addressed by the programme and summarized in this book. Then the action-research methodology is explained in more detail, and finally a profile is provided of the organizations that participated in it.

Core themes

This section sets out some of the core themes addressed by this book.[5] First, we highlight the shift from a supply-led to a client- or demand-led perspective. We then explore a shift in thinking about how to assess impact so as to inform policy and practice in a more timely, cost-effective and potentially reliable way. Third, we present a framework for classifying impacts, which also explains the way the book is structured and the contributions of each subsequent chapter.

Client-focused microfinance

Fundamental to the challenge of microfinance to increase its positive impacts is its ability to respond more directly to the specific needs of the clients it serves. The last few years have seen the beginnings of a fundamental shift in microfinance from a 'supply-led industry', inspired by a number of blueprint models of how access to financial services might be improved, to a more client-focused and demand-led approach (Woller, 2002; Sebstad and Cohen, 2001). The early growth of a new generation of MFIs responded to the success of a small number of pioneering organizations, including: BancoSol in Bolivia, BRI in Indonesia, FINCA in Latin America, Grameen Bank and BRAC in Bangladesh, and Inicjatywa Mikro in Poland. This phase of growth saw the replication of successful models of microfinance in a range of new countries and contexts. It was also characterized by a rapid growth in the number of organizations and clients served, and the value of funds managed. However, doubts also grew about the basis of this growth. In the rush for growth and financial sustainability, new MFIs risked failing adequately to adapt their initial blueprints to different contexts and clients.

One set of doubts about their performance arose from weaker than expected financial performance. The growth of microfinance has been not been as fast as many hoped, partially because many MFIs remained heavily dependent upon subsidies (Adams and Von Pischke, 1992). Moreover, much of the global growth in numbers of clients has been achieved by a relatively small number of 'high performers' in a few Asian countries (Morduch, 1999; Morduch 1998). Yet growth is also becoming harder. MFIs have increasingly found themselves competing head-to-head with each other, as well as facing high client exit and turnover rates. These problems have been a 'wake-up call', prompting many MFIs to review and redesign their services. The most fundamental lesson has been for MFIs to become more market-oriented: to design and deliver services that are better matched to the specific conditions, needs and preferences of clients in a highly segmented market.

A more market-led approach represents an important step forward for microfinance, but the issue does not end there. As markets have become more competitive, so have doubts concerning the social mission of MFIs. Despite the rhetoric, there is much evidence that microfinance has not, with important exceptions, reached significant numbers of very poor people. Rather, clients of microfinance are mostly clustered just below or above the poverty line (Mosley and Hulme, 1998). Although there is much value in supporting the livelihoods of moderately poor and vulnerable non-poor people, the lack of poverty focus amongst many organizations has also surprised many practitioners, and for many this is a second wake-up call (Daley-Harris, 2002). Similar doubts have also grown about the extent to which MFIs are achieving other social goals, such as empowering women and strengthening civil society (Johnson, 2005; Mayoux, 2001).

From impact assessment to social performance management

In addition to seeking to operate competitively in the market, most MFIs are set up with a specific social mission – ranging from improving access to financial services for enterprise growth, to reducing poverty, to empowering women. MFIs are increasingly using the term 'social performance' to refer to the effectiveness with which they translate such goals into reality. The 'social' here should be taken as short-hand for 'social and economic': any aspect of performance, in short, that goes beyond the financial performance of the MFI. To achieve such wider social goals they need to understand not just the market in general, but the characteristics of relatively poor people, whether to serve them directly as clients or to help them indirectly. In particular, social performance assessment places a poverty awareness lens over the client-focused eye.

Growing use of the concept of social performance also reflects a shift in thinking away from set-piece social-impact assessment studies, towards ways of institutionalizing assessment of outreach and impact on clients within routine operations of MFIs. During the late 1990s, a number of initiatives began to point this way, particularly the USAID-funded AIMS (Assessing the Impact of Microenterprise Services) project (Cohen, 2002; see also Chapter 3).[6] Impact assessment studies, while contributing importantly to public policy debate, were increasingly seen to be too time consuming, costly and complex to be routinely useful to practitioners (Hulme, 2000a).

However, it became clear that designing new and more practitioner-friendly impact or client assessment tools was only part of the issue; the bigger challenge was to integrate new tools and systems into MFIs' decision-making practices, both at operational and strategic levels (Simanowitz, 2001; Copestake, 2000). To be effective, decision-makers would need to understand the usefulness of information on clients – beyond their loan-repayment performance – in improving operations and achieving goals. They would have to be receptive to collecting the information and also be willing to make systematic changes in products and organizational processes in its light.[7] This is what the term 'social-performance management' (twinned to financial performance management and the idea of a double bottom line) is intended to reflect.

Table 1.1 elaborates on the concept of social performance management by comparing it with the more familiar concept of financial performance management. It also highlights areas of continued uncertainty and confusion, such as how compliance with social goals can be assessed in a way that is reliable, timely, useful, cost-effective and transparent.

Table 1.1 also emphasizes the importance of regarding social performance assessment as part of the management systems and organizational culture of MFIs. Central to this is the need for a regular flow of information. Occasional and uncoordinated studies can be useful, for example, where an MFI or its stakeholder wishes to understand a particular issue prior to making a major strategic decision. But they are generally more useful when linked to, or following up on, issues raised through routine monitoring. Indeed, a recurring theme of this book is that the 'cart' of externally funded impact assessment studies has often been placed in front of, and hence impeded, the 'horse' of routine internal client monitoring. Formal data collection and analysis has also often failed to connect with and complement informal processes and channels by which managers form their own view of their MFI's social performance.

Table 1.1 A comparison of financial and social performance management

	Financial performance management	Social performance management
Main goal?	Solvency of the financial institution	Achievement of wider social mission of the MFI – e.g. contribute to poverty reduction
How assessed?	Systematic bookkeeping and accounting. Market research	Monitor who clients are and assess value-added to them. Details are not clear – hence the subject matter of this book
What for?	To inform decisions about prices, products, service delivery systems and strategies	The same, but with a view to improving social mission as well – e.g. through a better fit with provision of complementary services
Cost-effective?	Part of the cost of doing business – a legal as well as a strategic requirement	Expenditure must be proportionate to potential benefits – norms on what is appropriate remain weak
How validated?	Internal and external audits	Internal quality assurance and external reviews – need for clearer guidelines on this

Types of impact and a brief outline of the book

The above discussion defines social performance in relation to an MFI's explicit social objectives. At the same time it is important to relate these to wider evidence of the multiple and unexpected impacts that microfinance services can have. Microfinance is clearly an intervention into people's livelihoods, but it also affects consumption behaviour and household relations. Because money confers general purchasing power or liquidity, it is very difficult to predict what its actual effects on the economic behaviour of an individual or household will be (Rutherford, 1999; Sebstad *et al*, 1995). But there may also be important influences at market and community levels (Johnson, 1998); it may have influences beyond the material domain (for example, on relationships, understanding, values, attitudes), and these may do harm as well as good. All microfinance has a wide array of social outcomes, even if these are not prioritized or even recognized by the MFI. And where these are not understood or part of the specific intent of the organization, the chances of them being negative is increased.

Imp-Act adopted a simple framework to categorize the different types of possible microfinance impacts (Kabeer, 2003a) and this has informed the structure of the book. First, impact depends upon who makes direct use of which services (breadth, depth, scope of outreach). Chapter 2 focuses particularly on this question, with special reference to depth of outreach relative to measures of poverty.

Next, we distinguish between (a) direct impact (value added or quality of outreach) on clients, their businesses and their immediate household and (b) indirect or wider impacts. With respect to direct impact, we further distinguish between material impact and other direct impacts. Direct material impacts are the subject of Chapter 3, and include changes in income and in assets. The latter includes changes in financial assets assessed through savings and debt. Other direct impacts include improvements in food consumption, health and education.[8] They also include less tangible individual effects, for example, on knowledge, skills, self-esteem. These are reviewed in Chapter 4. In principle, the list of direct impacts is near endless because any use of additional income for welfare purposes could be included. In other words, the outcomes are the result of choices made by clients and their households over how to utilize additional resources. In this sense, income changes are of instrumental rather than direct significance since it is the actual expenditure choices that determine welfare impact. Yet at the same time, because it is difficult to know all the choices that clients may make, material gain measured in money terms can be a useful proxy indicator.

Indirect or wider impacts go beyond clients to effect others, including family members, neighbours, employees, competitors, consumers and suppliers. They arise in part from induced changes in supply, demand and prices within markets, but they also include induced changes in ideas, attitudes, social organization and demand for public services. Chapter 5 explores evidence of such wider impacts, while Chapter 6 addresses the indirect effect of the growth of a new generation of MFIs on the wider financial landscape. Chapter 6 also complements the discussion of depth of outreach in this chapter with a discussion of breadth of outreach, here seen as overall growth of the market and changes in market shares.

All of the above is concerned primarily with current outreach and impact arising from the use of financial services. A major concern of the *Imp-Act* programme was also the extent to which MFIs themselves were building their *capacity* to have such impact, not just now but into the future. This capacity for sustained outreach and impact is not only influenced by financial performance, but also by many other aspects of organizational structure and behaviour. These are reviewed in Chapter 7. Finally, Chapter 8 looks more narrowly at how successful the MFIs in the *Imp-Act* programme were in institutionalizing systems for assessing and managing their social performance.

Chapter 9 provides a summary of overall findings presented in the book and suggests how social performance management of microfinance can be improved in the future. Our findings support what is perhaps the conventional wisdom that MFIs contribute positively to a broad range of development objectives, including poverty reduction, but less so than is often claimed – particularly with respect to depth of poverty outreach. At the same time, the book highlights the diversity and unpredictability of microfinance impact, as well as the scope for improving social performance by monitoring and managing it more explicitly and systematically. Much of the book consequently focuses on the processes by which impacts are created.

Methodology of the *Imp-Act* programme

Origins

Imp-Act was initiated by the Ford Foundation's Development Finance Affinity Group, comprising programme officers with a particular interest in development finance. The group began to discuss impact assessment as an area justifying a collective global activity in 1998. Ford Foundation was concerned to find ways to obtain better-quality information about the poverty reduction and developmental outcomes of its own investments in microfinance. But the group also recognized that, if they themselves commissioned independent studies of the MFIs they supported, they would encounter similar problems to those experienced by other donors. Instead they invited various organizations to produce concept papers on the topic and it was from the amalgamation of three of these that the idea of a global action-research project on a 'challenge fund' model emerged.[9] A one-year grant was approved for the consultation and design process, involving a range of stakeholders across the microfinance industry. This culminated in a workshop (in Brighton in June 2000) with about 50 participants, representing a broad range of MFI, networks, policy-makers and researchers.

The workshop reviewed the 'state-of-the-art' in microfinance impact assessment and provided space for participants to share their experiences and explore ideas for future activity, both collectively and within their own MFI. The identification of common themes (including reaching the very poor, increasing participation, institutionalization of impact assessment, and assessment of wider impacts) were an important part of this process. It also encouraged each participant to develop their own action-research project, taking into account these wider themes. Through this activity, a research agenda emerged that was centred on the needs and interests of practitioners, but located within broader industry debates and priorities.

Nearly 4,000 organizations were invited by email to express an interest in participating in the programme, and this communication was supplemented by several regional meetings. Several hundred written responses with expressions of interest were received. Organizations were then asked to demonstrate commitment and outline their priorities and needs for impact assessment. The final selection of participants also sought to achieve a reasonable geographical spread, as well as capture diversity of MFIs with respect to size, mode of operation and technical capacity. Prior receipt of grant support from the Ford Foundation was *not* a condition for participation.

Further refinement of proposals took place during the second half of 1999 through a series of regional workshops and exchange of comments between MFIs and the UK team, who made the final selection of 30 organizations.[10] Individual action-research projects lasted for three years, from April 2001 to March 2004. A UK team member was assigned to liase with each partner, though it was made clear that their role was to monitor progress and provide limited technical advice when requested and where appropriate, rather than to direct or to guide it. In this way *Imp-Act* intended both to foster MFI ownership and avoid any sense of the projects being linked to past or future funding.

Imp-Act aimed to offer a power reversal to the dominant model of externally focused and externally led impact assessment (Chambers, 1993); it sought to enable MFIs to be more proactive in developing their own learning systems, both to inform internal decision making and to satisfy the requirements of external stakeholders. In so doing, it also set out to test the assumption that quality and cost-effectiveness of impact assessment could be strengthened by linking it more closely to internal operations and strategic planning, and less closely to external funding and accountability.

Aims and objectives

The primary aim of the main phase of the *Imp-Act* programme was to improve the quality of microfinance services and their impact on poverty. This was sought by strengthening and developing social performance assessment systems appropriate to the needs of individual MFIs and their stakeholders. The objectives were then linked to activities, outputs and outcomes at the MFI and

Table 1.2 Anticipated outcomes of the *Imp-Act* programme

Activities	Outputs	Outcomes
MFI level	Ownership of projects by MFIs ·	Change in knowledge, attitude and practice of individual MFIs
MFIs implement action-research projects	Improved methodologies and understanding of social performance assessment	
	Improved understanding of MFI impacts and relationship to clients' livelihoods	
Programme and industry level	Practical testing of a range of approaches to social-performance assessment in a range of contexts	Changes in knowledge, attitude and practice of microfinance industry (non-participating MFIs, donors, policy-makers, academics)
Draw wider lessons and involve a wider range of stakeholders	Methodologies for assessing wider impacts relevant to MFI needs	
	Analysis and documentation related to key issues in microfinance	

industry level, as shown in Table 1.2. The specific objectives of the *Imp-Act* programme were:

- To develop and promote an approach that linked social performance assessment to existing staff work patterns, building on existing knowledge and experience, and producing results that could be easily used by management.
- To improve methodologies for assessing wider poverty impacts of microfinance, thereby contributing to improvements in poverty-focused design.
- To influence thinking and practice relating to the role of microfinance in poverty reduction.

The action-research process

Figure 1.1 shows the overall conceptual design of *Imp-Act* for its main three-year phase. The activities of the partner organizations formed the empirical foundation of the programme. Collaboration and cross-cutting issues were explored through thematic and methodological groups and regional collaborative efforts, and in this way contributed to the broader research objectives of *Imp-Act*.

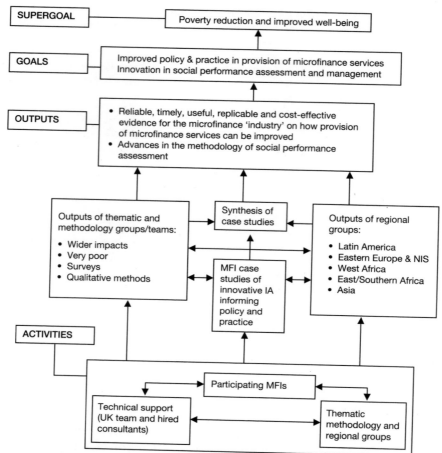

Figure 1.1 *Imp-Act* summary of the action-research process

Whilst the majority of the 30 partners had only limited experience of research, each was responsible for its own work. This did not mean that partner organizations had to undertake the research process themselves. Rather it was intended that they consult and then make informed choices about the information they needed and how to obtain it. Most used internal staff to some extent in the collection, analysis and reporting of data, but also contracted local and, in a few cases, international consultants. Many also used their existing national or international networks to gain support and advice. A limited amount of technical support was also provided by the UK management team, which also made a final review visit. The learning process was documented through quarterly reports to *Imp-Act*. These were summarized in final reports, with a revised version of many of these then published on the *Imp-Act* website. Despite these efforts, it is likely that a great deal of the individual and organizational learning that took place is not fully documented.

Support was also provided through global, regional and thematic workshops. These served as venues for training, sharing of experience between partners, and for planning collaborative work on cross-cutting issues. A final meeting was held in Bath in September 2004 to review draft chapters for this book, along with drafts of other *Imp-Act* publications, in order to ensure they reflected as far as possible the diverse experiences of partners.

Imp-Act's objective was partly to research the impacts resulting from the delivery of microfinance, but with an emphasis also on understanding the processes by which these are achieved, and how social performance of microfinance can be improved. *Imp-Act* was therefore designed as an action-research process, with emphasis on reflection and learning both within and between partner organizations.[11] The commitment to assessment studies and systems relevant to the needs and context of individual participants led to a decision not to seek standardization in the approaches of partner projects. Consequently, the action-research phase was *not* designed with common frameworks and processes. Whilst this allowed for an understanding to be developed about appropriateness and usefulness of different approaches, it means that comparative analysis (including in this book) has been more difficult. In this sense, neither *Imp-Act* nor this book should be seen as a systematic or representative study of the global impact of microfinance.[12] In seeking to highlight findings arising specifically from the *Imp-Act* action research itself, this book does not attempt to draw systematically on the vast secondary literature that is also relevant to the issues discussed.

Chapter 8 provides more information on what each participant attempted to do and how far it was successful. The list below provides an illustrative summary of the range of activities undertaken:

- Qualitative market research, primarily using focus-group discussions to better understand client needs, likes, dislikes, experience of using the MFI's services and reasons for leaving the programme.
- Base-line and, in some cases, follow-up surveys in order to monitor the profile of new clients and develop cheaper monitoring systems (including poverty assessment tools).
- Development of monitoring systems to track the changes in client profile over time, using a small number of client-level indicators related to the MFI's social objectives.
- Quantitative surveys using quasi-experimental design to provide statistically valid information about client impact. The majority of these surveys were based on the 'mid-range' AIMS impact survey tool (see Chapter 3).
- In-depth qualitative research designed to understand impact processes and expose reasons for patterns revealed through a survey or through monitoring.

- Institutional analysis looking at the effectiveness of overall organizational systems in setting social objectives, monitoring and assessing performance, feeding back this information to different audiences, and translating information into improved practice.

Reflection on lessons learnt was facilitated by visits (including exchange visits between partners organized at regional level) as well as regional and international workshops. Representatives of wider national and international workshops were also invited to attend these meetings as well. For example, SEEP (Small Enterprise Education and Promotion Network) (a Washington-based 'network of networks') was itself a programme participant, and members of its Client Assessment Working Group who had worked on practitioner-led assessment tools under the AIMS programme of USAID regularly attended *Imp-Act* workshops.

Finally, and in keeping with *Imp-Act*'s emphasis on useful research, great importance was attached to ensuring effective communication of experience and learning through the development of formal and informal dissemination mechanisms. In part this has been achieved through the programme process and the influence of the programme partners on their national, regional and international contacts. Also there was a strategy to engage key individuals and organizations in the microfinance industry. Finally, use was made of the more traditional dissemination channels, including a collaborative resource website, presentations at conferences and meetings, a series of practice and policy-orientated short notes, three special issue journals, a set of guidelines, a brochure, two books and various other outputs.

Further reflections on the research process

While the foregoing account of the *Imp-Act* research explains the rationale behind what was attempted, it does not acknowledge the full range of challenges and dilemmas entailed in involving a large, diverse and dispersed group of people and organizations in a common endeavour. A full account of these dynamics would be out of place here, however, brief discussion of them is warranted.

Perhaps the central difficulty resided in reconciling pressures for consistent structure (of themes, methods, guidelines, timetables) and responsiveness to partners' diverse priorities and capabilities (Copestake, 2005). The UK team itself reflected a variety of different views as to how the project should be implemented. Some argued for a more rigorous approach to commissioning research, while others favoured flexibility to encourage innovation and foster ownership within participating MFIs. This also reflected different priorities about the importance of generating systematic findings about the impact of microfinance on poverty vs. learning how to do this in a way that is more cost-effective for MFIs and the industry. Thematic working groups were formed partially to try to accommodate these different interests, but the differences also created confusion among participants about what was expected of them, particularly in the early stages.

A second and linked dilemma concerned the balance of responsibility for design of projects between MFI participants and the UK team. A central principle was established quite quickly that MFIs should have the greatest possible freedom to do what they wanted in order that findings would be as useful as possible to them. But this was not always consistently applied. For example, some asked for and received substantial technical guidance, some asked for it but got less than they wanted, and some found their work being questioned and challenged on grounds that they disputed. Attempts to coordinate activities at regional level sometimes helped, but also added to the complexity and confusion.

Third, some participants argued for a stronger hand in agreeing on standard methods and indicators (for example, linked to the Millennium Development Goals). Others resisted, and in practice the project never acquired the strength of leadership and direction that would have been required to standardize very far. Having committed during the initial phase to involve nearly twice as many MFIs as originally planned, the amount of technical assistance available to ensure uniform standards of implementation of agreed methods was also lacking. As a result, the project relied more on learning-by-doing and independent consultancy inputs. But such flexibility and local control was arguably essential to encourage adaptation to the diverse interests, needs, capacities and operating environments of each MFI.

Fourth, a latent dilemma in the project concerned the roles and responsibilities of individuals and organizations. Formal contracts were in all cases signed with organizations, but responsibility for making things happen generally rested with particular individuals. Inevitably, many of these key people moved on or were incapacitated in various ways, creating crises of continuity and communication. Although considerable effort was made to ensure a high level of institutional 'buy-in' at the outset, this did not always prove sufficient to overcoming these problems. Nevertheless, sufficient continuity of individuals (including Ford Foundation staff) was maintained over the three years for a shared culture of open, mutual and flexible learning to accrue. The willingness of Ford Foundation to be flexible about plans, timetables and budgets was also critical to building up and sustaining this ethos.[13]

The participating organizations

Imp-Act programme partners ranged in size and scale, in context and mission, and in geographical location. They included commercial banks, village and trust banks, a cooperative union, NGOs, not-for-profit MFIs, national, regional and international networks. They included both fully self-sustainable and donor-supported institutions operating under various degrees of government regulation. Some were relatively new and experimental research projects, others had been operating as established institutions for over 30 years. Our partners offer solidarity-group loans, village loans, individual loans of all kinds, voluntary and compulsory savings, microinsurance, transfer services, support to self-help groups, business development training, health and education training, and training and evaluation services to their own network members. Some of these characteristics are summarized in Tables 1.3, 1.4

Table 1.3 Performance indicators for selected MFIs.[1]

MFI	Active clients Dec 2000	Client growth[2] (%)	FSS[3] (%) Dec 2000	OSS[3] (%) Dec 2000	OSS[3] (%) Dec 2003	Avg. Loan Size[4]	No. of Staff	PAR[5] (%)
BRAC	2 993	16	111	124	127	49	10 711	6.1
CAME	14	179	91	115	133	224	47	0.1
CARD	35	217	102	104	134	204	290	0.0
CERUDEB	17	169	117	127	138	657	403	2.1
FINCA	179	43	89	100	112	194	1 261	3.2
FOCCAS[6]	13	23	36	41	80	37	55	2.0
FPC	14	8	n/a	n/a[10]	n/a[10]	–	60	–
KDA[7]	7	312	92	106	n/a	72	60	4.0
LAPO	9	157	n/a	n/a	119	47	32	–
ODEF	9	21	100	109	n/a	358	68	0.1
PRIZMA	3	298	92	107	134	569	32	0.3
PROMUC	13	118	n/a	n/a	117[11]	107	43	–
ProMujer Peru	3	544	18	19	135	58	12	0.0
SAT[8]	17	117	74	144	115	80	67	7.6
SEF[9]	12	80	65	66	99	76	94	2.1
SHARE	31	331	74[12]	99	118	78	273	0.0
UMU	8	278	98	105	126	94	83	0.5

Notes: [1]Unless otherwise indicated data reflects the status of MFIs in December 2000, before the start of the programme, and so do not reflect its influence. The second and fifth column of figures have been included to portray a picture of growth in partner MFIs over the action-research period. [2]Refers to percentage change in number of active clients between December 2000 and December 2003. [3]FSS and OSS refer to financial and operational self-sufficiency respectively. [4]Figures are US$ at 2000 exchange rates and prices. [5]Portfolio at risk (>30 days), December 2000 unless otherwise noted. [6]March 2001 figures. [7]FSA Programme only. [8]Refers to group loans only. [9]June 2001 figures. [10]Consolidated figures not available but OSS was greater than 100 for all branches on both dates. [11]December 2002 figures. [12]March 2000 figures.

Table 1.4 Mode of operation of participating MFIs (December 2003)

MFI	Products[1]	Rural	Women	Screening or targeting methods	Linkages[2]	Reg.[3]
BRAC	Group loans, voluntary savings	Mixed	100%	Geographic targeting, Rapid Rural Appraisal and PWR	Enterprise skills and health training	Yes
CAME	Group loans	Urban	85%	Market Research	Life insurance, client training	No
CARD	Group loans and voluntary savings	Rural	100%	CASHPOR housing index	Training and consulting	Yes
CERUDEB	Loans, savings, fund transfer services	Rural	38%	None	Insurance	Yes
CYSD[4]	n/a	Mixed	100%	Geographic and poverty targeting	Livelihoods and community development promotion	No
DEMOS	Group and individual loans, SME loans	Mixed	52%	Means testing	Business training	Yes
FINCA INT.	Village-bank loans, savings, insurance	Mixed	96%	None	None	No
FOCCAS	Group loans	Rural	100%	None	Credit with Education – health and business training	No
FORA	Individual and group loans	Urban	72%	None	None	No
FPC	Group loans	Rural	90%	None	None	No
INTEGRA[5]	Individual and group loans	Mixed	63%	Geographic targeting, mean testing	Business training	Yes
KDA	Financial services associations (FSA)	Rural	42%	None	None	Yes

Table 1.4—*continued*

MFI	Products[1]	Rural	Women	Screening or targeting methods	Linkages[2]	Reg.[3]
LAPO	Group loans, voluntary and regular savings	Mixed	95%	Poverty screening through participation form	Business development services, health, gender, environment, leadership training through LADEC	No
ODEF	Group and individual loans, savings, insurance	Mixed	65%	Geographic targeting	Training	No
PARTNER	Individual loans	Mixed	56%	None	None	Yes
PRADAN	Livelihood promotion, including SHGs	Rural	100%	Geographic targeting and wealth ranking	Livelihoods promotion	No
Promujer	Communal bank and seasonal loans, voluntary and compulsory savings	Urban	100%	Targets the poor, but does not use targeting tools	BDS, health and education training	No
PRIZMA	Individual and group loans	Mixed	100%	Geographic targeting, poverty scorecard	None	No
SAT	Group and individual loans, voluntary and compulsory savings	Rural	92%	None	Basic business training	Yes
SEF	Group loans	Rural	99%	Participatory Wealth Ranking	None	Yes
SHARE	Group loans, savings	Rural	100%	Geographic and means test	Training	Yes
UMU	Loans, savings, insurance, fund transfer	Mixed	48%	None	None	No

Notes: [1]Refers to financial services provided by the institution; [2]Refers to linkages to non-financial services within the institution; [3]Refers to whether or not the institution is externally regulated; [4]Refers to SHG programme only; [5]MED programme only.

and 1.5. At the end of the programme each partner produced a four page summary of its activities and lessons learnt. These are available on the *Imp-Act* website, www.*Imp-Act*.org.

The following is a very brief description of the organizations that managed financial contracts under *Imp-Act*. First to be described are the specialized MFIs, most of which started out as non-profit NGOs. Then the other organizations are described, which are mostly networks or training and support NGOs.

Microfinance institutions

BRAC (Bangladesh Rural Advancement Committee), in Bangladesh, is a large not-for-profit development organization with the twin objectives of poverty alleviation and empowerment of the poor, especially women, in rural areas. BRAC takes a holistic approach, emphasizing income generation and social development. Established in 1972.

CAME (Centro de Apoyo al Micro Empresário), in Mexico, provides financial services to small businesses and microenterprise operators in south-east Mexico City, principally using a village-banking methodology. Established in 1993.

CARD (Centre for Agriculture and Rural Development), in the Philippines, is a poverty-focused microfinance institution that provides credit and savings services through both a solidarity-group lending methodology and the Credit with Education programme. It offers services through a set of mutually reinforcing institutions, including CARD Bank, CARD NGO and CARD MBA. Established in 1986.

CERUDEB (Centenary Rural Development Bank Ltd), in Uganda, is a national commercial bank with a strong sense of social purpose that aims to provide financial services to all Ugandans, including low-income and agricultural clients. Established in 1982.

FINCA (Foundation for International Community Assistance) International, based in the USA, works through a network of locally managed, self-supporting institutions in 19 countries, offering village banking and savings services to poor families. Established in 1985.

FOCCAS (Foundation for Credit and Community Assistance), in Uganda, combines village banking and Credit with Education methodologies to provide financial and educational services to poor rural women in Eastern Uganda. Established in 1995.

FPC (Funding the Poor Cooperative), in China, an experimental project of the Rural Development Institute of the Chinese Academy of Social Sciences, uses a group-lending methodology to provide access to financial services for the rural poor in the Henan and Hebei Provinces. Established in 1994.

Table 1.5 Network characteristics (December 2003)

Network	Country	Members	Clients of network services members (thousands)	Trng/TA[1]	IA/MR[2]	Res.[3]	Advoc.[4]	Diss.[5]	Other
CMF	Nepal	63	65	X	X	X	X	X	Study tours
COVELO	Honduras	21	131		X	X	X		Financing
FINRURAL	Bolivia	14	188		X	X		X	
MFC	Poland	86	280	X	X	X	X	X	Exchange visits
SEEP	USA	55	22,829	X		X	X	X	
PROMUC	Peru	11	28	X	X	X			Leveraging financial resources

Notes: [1]Training and technical assistance services; [2]Impact assessment and market research services; [3]Other research activities; [4]Local and regional advocacy at the donor and policy-maker level; [5]Dissemination of best practice information within the network and the microfinance industry.

KDA (K-Rep Development Agency), in Kenya, is a microfinance research and innovations company whose main focus is in expanding the access of financial services to those who traditionally have not been served by formal financial institutions. Established in 1984.

LAPO (Lift Above Poverty Organization), in Nigeria, works with the poor using solidarity-group lending and savings methodologies, in concert with non-financial services such as training and awareness-raising. Established in 1993.

ODEF (Organización de Desarrollo Emresarial Femenino), in Honduras, offers financial services through communal- and individual-lending methodologies. ODEF is a member of the national network, COVELO. Established in 1992.

Promujer, in Peru, is part of the US-based not-for-profit organization that seeks to empower women through the provision of financial services, as well as programmes on health, family planning and child development. Established in 2000.

SAT (Sinapi Aba Trust), in Ghana, provides financial services to poor people using Trust Bank and individual-lending methodologies. It is supported by the Opportunity International network. Established in 1994.

SEF (Small Enterprise Foundation), in South Africa, uses a group-lending methodology to provide sustainable financial services to poor women in the Limpopo Province, one of the poorest regions of the country. Two programmes run in parallel, one designed specifically for very poor clients who are identified using participatory wealth ranking. Established in 1993.

SHARE (Society for Helping Awaken Rural Poor through Education), in India, is one of the world's fastest-growing MFIs. It provides both financial services and training to poor and very poor women in Andhra Pradesh. Established in 1989.

UMU (Uganda Microfinance Union), in Uganda, is the fastest-growing MFI in the country. It offers flexible group-lending services to microentrepreneurs and low-income groups. Established in 1997.

Other institutions

CMF (Centre for Microfinance) is a network that aims to strengthen the capacity of MFIs in Nepal to enable them to serve their clients sustainably, especially poor women. CMF provides training and technical assistance, undertakes research and promotes best practices amongst donors and policy-makers. Established in 1998.

CYSD (Centre for Youth and Social Development) is a poverty-focused NGO in India. It promotes microfinance through a self-help group model as part of its integrated development services to improve the lives of the poor and excluded in Orissa through community organization and rural institution building. Established in 1982.

FINRURAL (Association of Financial Institutions for Rural Development) is a national network of 14 microfinance institutions in Bolivia. Most of its members have a strong commitment to working in rural areas, many (including CRECER and Promujer) provide complementary non-financial services, and are not registered as formal financial institutions. Established in 1993

MFC (Microfinance Centre) is a trust based in Poland with institutional members across Eastern Europe, the Balkans and Central Asia. Its main role is to provide these members with technical support services. Members who became involved with *Imp-Act* include DEMOS (Croatia), FORA (Russia), Inicjatywa Mikro (Poland), INTEGRA (Slovakia and Romania), PARTNER and PRIZMA (Bosnia and Herzegovina). Established in 1997.

MicroSave is based in Kenya. While the organization did not receive financial support under *Imp-Act*, it was an important contributor to regional activities in Africa.

PRADAN (Professional Assistance for Development Action) is an NGO in India that helps support sustainable livelihoods for the rural poor and socially disadvantaged, and includes support and training self-help groups in its integrated-development approach. Established in 1983.

PROMUC (Promoción de la Mujer e la Comunidad), in Peru, is a partnership of NGOs concerned with microenterprise development as a strategy for poverty reduction and the empowerment of women. At the end of 2003, 12 NGOs were active members, of which 11 operated village or communal banking programmes under a common brand, *La Chanchita* (The Piggy Bank). Established in 1994.

SEEP (Small Enterprise Education and Promotion Network) is a USA-based network of microenterprise promotion agencies, many of which either sponsor MFIs or have their own MFI programmes. Members include Accion, Care International, Freedom from Hunger, FINCA, Mercy Corps, Opportunity International and Plan International. Established in 1985.

CHAPTER TWO

Sustainable poverty outreach

Martin Greeley

Introduction

Most MFIs have a mission mandate to reduce poverty, and the principal means by which they seek to fulfil it is through providing financial services to poor households. It seems self-evident that they should know whether the households they serve are actually poor or not. Poverty outreach assessment is a central component of social performance assessment, and the arguments in this chapter link closely to subsequent chapters.

This chapter provides an overview and commentary on the state of poverty outreach within microfinance generally, including its relationship to financial sustainability and options for poverty measurement and targeting. It also reviews how some of the *Imp-Act* partners have gone about assessing their poverty outreach and with what results. It emphasizes not just poverty outreach performance *per se,* but also how the selected MFIs are linking this work to organizational learning and change. The main conclusion of the chapter is that while there are a range of appropriate approaches to defining and measuring poverty outreach, there is a growing consensus that routine monitoring of poverty using carefully validated proxy poverty indicators is central to improved social performance.

An overview of industry experience

Poverty outreach and financial sustainability

Empirical indications are that the poorest can benefit from microfinance in terms of both economic and social well-being, and that this can be done without jeopardizing the financial sustainability of the MFI. While there are many biases presented in the literature against extending microfinance to the poorest, there is little empirical evidence to support this position. However, if microfinance is to be used, specific targeting of the poorest will be necessary. Without this, MFIs are unlikely to create programmes suitable for and focused on that group (Morduch and Haley, 2002).

The substantial variation in targeting performance within specific programme types and specific targeting methods suggests that differences in implementation are also important factors in determining the success of targeting to poor individuals (Coady *et al*, 2004). The key development feature of microfinance is in the innovations – in products, terms, transaction costs and risk – that enable MFIs to provide financial services where banks have failed. From the earliest development of these models, in Bangladesh, Bolivia and elsewhere, these innovations were specifically identified as a means to achieve poverty reduction. Their success has led to expansion and to increasing financing needs. This in turn has prompted increasing attention to financial sustainability and to the relationship between specialized micro-finance institutions and the regulated financial system. It has opened up linkages with the formal financial sector, which had retreated rapidly from rural areas with the advent of liberalization in financial markets. All MFIs face pressure to achieve a financial performance that allows them to make this linkage so that they are not dependent on continuing donor support.

Several recent articles (Greeley, 2003; Woller and Schreiner, 2002; Morduch, 2000; Rhyne, 1998) review how the microfinance industry has analysed relationships between the two core drivers: outreach to poor households and financial sustainability of MFIs. In recent years, the latter has come to dominate the agenda. The preoccupation with financial sustainability has grown in part out of concern with how to expand and sustain direct access to services among poorer people. But it has also been conflated to some degree with a different goal – to contribute to financial sector deepening necessary for broad-based economic growth. For many MFIs, this shift has threatened their social mission to serve poor households.

Many of the *Imp-Act* partners, reflecting this wider problem, have com-plained that their focus on poverty reach has been sacrificed at the altar of sustainable microfinance. According to one West African partner, 'As SAT transforms itself from an NGO into a formal financial institution, there is the tendency for mission drift (focusing more on profit and less on helping the poor)'. This comment is typical of a widespread view among *Imp-Act* partners. The trade-off and the reality of greater pressure to achieve financial sustain-ability have been very widely recognized within the industry for a number of years. It is well known that targets influence activities, and MFIs have certainly been persuaded to focus their activities on the financial sustainability goal, despite their avowed commitment to poverty outreach (Mathie, 2001).

MFIs who have shifted from an emphasis on direct poverty outreach towards a financial system deepening perspective can point to potential poverty reduc-tion through the creation of an enabling environment for private sector growth. By addressing financial market failure, MFIs can allow entrepreneurs to access investment loans, and by providing insurance and savings services they can mitigate the risks associated with such borrowing, or indeed, any risk to livelihoods. They can argue that increasing the size of the industry should be the priority because all neglected households, *including* poor households, benefit from the financial markets and growth created. But while it is widely accepted that growth in mean income per head generally increases income per head of the poorest, the literature also highlights the large variation in this relationship (Thorbecke, 2004; Dollar and Kraay, 2000).

Not all growth is pro-poor growth and so the case for abandoning direct outreach as a social performance goal in favour of indirect impact is at best highly controversial.[1] And just as there is a need for stronger empirical evidence on indirect poverty impact via general financial sector development and growth, so there is a need for better understanding of the scope for poverty reduction through explicit strategies of providing financial services directly and sustainably to poorer people.

Defining poverty

This leads to the issue of poverty definition. World Bank figures for the turn of the millennium indicated that over one billion people globally were under the one 'dollar-a-day' poverty line, and over two and a half billion were below a two-dollar line. Depending on country context, these are the people most MFIs refer to when they identify poor people as their market. At the tail end of this distribution lie very poor, often destitute people who are unlikely (almost by definition) to be able to service any kind of loan or use the extra liquidity productively. MFIs would be taking substantial risks with the quality of their portfolio if they deliberately targeted this 3 to 8 per cent of households whose chief use of loans is to satisfy today's hunger. Indeed, there is evidence, including *Imp-Act*-commissioned research (Rangacharyulu, 2004), that they are excluded from MFI operations – including from MFIs that have effective poverty targeting instruments. Sometimes such exclusion is shown to be institutionally determined by staff operational practice or by product terms and conditions. Sometimes it is self-exclusion – fear of debt and repayment difficulties – and sometimes other MFI members are responsible.

MFIs with good research records, such as BRAC in Bangladesh, are fully aware of these households and have alternative programmes, with strong social development inputs, to work for their well-being. They recognize that microfinance is not suitable for every category of poor household and that for the poorest, in particular, loans will harm rather than help. The poorest may well benefit from flexible savings products, however. But this group is a small minority of those one billion plus households living on less than a dollar per day. Most households below this mark are economically active and capable of managing loans to strengthen their livelihoods.

Conventionally, poverty has usually been defined in terms of income short-fall compared to a standard.[2] Income poverty may be the obvious candidate for assessing poverty outreach but it is quite limited for two reasons. First, income increases for the poor are instrumental; that is, they are important not because more cash in hand is intrinsically good but because such increases mean the poor can buy food, clothes, health care and education. Deprivation in these and other aspects of well-being are the real essence of poverty. Income increases give households powers of choice[3] over which of these aspects of well-being they address.

Second, there are other objectives – characteristics of poor people, households and communities – that MFIs might choose to address in their social mission. Low income might be correlated with most of these other poverty characteristics but it need not be. MFIs may have specific social targets such as: social and political empowerment of women; developing social capital within conflict-affected communities; or developing community capacity to address food, health and education problems. Such programmes may perform poorly on household income-based measures of poverty outreach. However, there is no readily agreed set of poverty characteristics that constitutes a complete set. In practice, therefore, it may be difficult to assess whether a particular mission is directly poverty focused or represents what, in donor terminology, is referred to as either an indirect or enabling approach to poverty reduction.[4]

Targeting methods

Given the diversity of definitions, a critical issue is *how* MFIs can most effectively and sustainably identify and serve different categories of poor people with specific characteristics that correspond to their social mission. The term targeting can be used here in both an 'exclusionary' and 'inclusionary' way.[5] MFIs can target to exclude those that do not meet a criterion (for example, households owning more than half an acre of crop land) or they can target to include households with some specific characteristics (for example, households that rely on wages from agricultural labour). This is a distinction between hard and soft targeting; between programmes that have a hard target of *only* poor people and those with a softer target of *some* poor people.

The achievement of financial self-sustainability may be slower with exclusionary targeting because average loans are smaller. These extra costs can be absorbed through improving repayment performance; through staff serving higher numbers of clients, acquiring skills in use of targeting instruments and being given incentives to apply them; and through gradual increase of services provided, including increases in average loan sizes over time. With inclusionary or soft targeting, the extra costs of the portfolio of the poor can also be cross-subsidized if necessary with the (potentially) higher profits from loans to the not so poor. This is not possible with hard targeting. In both cases, cost absorption and cost reduction practices depend on organizational efficiency and learning in the use of targeting instruments, product development and portfolio management. Developing these practices is at the core of the social performance management agenda.[6]

MFIs practice both of these approaches. In South Asia, hard targeting is quite common, especially amongst those MFIs modelled on the Grameen Bank. This may be because in many parts of South Asia targeting is relatively easy. There are large numbers of readily identifiable poor households living close to each other. In other parts of the world, the approach of those that do target tends to be inclusionary only, for example, 'female entrepreneurs living in slums'. This category will include many poor women and their households, but does not actively exclude anybody who does not meet these criteria. This will often be the only viable strategy for an MFI to adopt for a number of reasons apart from any direct effects on loan portfolio. For example, in small communities it may be inappropriate or difficult to exclude non-poor households. It also may be advantageous to the poor to include such households if, for example, it facilitates their access to knowledge or to markets, perhaps through the non-poor and the poor being in the same solidarity groups.[7] However, inclusionary targeting is more prone to mission drift unless actual poverty outreach is monitored.

In defining outreach strategy, the context-specific analysis of poverty that is underlining the strategy is of paramount importance. The analytic focus on the household and its well-being characteristics are of course common to international statistics and national assessment of poverty. But, in some contexts, the approach to poverty reduction by service delivery agencies such as MFIs is strongly informed by structural assessment of poverty causation. In Latin America, such analysis often results in a programme focus on the informal sector, urban slums and remote, rural areas. In Eastern Europe, the recovery from civil conflict and the 'new' poverty affecting displaced formal sector workers during economic and political transition drives targeting strategy.

In these contexts, MFIs may perceive their role as part of broader political processes of engagement with structural conditions underlying poverty causation. For example, in Bolivia, microfinance has been a focal point of political agitation in the recent economic crisis. In such circumstances, it is clear that direct poverty outreach is only a very partial assessment of the potential contribution of MFIs to poverty reduction. This is an important caveat to the argument that direct poverty outreach is the 'right' approach to fulfilling an MFI's poverty reduction mandate. However, 'poverty reduction success' from MFI engagement with economic and social inequalities[8] that are structural in nature is necessarily difficult to determine. Without evidence on direct poverty outreach such MFIs will have difficulty in establishing their performance on poverty reduction.

There are three characteristics of a 'good' poverty indicator. It should be objective, verifiable and easy to collect. These are not easily satisfied. For example, self-assessment of poverty is challenged by the first condition, informal reliance on MFI field staff judgements by the second, and a money-metric measure by the third. Instead, many MFIs use other household characteristics that are easy to identify and correlate with income poverty. Possible proxies for income poverty include housing, dress, education and occupation, for example.

There is a large literature on proxy indicators of household poverty because this is an interest that extends into many development arenas.[9] There are many candidates and local knowledge is needed to specify them accurately. One example is the use of a housing index, an approach promoted most prominently by CASHPOR, an agency supporting 'Grameen clones' in Asia. A weakness of this index is that it relies on one dimension of poverty and index results may be misleading (Simanowitz *et al*, 2000). A second example is the use of a food security question, or questions, developed by the US Department of Agriculture, and adapted for microfinance more widely by Freedom from Hunger. Experience, in the Philippines and elsewhere, suggests that local adaptation is critical to make the indicator effective. Rather than choosing one proxy, there is a strong case for monitoring a set of them, and doing so systematically at client intake as well as subsequently. This approach has the potential to give very accurate estimates of poverty outreach and can also greatly aid impact assessment (see Chapter 3).[10]

The household (as the commonest unit for pooled-consumption decisions) is the most common unit of analysis for poverty assessment and this has been implicit in the discussion so far. However, many MFIs with a social mission do not target poor households as such. One widely used alternative indirect approach has been to rely on characteristics of the MFI services (such as value of loans) as a proxy indicator of the poverty status of clients. This has been shown to be flawed (Dunford, 2002) as a general basis for poverty outreach. Loan size is often a poor guide to client poverty status. Richer clients may take small loans simply because that is all the MFI offers. In some circumstances though, loan size can be deliberately used as a product-based form of seeking poverty outreach. This would be true where the MFI has reason to believe that only poor households would actually use the small loan sizes they offer. Other product-based poverty outreach methods could include requirements to attend meetings, to undertake collective tasks or to repay in a certain way. These product-based methods would need validation against a poverty benchmark to be credible. Moreover, the relationship between MFIs and their potential clients is dynamic and there is no guarantee of consistency of outreach through product-based targeting.

Many MFIs also target by gender. Some do so in combination with poverty outreach measures related to income, and almost all have some other form of outreach indicator beyond a focus on women. Targeting services geographic- ally or by occupation is common and very often a client target group may be defined as 'poor women in . . . or doing. . .'. Targeting women is more likely to be sensitive to poverty than targeting men because more women are poor. Targeting women is also likely to be better for poverty reduction because of the ways in which income is used by women for improving the well-being of household members, especially children. Intra-household income distribution is likely to improve by providing services to women in preference to their partners. This may still be true even when women are effectively acting mainly as conduits to transfer loans from MFIs to men. Very often, this role will enhance women's voice in both investment and consumption decisions. Nevertheless, as a poverty outreach indicator, gender targeting has obvious limits and would need validation by other methods to clearly establish direct poverty outreach.

Another common method of indirect poverty outreach is to target geographically. For example, the rural programmes of CYSD and PRADAN in India target poor parts of poor districts in poor states. The absolute poverty of most households in these places makes it a certainty that a high proportion of clients are poor. However, not all geographical targeting is so clear cut. Moreover, there is some evidence from some programmes that within regions that are poor by national standards, MFIs tend to work with the less poor. Thus, geographic targeting may be a good start on poverty outreach but it will not generally be sufficient to ensure direct poverty outreach. As with other methods of indirect poverty targeting, it is necessary to complement such approaches with more direct measures to establish strength of direct poverty outreach

The methods described above are all forms of proxy means testing. Determining how reliable, effective or credible a proxy indicator of 'means' is typically requires an assessment of how well it identifies households that are poor by a money-metric measure such as a national poverty line. Indicators that exclude households that are income poor suffer from 'type one' errors or false negatives; indicators that identify households that are not income poor suffer 'type two' errors or false positives. Most proxies suffer from both errors and the purpose of experimentation prior to selection of indicators is to minimize both, usually with some implicit cost constraint relating to the time it takes to collect information on the proxies.

As concerns about mission drift within the industry have multiplied, so the search for good proxy indicators has intensified. Several networks, including ACCION, FFH, Opportunity International and SEEP, have encouraged partner MFIs to assess depth of poverty outreach systematically – many in collaboration with the *Imp-Act* programme. These are discussed below. Two other initiatives have been particularly important. First, CGAP (Consultative Group to Assist the Poor) has developed a means test approach, the CGAP Poverty Assessment Tool (PAT), based on relative, as opposed to absolute, poverty.

Second, US legislation is in the process of being phased in that requires USAID's microenterprise programme to demonstrate that at least 50 per cent of benefiting households are very poor. The Centre for International Research on the Informal Sector (IRIS) has been commissioned to test how well a range of proxy indicators in current use correlate with income-based poverty Living Standard Measurement Survey estimates.[11] The aim is to develop at least two approaches to MFI poverty assessment that fulfil the three conditions identified above (objective, verifiable and easy to collect) of a good poverty outreach indicator. The chosen indicators should be both practical and accurate and establish clearly whether MFI clients are above or below the dollar-a-day poverty line.[12] This is a fairly strong form of inclusionary targeting. Its ramifications for the industry, specifically whether all MFIs will seek to comply and whether other donors will set similar standards, are not yet clear. However, this is a welcome initiative because, as the discussion above has indicated, income-based poverty outreach is indispensable for MFIs to have confidence in their targeting of absolute poverty. Several *Imp-Act* programme partners have also been examining their depth of absolute poverty outreach using LSMS, or similar comparisons, and trying to develop suitable proxy indicators.

Experience of *Imp-Act* partners[13]

However, a significant change has already taken place. This pertains to the return of the organization to social dimensions of client-centred service rather than a concentration on clients' fees for service delivery. The former brings responsiveness to the clients in line with their cultural values, while the latter keeps a transactional mode that strains client–field staff rapport. The staunch attention of the institution on reducing costs and PAR, the rush for expanding outreach and portfolio, and staff performance-binding efficiency and productivity ratios clouded the basic human touch of personal concern for client welfare (CARD, 2004).

Imp-Act partners have undertaken a wide variety of activities to strengthen knowledge about their outreach and to institutionalize more effective and reliable poverty monitoring and assessment. They have found the research timely. The pressure to achieve financial sustainability that has been felt by most of them has led to concerns from partners, board and management that they are suffering from mission drift. The activities have principally involved assessment of targeting methods and developing organizational learning to improve performance on outreach. Organizational learning from these activities is the subject of later chapters. Here we are more concerned with the actual tools used for outreach assessment, the results and their implications.

Table 2.1 summarizes some of the main outreach assessment approaches of *Imp-Act* partner MFIs. Nearly all of them used some form of target group related to poverty status. In seven cases (BRAC, CARD, LAPO, SAT, PRIZMA, SEF and SHARE) household-level proxy indicators of income poverty were used. In other cases, targeting was by geographic area or a locality, such as shantytowns or a particular occupation group. Gender targeting is common though not universal. These geographic and occupational targets were usually selected on the basis of local patterns of poverty and gave MFIs some confidence that their outreach was to the poor. But the widespread concerns about mission drift and the commitment to their social missions has prompted partner MFIs within the *Imp-Act* programme to test this underlying belief and to assess more rigorously the strength of their poverty outreach.

This work was led by those within the 'Very Poor' thematic group (BRAC, CYSD, KREP, LAPO, PRADAN, PRIZMA, PROMUC, SEF and SHARE, with important inputs also from CARD, FINCA and SAT). This thematic group met four times during the research phase and their experience guided the overall programme with the broad objective of strengthening organizational

Table 2.1 Summary of poverty outreach approaches used by *Imp-Act* partners

Partner	
BOSVITA	Refugees and local population (43 per cent below national poverty line[1])
BRAC	Targeting through land holding and occupation; women
CAME	Geographic; the economically disadvantaged. CAME does not emphasize poverty so much as exclusion and marginalization. Their *Imp-Act* survey suggests that clients are not among the poorest inhabitants of CAME's area of operation
CARD	Housing, food security, education and assets. Means test form to screen clients on entry
CERUDEB	Non-targeted
CMF partner SACCOS	Geographic
CYSD	Geographic
FINCA	No exclusion but targets women (95% plus of their village bank groups)
FINRURAL	Their partners include those who are effective in targeting poor women in the urban informal sector e.g. Promujer (Bolivia), and those who target poor rural and urban women e.g. CRECER – other partners have limited depth of outreach
FOCCAS	Poor families in rural Uganda
FPC	Geographic
K-Rep	Various groups excluded from formal financial service access
LAPO	Various income-related criteria via participation form
ODEF	Clients with small and micro-businesses – scored in regulatory assessment of private finance institutions
PARTNER	Low-income and war-affected population (43% below national poverty line[1])
PRADAN	Geographic
PRIZMA	Poor and low-income women and their families
PROMUC partners	Poor women, mainly urban, and targeting poor areas
Promujer, Peru	The majority of their clients are female vendors who work in the informal sector
SEF	Participatory Wealth Ranking for their targeted programme; women
SHARE	Targeting through land holding and occupation; women
SAT	Economically disadvantaged women (80%)
UMU	Self-selection

Note: [1]Based on a sample survey of 1,742 clients in 11 MFIs in Bosnia-Herzegovina of which 137 were from BOSVITA (an MFI that has now merged with PARTNER) and 230 from PARTNER.

performance on poverty outreach through improved assessment and institutionalization of improved practice. They made important research contributions on assessing poverty outreach in two ways. First, several of them used the CGAP relative poverty assessment tool. Second, an overlapping group tried to validate their poverty outreach approach against national and international (dollar-a-day) measures of poverty.

Relative poverty: results from Imp-Act CGAP studies

In order to establish more transparency in depth of poverty outreach by MFIs the CGAP method uses a sample of non-clients and new clients to collect data on a core indicator of poverty and on a range of other household characteristics thought to be associated with poverty. The basic approach, which involves a technical process requiring specific expertise, is to construct a poverty index and then score individual households with it, thus enabling an assessment of poverty outreach. The core indicator is expenditure on clothing and footwear because surveys show that they appear to have a reasonably stable share of total expenditure. Information on other characteristics is in four domains: human resources, dwelling, assets and food security. There is a range of indicators in each domain and these are assessed using principal components analysis (PCA). The presumption is that the indicators have been selected because they capture an underlying dimension of poverty.

The method involves running cross-tabulations between the core poverty indicator and the indicators in each domain to establish which are correlated. These are then used in the PCA, which is essentially a data-reduction technique. The method creates a new variable, which is a composite based on the commonalities between the individual variables. In other words, it is a measure that combines information about different dimensions of poverty that together 'explain' the state of poverty of the household. In practice the PCA requires many iterations with different clusters of variables to establish the best set; this is that set for which the component loadings – the correlation between the composite 'poverty index' and the individual variable – are most significant. The model's strength is assessed by examining the amount of total variance among the indicators that is captured by the composite indicator.

Assuming the variables have been well chosen then the first principal component should be identified as a measure of poverty. Initially, this is really a subjective assumption. It is then tested by looking at the partial correlation between individual indicators and the core measure of poverty. Once the strongest index has been identified,[14] it is then used to give each household in the sample a poverty score. Based on the sample of non-clients, the scores are grouped into three terciles of relative poverty (each containing 33.3 per cent of the population). The scores of new clients in the sample are then used to assign them to these terciles and comparison of the distribution forms the basis for assessment of outreach performance. The method was applied by seven *Imp-Act* partners and the results are summarized in Table 2.2.

Table 2.2 *Imp-Act* partner results from the CGAP PAT

MFI	Share of clients in each poverty tercile		
	Lower tercile Poorest (%)	Middle tercile Less poor (%)	Upper tercile Least poor (%)
CYSD	17.8	26.6	55.6
LAPO	34.5	35.5	30
PRADAN	31	43	26
PROMUC	37	39	24
PRIZMA	26.2	37.2	36.6
SEF[1]	32	37	31
SHARE	58	38.5	3.5

Note: [1] Information refers to SEF's combined operations, comprising more and less strongly targeted programmes.

The apparent message from these results on relative poverty is that most *Imp-Act* partners, with the important exception of SHARE, are struggling to be very finely targeted. Yet this is grossly misleading. Of the various qualifications to be made to that assessment, the first and most significant is the importance of context. The tool compares the poverty status of households in an MFI programme to a randomly selected group of neighbouring non-participants. No information is available to relate these results to national or international indicators of poverty status. The fact that it is relative poverty that is being assessed means that the results can only be properly interpreted for depth of outreach in the light of knowledge about geographic targeting. In other words, how poor are the areas studied in relation to national and international measures of poverty, such as the dollar-a-day measure?

The CYSD results (Vyasulu, 2003) are a clear example of why these raw results are misleading. The CYSD rural programme areas for this study were remote tribal villages in western Orissa, which are almost the poorest in India using national poverty line standards. In these areas, even those in the top tercile of the poverty distribution locally are amongst the poorest households nationally. This is almost equally true for PRADAN. In both these programmes the mandate is to work with whole communities of very poor and economically and socially marginalized people. This crucial issue is also highly relevant to SEF, which also works in a very poor province and almost certainly does better at targeting by national poverty line standards than the relative poverty results indicate.

By contrast, the results for PRIZMA, PROMUC and SHARE probably over-estimate outreach measured by national poverty lines. Again, examining geographic targeting is crucial. In these three cases the organizations are working in areas that are less poor by national standards. For PROMUC, the study shows that their areas of outreach are in the top two quintiles of the national distribution of poverty. In the case of PRIZMA their performance in terms of the national poverty line shows a pattern of outreach biased towards the better off that is even more marked than the numbers in Table 2.2 indicate. For SHARE, comparison with the national poverty line (Rangacharyulu, 2004) showed that only 39 per cent of new rural clients were in poverty compared to 58 per cent in the bottom tercile based on relative assessment. The figures for urban areas showed the opposite, however, with nearly four-fifths of new clients being below the poverty line.

Whilst it is clear that there are intrinsic biases in the tool because of its focus on relative poverty, the tool is nevertheless a good indicator within that constraint. It was not clear when developed just how serious this might be for comparative assessment of outreach. The discussion above suggests that the relative nature of the results is in fact a primary and serious limitation for an accurate assessment of targeting. The CGAP manual does discuss a partial way forward through determining first, via expert panel assessment, how poor the region of MFI operations is nationally (Ratio Three in the CGAP manual). Second, (Ratio Four) it takes the ratio of the country Human Development Index (HDI) to the average HDI for developing countries to score the absolute poverty of the country in question. The manual acknowledges that, to move towards an absolute measure, these two last steps need further work.

A second limitation concerns the reliability of the accuracy of the core indicator: expenditure on clothing and footwear. This information is collected through the survey using recall over a year of such expenditure for each individual household member. Clearly, despite the emphasis on the need for accuracy in the CGAP manual, there is considerable scope for miscalculation. Hence, the test of correlation of other potential poverty indicators is subject to some unknown degree of non-sampling error. It is also the case that some dimensions of poverty may correlate poorly with most others and perhaps be rejected from the composite because of this.[15]

A third and important limitation is that the tool is essentially designed as a means of external verification of outreach. Indeed, at one point, the manual suggests that MFI staff should not be told too much about what questions will be asked of their clients in case they influence their responses. MFIs may well wish to be seen to be serving the poor, regardless of what they are actually doing. The methods used – through sample selection, questionnaire design, data collection, analysis and interpretation – require specific skills and will usually involve the use of external consultants, and indeed this is the presumption in the manual. This lack of staff engagement in the process limits the utility of the tool as a vehicle for organizational learning.

The *Imp-Act* partners involved in the CGAP study are all strongly committed to poverty outreach. Their common problem has been a combination of pressure to move towards a financial sustainability target, a lack of knowledge of how their programme methods affect poverty outreach, and limited knowledge of how they might cost effectively combine poverty outreach and financial sustainability. Their engagement in the CGAP study was aimed at helping them respond to these issues through enhancing their knowledge on outreach performance. The results were mixed and further research showed the limitations of the relative poverty measure. The key conclusion of this research is that it clarified the need for indicators that were valid in terms of absolute poverty. This is the approach being adopted in the USAID-supported work referred to above, which is collecting income poverty data at the same time as potential poverty proxy indicators to allow a rigorous assessment of their reliability.

Absolute poverty measures: experience of six Imp-Act partners

The *Imp-Act* results reported below are based on absolute income poverty assessment. However, a fundamental emphasis in *Imp-Act* work is its closer integration with operations (for example, routine monitoring and MIS (management information systems)), in order that the activity is incorporated into organizational decision making (see Chapter 8). Six case studies are presented here.

FINCA

FINCA's global activities on outreach, partially funded through *Imp-Act*, reflected a concern over growing client desertion rates and a suspicion of mission drift towards non-poor clients. They had conducted assessments in a small number of countries three times earlier (in 1997, 1999 and 2002). This experience had taught them a great deal about survey technique and, crucially, had developed knowledge about specifying appropriate indicators. A major innovation in the 2003 round was the use of handheld computers (palm pilots) for data collection in the field. They used student interns from universities in the USA to work in 11 countries and, remarkably, the whole operation of evaluating the social mission of FINCA country programmes took just two months.

FINCA selected ten simple indicators for measuring 1) the poverty levels of new clients entering FINCA programmes and 2) the principal programme impacts on the well-being of their households. It has always been the intention to integrate these indicators into FINCA's management information system, but this is for the next stage of activity. The questions on poverty levels were on a simple but well-designed form (see Figure 2.1), and once data was collected the palm pilots were programmed to sum and translate the data into daily per capita expenditure (DPCE) figures. These were then compared to different money-metric poverty-level estimates, but the most reliable were the comparisons with the national poverty line.

When national poverty lines were used, expressed in local currency, it was found that 17 per cent of FINCA's new clients were very poor, 18 per cent were moderately poor and 65 per cent were non-poor. New clients and non-clients had very similar daily per capita expenditures in most countries. These two results suggest mission drift away from the poorest, *not* because the poorest are

1. No. of adults who earn income	2. No. of family members	3. Expenditure on food	4. Expenditure on education	5. Expenditure on health	6. Expenditure on housing	7. Expenditure on utilities
8. Expenditure on transport	9. Expenditure on fuel	10. Expenditure on clothing	11. Other expenditure	12. Total monthly expenditure	13. Daily per capita expenditure	14. Level of poverty

Figure 2.1 FINCA expenditure assessment and poverty scoring

being left behind in communities that FINCA serves, but because service outreach appears to be drifting towards only moderately poor communities. The key message for learning on outreach from these results was how FINCA's social mission had been neglected. The research department at FINCA international, who organized the research, have made nine recommendations around organizational learning as well as identifying additional research tasks, including further work on validating the indicators used and the methods of data collection.

BRAC

This is a very large NGO with more than two million clients. It has consistently employed targeting mechanisms and over the last decade has conducted three major rounds of assessment on outreach and impact. Its mission goals are poverty alleviation and empowerment of the poor; their development approach seeks to be holistic, recognizing the need to create an enabling environment and address the multiple dimensions of poverty. The impact research has sought scientific rigour and reliability and it is purposeful, with the aims of capacity building and programme improvement through knowledge about change in the lives of clients.

BRAC used a combination of household surveys, village profiles, participatory methods and case studies. Targeting criteria were related to land holding and husband's occupation (new entrants are all female) as a wage labourer; both are commonly used in Bangladesh. From the very first survey (1994–95) they found that over 80 per cent of their member households were correctly targeted. BRAC achieve this through preliminary surveys in new villages and rapid listing of potential entrants to their Rural Development Programme (RDP). Their own staff are well trained and in each zone there is abundant experience in programme expansion and the related targeting task. BRAC estimates a marginal additional cost involved in targeting, but this has not been quantified except in a 'guestimate' of how it affected the achievement of self-sustainability. This is in the order of five years but is vague. In truth, targeting in Bangladesh is not that difficult. The proportion of poor people has been falling significantly as economic reforms and technological progress in agriculture have had effect, but even so the targeting criteria mentioned (land and occupation) are accurate, easy, not sensitive, verifiable and have been shown to be associated with low levels of household income per head.

BRAC has its own research and evaluation division that has undertaken these assessments, sometimes with inputs from local and international consultants. They are widely regarded as scientifically sound. They have been important in helping BRAC identify a category of the very poor at the lower end of the spectrum that has been relatively neglected in programme operations. BRAC has established that other services are required to work with these households to strengthen their livelihood levels and options, prior perhaps to joining an MFI. For this programme, where stipends and asset transfers are initially involved, they have developed a very stringent model to ensure accuracy of targeting. This targeting cost is one of the additional costs associated with this programme (called Challenging the Frontiers of Poverty Reduction) and is a good example of how targeting costs can vary with the socio-economic profile of the group being targeted, even within the same communities.

Perhaps more fundamental though is how BRAC has used knowledge of poverty conditions to identify new programming needs. Recognizing that its mainstream programme, successful though it has been shown to be in poverty reduction, does not include the poorest, the NGO has invested in the development of a wholly new programme that is responsive to the needs of the very poor. This is an important example of organizational learning around a social performance agenda and underlines the need for accurate assessment of poverty outreach to strengthen social performance.

LAPO

LAPO use a 'participation form' on client entry to record information (see Figure 2.2) about new clients; they also use this as a screening mechanism to ensure their focus on poverty. Their poverty definition is based on scoring answers to eight questions.

LAPO scored these answers, weighted them and assigned cut-off values to three categories of poverty status in an essentially subjective way. Their *Imp-Act* research allowed them to compare this index with the results from their CGAP PAT study. They were thus able to test the validity of their methods and use sensitivity analysis to find the best combination of scoring, weighting and categorizing. As shown in Table 2.3, the results on the existing scoring method showed a 30 per cent misspecification error.

Further statistical review by a consultant identified a much more appropriate use of the data from the participation form. By narrowing the scoring basis down to just the first five of the questions, using equal weights and three categories, the misspecification error was reduced from 30 per cent to 10 per cent.

Poverty status questions
1. What is your marital status?
2. May I ask about your approximate level of education?
3. What is your occupation?
4. What is the interior and exterior walls/flooring condition of your dwelling house?
5. What is the sleeping arrangement like in your household?
6. How steady is your total household income?
7. How regular is the daily feeding of your household?
8. How often do you cook special food for your household?

Figure 2.2 LAPO's participation form

Table 2.3 Specification error rate for the LAPO participation form compared to the CGAP PAT

Error type	Number	% of total
Least poor specified as less poor	16	9.3
Least poor specified as poorest	0	0.0
Less poor specified as least poor	5	2.9
Less poor specified as poorest	0	0.0
Poorest specified as least poor	0	0.0
Poorest specified as less poor	31	18.0
Total specification errors	**52**	**30.2**

LAPO have used these results to reform their participation form to allow more accurate targeting and to provide a reliable basis for monitoring impact. They have also conducted comparative analysis of results from different branches to investigate operational performance because significant differences were observed. They are now strengthening their staff training and operational procedures to improve their poverty outreach performance.

PRIZMA

This organization has embraced social performance and financial sustainability as its core values since its inception. One of its chief strategies has centred on measuring and deepening outreach in an overall environment of poverty, vulnerability and increasing inequality. PRIZMA seeks to address this strategy through leadership, organizational culture, incentives and management information systems. On poverty reduction a specific concern under the *Imp-Act* programme was to: 1) measure and deepen outreach; 2) improve service quality and institutional performance; and 3) measure and improve social impact.

To meet its first concern, PRIZMA developed a 'poverty scorecard'. The scorecard is a composite measure of household poverty based on some of the strongest and most robust non-income indicator proxies for poverty in Bosnia-Herzegovina. This was established through triangulation with the 2002 Living Standards Measurement Survey, United Nations Development Programme (UNDP) data, a CGAP poverty assessment and findings from internally led focus-group research. The CGAP comparison established that nearly 64 per cent of new PRIZMA clients were among 'moderate poor' and 'poorest' terciles, but PRIZMA wanted to improve on that depth of outreach, hence the development of the scorecard.

The action-research purpose was to ensure that their scorecard was accurate and credible, adaptable, verifiable, cost effective, embedded in the institution's existing operations and complementary to market research. It was also designed to provide the basis for impact monitoring. Testing revealed that eight relatively strong indicators yielded a score that was very robust. More or fewer indicators could be employed, but eight effectively balanced cost with accuracy. Given that PRIZMA operational staff were already collecting four of the final eight scorecard indicators selected, the additional data collection is very modest.

The scorecard (see Figure 2.3) is comprised of two sets of indicators. The first three – education level, residence and household size – reflect poverty-risk categories or accuracy of poverty targeting. The second group of four indicators, in addition to measuring initial poverty status, will also be used to assess change in household poverty status. PRIZMA's use of the scorecard is wide-ranging and includes: managing human resources; segmenting the market; monitoring client dropout; developing products and services; positioning the organization strategically; improving efficiency; and managing credit risk.

The organization's intention was to assess clients' poverty status relative to non-clients across different segments of its clientele, to understand who is being served (who joins, stays and leaves) and to refine targeting strategies, client and staff incentives, and product attributes. Second, it wished to report on clients' poverty status in absolute terms, in relation to the national poverty line and the widely referenced international poverty benchmarks of US$1 and US$2 per day. Figure 2.4 compares household scorecard results to poverty status according to the LSMS survey results.

Figure 2.4 shows very clearly that PRIZMA's scorecard is a robust indicator of poverty. In terms of the cut-off for poverty targeting, the graph shows that, within the households in the LSMS survey that scored two on the poverty scorecard, 47 per cent were below the poverty line. Other data descriptions show that nearly 59 per cent of those that scored two or below were in the

		Indicator		0	1	2
Poverty risk		**Education**	What is the education level of female household head/spouse/partner?	*≤ Primary*	*> Primary*	
Poverty risk		**Residence**	Where is residence?	*Rural/Peri* *≤ 10,000*	*Urban* *> 10,000*	
Poverty risk		**Household**	What is household size?	*≥ 5*	*< 5*	
Poverty risk	Change	**Household Assets**	Does household possess a stereo CD player?	*No*	*Yes*	
Poverty risk	Change	**Transport Assets**	Does household possess a transport vehicle?	*No*	*Yes*	
Poverty risk	Change	**Meat Consumption**	On average, how often does household consume meat each week?	*Rarely* *0–2* *times/week*	*Sometimes* *3–5* *times/week*	*Often* *6+* *times/week*
Poverty risk	Change	**Sweets Consumption**	On average, how often does household consume sweets with main meal each week?	*Rarely* *0–2* *times/week*	*Sometimes* *3–5* *times/week*	*Often* *6+* *times/week*
		Poverty status score (0–9)				
(Poor and very poor 0–2 • Vulnerable non-poor 3–4 • Non-poor 5+)						

Figure 2.3 PRIZMA poverty scorecard

lowest LSMS poverty tercile and over 92 per cent were in the bottom two terciles. There was just over 3 per cent false negatives – households that scored five or above on the scorecard but were in the lowest tercile by income.

PRIZMA's own results on its poverty outreach (2,617 clients) at the end of 2003 showed a mixed performance by urban and rural difference and especially according to geographic difference. Overall, PRIZMA was not achieving poverty scores even proportionate to the national population and the depth of outreach was not satisfactory, as shown in Figure 2.5.

PRIZMA is now confident that the poverty scorecard can be used in a leadership, management and organizational learning strategy to target poor

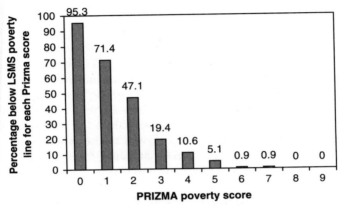

Figure 2.4 Comparison of PRIZMA poverty score with LSMS poverty line: percentage below LSMS poverty line for each PRIZMA score (on 2002 LSMS national sample)

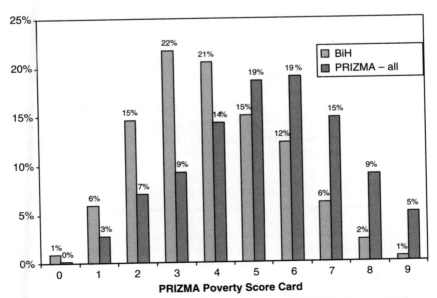

Figure 2.5 Scorecard distribution in LSMS sample and PRIZMA client portfolio

households more effectively. More broadly, the poverty scorecard is a tool to generate information. This information can be used as part of an organizational learning strategy not only to better *find* poor households, but to improve outreach and impact by designing products, services and delivery systems that better meet the needs of poor households. Crucially, PRIZMA projects extensive financial benefits from knowing their clients and their needs through a substantial reduction in client exit, which, as is common in the East European region, is a prime threat to MFI viability.

SEF

Through its Tšhomišano Credit Programme (TCP), SEF works to consciously identify and reach the very poorest households, and uses a rigorous methodology to identify the poorest in target communities. Implementation of TCP in a community begins with a detailed poverty targeting process using participatory wealth ranking (PWR).[16] A cut-off line is established that is equivalent to the level of the poorest 30 per cent of households in the province. All households below this line are eligible for inclusion in the programme. Ensuring that TCP remains open to the poor and that staff incentives and operational sustainability pressures do not cause mission drift is a major organizational imperative.

The accuracy of PWR targeting was tested as a relative poverty-targeting tool by using the CGAP PAT. The results, as shown in Table 2.4 were good but did show a 10 per cent group of false positives, indicating 90 per cent accuracy of targeting. Also revealed was a 21 per cent group of false negatives, indicating that about a fifth of poor eligible households were being excluded.

SEF also operates another programme in Limpopo province that is not targeted other than geographically (Limpopo is the poorest province in South Africa). This was in fact SEF's original programme and their concerns about its weakness in poverty outreach prompted the development of TCP. A comparison of this non-targeted programme (the MCP) with TCP and with the CGAP PAT results are given in Figure 2.6.

The differences in poverty outreach are evident and led the authors of the report on poverty outreach at SEF to conclude that 'poverty alleviation programmes need to be accompanied by a targeting strategy and a programme structure appropriate to the needs of the poor. A poverty targeting strategy

Table 2.4 SEF match between the PAT and the PWR

Error type	Number	% of total
% of households considered poor by the PAT and poor by the PWR	118	59
% of households considered non-poor by PAT and non-poor by the PWR	18	9
% of households considered poor by the PAT and non-poor by the PWR	43	21
% of households considered non-poor by PAT and poor by the PWR	20	10

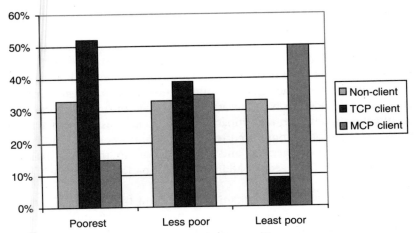

Figure 2.6 Clients and non-clients in SEF microcredit programmes

appears to be a central component in ensuring that the most vulnerable people are drawn into a poverty alleviation programme' (Van de Ruit *et al*, 2001). The authors also compared the CGAP PAT results to national money-metric poverty lines and found that there was strong overlap with 60 per cent of the dollar-a-day poor and 40 per cent of the poor by the national poverty line being in the bottom two terciles of the CGAP distribution. This of course also implies a high degree of correspondence between the targeting by SEF's PWR and dollar-a-day poverty. The research demonstrates that TCP was an effective response to the concern that the main programme was not reaching the poor. SEF is now examining ways of strengthening its monitoring activities to ensure continued effective outreach and to provide the basis for impact assessment.

CARD

During its participation in the *Imp-Act* programme, CARD focused on the development of an information system that integrates data on poverty outreach into management information systems. Through an organization-wide workshop they reviewed five previous impact assessment studies, four of which were entirely external, and examined their learning experience. The assessments were generally positive on outreach and impact, but the CARD database, compiled from membership and loan application forms, did not address outreach effectively or key areas of impact. CARD's founding philosophy is rooted in economic empowerment of the poor, thus resulting in the wish to improve performance on outreach. In embarking on a project under *Imp-Act*, CARD effectively committed itself to making social performance as important as financial performance. The former could bring about responsiveness to the clients in line with their cultural values, while the latter was leading to a transactions mode that strained the rapport between clients and field staff.

CARD's target market is poor women in households with per capita income of less than P1,500 (US$27.6), marketable assets below P150,000 (US$2,760), and a poor score on their housing index. It was neither clear that these were being applied properly nor that the information could be used to monitor client welfare. CARD was therefore appreciative of the potential gains from integrating outreach and impact into their client assessment activities. However, CARD is also committed to efficiency and low costs, and engaged in a process of re-engineering and simplification to this end. It had to reconcile this with the need for additional information on outreach and on impact.

After discussion within the organization around the choice and value of specific approaches, the CARD board eventually came up with four criteria that the indicators had to fulfil: 1) only three to four impact indicators that could be tracked over time; 2) a strong preference for impact information directly useful for improving organizational performance; 3) a focus on understanding CARD's impact at the community level; and 4) addressing the ultimate concern of how to move clients out of poverty.

The focus on progress on poverty reduction required reliable indicators on poverty levels at entry point. In addition to income, they reviewed indicators in four domains:

- Food security – one question, with four standard responses, was asked for respondents to indicate their perceived food security condition.[17]
- Housing index – includes roofing material, structure and size, which enumerators observed and rated according to a given scale.
- Education of school-age children – names of clients' children were reported along with their respective ages and educational levels or attainment.
- Productive assets – a list of assets used for income-generating activities was recorded with the corresponding estimated present cash value of each.

Results of the analysis of the housing index scores showed that 71 per cent of new client respondents scored below six (CARD's housing index cut-off), while 29 per cent scored above six. Based on this poverty-screening tool alone, CARD may have admitted 29 per cent non-poor clients. The single-question food-security tool with the four-level scale was found to be insensitive as a targeting tool. Results were similar across all years of membership in CARD. About 70 per cent of all respondents chose the level 'enough quantity, but not always the kind we want'. This is equivalent to households having barely adequate food or feeling food insecure without hunger. Only 12 per cent revealed they often did not have enough to eat, that is, they were food insecure with hunger.

Only 25 per cent of new client respondents estimated their per capita monthly income to be not more than P1,500. Using the national poverty threshold of about P1,000 this means that only 23 per cent of the respondents' families were classified as poor households. In terms of per capita income per month, therefore, CARD has admitted 77 per cent of the non-poor. Most (95 per cent) of new clients possessed productive assets valued at no more than P150,000. On this criterion alone, most of the new clients qualified as poor. On the last indicator, national data showed there was little difference in the proportion of children not in school in the highest 60 per cent of the income strata compared to those in the lowest 40 per cent.

Although results were mixed, comparisons between older and newer clients confirmed the appearance of mission drift. CARD determined to tighten their screening criteria (means test) on entry. To start with, management reinstated the policy of only accepting clients who could pass all three of their poverty screening criteria. Previously, CARD had allowed the entry of those who passed two out of the three screening tests. Second, in association with IRIS, CARD re-examined their poverty indexes and are now engaged in a scientific assessment to establish which of these 'easy-to-collect' indicators are most associated with poverty according to accurate data on per capita expenditure. They have already adapted their membership and loan application forms to record information on outreach and impact, and these will be further refined in accordance with the further research on their indicators. Through their partnership with the Microfinance Council of the Philippines, CARD's experience and the benefits of their focus on cost-effective social performance assessment as an institutional learning and growth stratagem have been shared nationally.

The research of these partners collectively represents a significant contribution to our knowledge about the assessment of absolute poverty and the opportunities for organizational learning based on it. As argued above, it is important to be able to assess direct poverty outreach in order to make meaningful statements about poverty performance. These MFIs have responded to this challenge and have gone through careful processes to develop meaningful data on outreach. They have done this primarily to improve performance rather than to be able to demonstrate to donors or others their poverty outreach. In several cases the work was energized by the belief that mission drift was occurring, a belief that was usually proved to be true.

Conclusion

The chapter first reviewed key issues on assessment of poverty outreach and then presented evidence from *Imp-Act* partners on measuring and monitoring depth of outreach. As the review demonstrates, many different forms of poverty outreach are attempted by MFIs. These vary both with respect to the concept of poverty adopted and to operational means for addressing the corresponding market segment. The chapter argued that without some form of deliberate inclusionary process (targeting) MFIs cannot easily justify any claim to be working with or for the poor.

The core mission of most MFIs is direct strengthening of the economic agency of poor households through financial services, but many *Imp-Act* partners have a sense of mission drift as they respond to concerns about their financial sustainability. Many have recognized that ensuring the inclusion of poor clients requires targeting to be validated through methods of assessing client poverty on entry.

The second half of the chapter described the research experiences of six partners on assessing depth of outreach and the processes of organizational learning on poverty reduction that the research engendered. The varieties of experience described in the case studies underline the importance of context in defining and developing a social performance agenda. Nevertheless, certain key commonalities can be extracted from these studies:

- MFI ownership – all these cases were driven by organizational desire to fulfil social mission.
- Commitment to depth of outreach – there was recognition that there was no substitute for knowing that client households were from the target group as assessed through national or international monetary poverty measures.
- Scientific approaches – there was recognition that income proxies are the most appropriate and cost-effective approach to the assessment of depth of outreach and that careful and rigorous research is required to develop the right proxy indicators for the specific context.
- Organizational learning – all the MFIs showed a high degree of commitment to using poverty outreach results to strengthen operations. New products, staff incentives, training and improving their MIS are all examples of organizational change that MFIs have adopted to fulfil their social performance mandate.
- Monitoring – all organizations sought to develop indicators that would serve to assess depth of poverty upon entry and that could also be used relatively easily to assess client progress over time.
- Networking – in developing their work programme and identifying improving practice, MFIs benefited from the *Imp-Act* network of activities on this agenda as well as from their partnerships with other networks, both national and international.
- Cost-effectiveness – all organizations were very sensitive to the need for developing assessment of depth of outreach in ways that are financially and organizationally sustainable.

These common elements are at the heart of improvement on social performance assessment for most MFIs. This social performance agenda is directly concerned with integrating financial sustainability concerns with poverty outreach. There is a trade-off with financial sustainability but organizational learning and innovation can improve the odds in the battle and create win-win situations. The experiences of *Imp-Act* partners illustrate the justification for concerns about mission drift. The partners demonstrated a concern with improving poverty assessment through approaches that will strengthen their pursuit of their social missions.

CHAPTER THREE
Direct material impacts

Martin Greeley

Introduction

The microfinance industry has embraced the concept of client assessment as a means to strengthen organizational performance. This has been widely understood as a shift away from a supply- or product-led approach to a demand- or market-led approach. New approaches to market research have been developed to help MFIs identify client demand and improve the range and relevance of financial products. For MFIs concerned with poverty outreach, this market research will be of little use if it does not segment the specific product needs of poor people. The poor represent a market opportunity for MFI services to demonstrate competitive advantage and commercial value, but to achieve this requires appropriate forms of client assessment.

Within the *Imp-Act* programme, this type of client assessment and the organizational capacity to respond that needs to go with it are termed social performance management. Most MFIs define their social performance in terms of their poverty outreach and impact. Chapter 2 has shown that this requires knowledge of client poverty status and what this requirement entails. As reflected in the Chapter 2 case studies, this is the bedrock of a social performance management system for poverty-focused MFIs.

In this chapter, we report on the experiences of *Imp-Act* partners in proving and improving through client assessment. The material shows both the performance of *Imp-Act* partners with respect to impact on client welfare and the ways in which knowledge of clients can direct organizational learning on poverty-focused service delivery. The next section provides an overview of the relevant general literature on impact assessment and microfinance, with a particular emphasis on the purpose of such studies, tools, methodological challenges and prevailing wisdom.[1] The third section reviews selected experiences and findings of eight *Imp-Act* partners. There are two conclusions that arise from these experiences. First, the evidence is consistent with the prevailing consensus that impact of microfinance on income and poverty is generally positive, but that this is hard to prove rigorously. Second, the reports from the *Imp-Act* partners demonstrate that real and significant organizational changes resulted from the findings as these MFIs set about institutionalizing social performance assessment within their programmes.

An overview of industry experience

Approaches to impact assessment

The assessment of MFI impact has been driven by two distinct audiences and purposes: an external audience, seeking credible evidence to justify its investment in microfinance; and an internal audience, seeking reliable evidence as a means to improve services. These two drivers have also influenced impact assessment methods – external audiences generally requiring more rigorous methods than the MFI staff, for whom formal impact assessment is just one source of evidence to inform programme changes. For this reason the two drivers have also been referred to as 'proving' and 'improving' agendas, although this is misleading to the extent that reliability of evidence is important in both, and both aim to improve policy and practice.

The external or proving agenda has been dominant until recently. In the light of strong claims by the global industry on poverty reduction, it has generated an enormous literature. MFIs themselves have often regarded such studies (often implemented by independent consultants with relatively little staff involvement) as an intrusive examination of their claims. The internal or improving agenda is less well developed and this is reflected in a thinner literature. It is distinguished from the proving agenda in two key respects: first, it is typically implemented by MFI staff themselves; and second, the knowledge generated is consciously and systematically directed to the refinement of service delivery.

The *Imp-Act* programme has been influenced by both agendas. However, from its inception in 1998, its emphasis has been on action research to strengthen the internal improving agenda. Intellectually, it draws heavily on an actor-oriented sociology of development (Long, 1992), the philosophy of participatory action research, and the challenge offered by the question, posed originally by Robert Chambers (1997), of 'whose reality counts?'. By better understanding of the livelihood options and constraints of poor people, as perceived by the poor clients themselves, MFIs can more effectively address poverty reduction through adapting their financial services and through identifying non-financial constraints that delimit the potential effectiveness of their products.

The improving agenda is important for financial sustainability. For example, many MFIs suffer from high exit rates, which are costly. Improving staff–client relations can also help to improve repayment rates. But the improving agenda is also important for poverty reduction. As elaborated in Chapter 2, the trade-off between poverty outreach and financial sustainability is real; other things being equal, it costs more to lend to the poor than to the non-poor. MFIs, under pressure to demonstrate financial sustainability, have suffered from mission drift away from poor households. By improving their knowledge of client's livelihoods and the role of financial services, MFIs can address this trade-off.

In some contexts, where there are many poor people with well-known livelihood strategies and needs, the trade-off has been shown (by SHARE in India, for example) to be manageable with effective leadership and commitment to a social mission throughout the organization (Todd, 2001). SHARE accesses commercial funding that would not be forthcoming if they were not profitable, yet at the same time they have an impressive record on poverty outreach.[2] In other contexts managing the trade-off is more complex, such as in South Africa where staff costs are high, the local economy is depressed and there is a weaker knowledge base on livelihood strategies for the poor. But, as SEF have demonstrated, the trade-off can be managed through attention to an improving agenda (Baumann, 2004).

Choice of assessment methods

'If practitioner organizations have the institutional will, resources and skill to carry out a multi-year longitudinal impact evaluation with comparison groups, this would be the best, most valid, and most widely accepted approach' (AIMS-SEEP, 2000). Many *Imp-Act* partners took as their starting point the tool kit developed by the SEEP network under AIMS, the USAID microenterprise programme. These tools were groundbreaking in their approach to impact. They charted a new direction by focusing on the needs of MFI practitioners. Developed by and for practitioners, the tools emphasized the case for collecting data that was reliable, useful, timely and cost-effective, with academic standards of rigour.

The AIMS-SEEP manual (2000) has five tools: the impact survey; the client exit survey; loan use and savings strategies over time; client satisfaction; and client empowerment. Two are quantitative and three are qualitative. They are described as mid-range tools. The manual provides a conceptual framework for assessing impact and a thorough discussion of the options on methods. As the quotation above indicates, the authors were very aware of the value of comparison groups and longitudinal data. However, their purpose was not just to focus on precision, but also to develop methods that were practical, cost effective and relevant. They steer a midway between the precise and the useful in their development of indicators, instruments, training and analysis. They also emphasize the importance of context and the need to refine the tools to account for the specific mission and circumstances of individual MFIs.

The *Imp-Act* programme shared a similar focus. It saw opportunities to push further with the agenda of organizational learning and the challenge of adapting and using these and other tools to meet both internal and external data needs. The AIMS-SEEP manual is very clear on being a practical tool for MFIs. The manual and the work of *Imp-Act* have highlighted the many and very real process issues entailed in measuring impact usefully. But this does not mean that deeper methodological issues, highlighted by many authoritative reviews, somehow go away.[3] The challenge is to find ways to minimize and manage the difficulties, rather than achieve the almost impossibly expensive task and complex scientific challenge of completely solving them.

One example is the attribution problem of how to be sure that observed changes to impact indicators occur as a direct result of MFI services. The usual approach to this problem is to use a control or comparison group, that is, a set of individuals and their households that are comparable with members and their households in every respect except that they do not receive MFI services. However, this introduces the problem of selection bias. Without random assignment of services between potential clients there will always be a good chance that there are significant underlying differences, such as entrepreneurial talent, between the client and control group.[4] For independent observers of microfinance this problem can completely undermine the validity of a study. But for practitioners who are closer to the ground, and have direct experience of the context, it is one factor that has to be taken into account in assessing the validity of findings relative to other sources of evidence.

Education and skills, assets, occupation and enterprise type and age, poverty status, member age, family size, sources of loans, patterns of savings (beyond MFI services), access to infrastructure and distance to market are some of the commonest variables thought to be important in specifying an appropriate control group. If all such sources of difference between the control and the members are tested and are shown to be insignificant, then the problem of selection bias can be disregarded. However, it is difficult, as our case studies testify, to achieve this, especially because only some of these variables can really be known prior to inclusion in a survey. In addition, there is no firm standard to determine degrees of accuracy in reported results or how to assess more qualitative data that can inform the judgement of reliability.

Sometimes the control group is a random selection of eligible non-members from the locality or a neighbouring village; often new members are used as a control to compare with existing members. Both approaches are fraught with problems in ensuring that the two groups are comparable in all essential respects except receipt of financial services.[5] Nevertheless, it is the preferred method for most MFIs because, carefully done with a discussion of the attendant risks and how they were addressed, it does provide a basis for evidence on welfare differences between the groups that may be attributable to financial services provided to one and not the other group.[6]

Similarly, the problem of fungibility is effectively addressed if the sources of funds and expenditure patterns of the two groups are essentially similar prior to receipt of MFI services, so that the additionality of those services is established. *Imp-Act* partners have used control groups, often new members as proposed in the AIMS-SEEP manual, to address the proving agenda but have put most effort, as the second half of this book discusses in detail, in to the organizational learning agenda to improve social performance.

MFI impacts: the state of knowledge

The growth of the global microfinance industry has been accompanied by many impact studies of all shades of scientific quality. Among the most rigorous is a World Bank study in Bangladesh, described by Khandker (2003) and Khandker and Pitt (2002). This used cross-sectional data with a control group and then added a re-survey to create a two-period panel data set. Particular care was taken to deal with the problems of method discussed above. The results, on three major Bangladesh programmes, demonstrate a substantial improvement in income for the very poor and the existence of spillover effects to non-clients in the programme villages. A range of direct and wider impacts in the social domain was also identified. However, this World Bank study entailed the use of a long questionnaire and many person-months of data processing and analysis; it does not represent a model for others. It is valuable in showing the resources required to develop results that pass the 'science' test and confirms that the tenor of results from less sophisticated studies, showing positive impact, is supported when rigorous methods are adopted.

Whilst many other studies have documented individuals using microfinance to move out of poverty, the more common story is of more marginal improvement.[7] BRAC (1996), in a well-designed study, showed that the level of economic vibrancy in the local economy is a key determinant of these differential outcomes. *Imp-Act* results, for example from the Philippines, have shown the same problem of only marginal improvement for many female clients and raise the question of the existence of a 'glass ceiling' for women borrowers in some occupations.

A comprehensive survey of studies by Morduch and Haley (2002) concurs with a generally positive view that microfinance does contribute directly to the achievement of six of the eight Millennium Development Goals. It is based on evidence in relation to impacts on income and assets including housing and sanitation, education enrolment, female status and health-seeking behaviour. Ultimately, sustained poverty reduction for the household depends on improvements in labour productivity in order to expand the material basis of livelihoods; injections of working capital will not automatically deliver this, though of course they can.

A contrasting set of studies, reported in Lont and Hospes (2004), provides detailed evidence from anthropologists and sociologists on the ways in which MFI services fit into household livelihood strategies. The authors are generally critical of the failure of impact studies to locate their findings in broader analyses of household livelihood strategies.[8] In several cases, the broader functions of the organization through which clients receive services are identified as more complex and multi-functional than a simple vehicle for service delivery. These organizations include, or are moulded on, religious societies, burial societies and labour groups as well as purposive microfinance groups established by external agencies. They are embedded in broader social arrangements, thus the bolting on of financial services, building on existing social capital, can cause conflict and undermine that social capital as well as produce negative outcomes for the sustainability of the financial services (Hospes and Prosé, 2004; Smets and Bähre, 2004). These studies of livelihood and microfinance support the *Imp-Act* emphasis upon developing greater knowledge of clients to improve organizational performance, but also encourage recognition of the social context in which services are delivered and how these help determine impact.

Imp-Act *partner results*

We have referred above to the *Imp-Act* programme emphasis on improving by organizational learning about what clients need and how to deliver it. As an integral part of that learning, several partners made a serious attempt to assess direct material impact in ways that paid attention to the difficulties discussed above. The commonest indicators used were sales, turnover, gross income and profits for the main enterprise financed by the loan. MFIs added to this more context- or programme-specific data, such as employment generated, business location and restocking expenditure. The most widely used approach was to adapt the impact assessment survey and the loan use and savings tools from the AIMS-SEEP manual. Others relied on survey instruments that they developed themselves in collaboration with university partners.

In broad terms, the main conclusion from these results was that MFI financial services had contributed to an improvement in economic conditions as reflected in improvements in incomes and assets. This was true for all MFIs but not for all branches and certainly not for all clients. Data are not available to produce comparable figures on the extent of income poverty reduction. This chapter reports on findings and implications from eight studies.[9]

PROMUC

PROMUC is a Peruvian network of 12 NGOs operating community banks called *La Chanchita*. These are both rural and urban and are mainly directed towards women operating small enterprises, mainly in trading and agriculture, depending on geographic area. PROMUC undertook a variety of impact assessment activities including use of the QUIP (*Imp-Act*, 2004b) approach, use of adapted AIMS tools on client satisfaction and dropouts, focus group discussions, individual interviews and a survey.[10] The qualitative research is particularly valuable in providing insights on why change occurs, especially explanations of why some clients experienced negative changes and others more positive changes, but it does not provide a sufficient evidence base on impact, without being complemented by more representative survey data.

The quantitative survey was conducted in two rounds (August and September 2001 and August and September 2002) to examine the quantitative impacts of microfinance programmes with two partners, Alternativa and Araiwa. PROMUC interviewed 769 clients in the first round and 607 non-clients as a control group. In the second round the organization was able to re-interview 547 clients and 391 of the original control group, falling to 388 after merging and cleaning the data set. Using this data set of 935 observations, one particularly useful assessment examined changes in four material impact variables for each household: changes in enterprise sales and profits, family income and individual monthly income.

The statistical analysis tested whether the differences in change were themselves significantly different between the clients and the control group. The analysis showed that both family and client income variables were significantly different. Client households had seen larger increases in incomes.[11] However, the coefficient on profits was not significant in the regressions, even after outliers had been eliminated, and the coefficient for enterprise sales was only weakly significant. Only one variable, change in quality of business management, was negatively associated with membership and it is not clear from the reports why this is so, though one explanation suggests that clients were starting from a higher level of management.

The analysis went on to examine whether the differences between members and the control group were possibly explained by initial differences or selection bias, that is, heterogeneity between the control and the clients. This analysis found some factors, such as age, partner's income and access to family credit were significant in explaining change in individual monthly income, but the coefficient on membership remained large and significant. Assuming that the variables tested captured all the relevant sources of heterogeneity, these results provide a strong evidence base for the positive impact of these two programmes.

One potential limitation was the high attrition rate between survey rounds, as high as 43 per cent for the control group in one area. This is cause for concern if there is a systematic reason for omission, for example, business failure and unwillingness to discuss that failure, since it could bias the reliability of the coefficients for either of the samples. However, tests[12] of key characteristics did not establish any significant differences between those clients with one round of data and those with two and, specifically, the attrition cases were not likely to be poorer. Through conducting tests such as this, and more generally through attention to methodological concerns as described in their various papers, PROMUC is one of the few *Imp-Act* partners whose results might be regarded by most as technically sensitive to the conceptual problems of accurate impact assessment discussed earlier.

The PROMUC reports also state that 62 per cent (Alternativa) and 75 per cent (Araiwa) of the sample members were above the poverty line. The CGAP poverty assessment (see Chapter 2) had established that within their regions of work the selection of clients was directed towards poorer members, which suggests that PROMUC consortium members are not working in the poorer regions of Peru. It is not appropriate, therefore, to assess the very real gains by members as poverty reduction according to a dollar-a-day definition. PROMUC is one of the four *Imp-Act* partners that attempted an estimate of the poverty level of their clients as a part of assessing impact and the results underline the importance of knowing the poverty status of clients at entry.

CARD

CARD has over 100,000 clients in the Philippines and is operationally self-sufficient. Originally an NGO, CARD became a registered bank in 1997 and operates essentially as a Grameen replicate. In the Philippines, traditional impact assessment is seen as an activity by and for donors, however, CARD developed its activities in close association with the Microfinance Council of the Philippines (MCPI)[13] and their participation in the *Imp-Act* programme was designed not just to allow them to effectively monitor their own social performance, but to promote country-wide learning on impact assessment.

CARD used a monitoring form, labelled a means test, as a pilot client entry form. Through using it with older clients and taking recall data, the organization was able to examine programme impact. It used five indicators on a sample of 591 members selected proportionately in different age-of-membership cohorts. The survey produced findings by cohort on housing condition, food security, per capita income, value of productive assets and school attendance. Only two of these, per capita income and housing, showed positive results in the comparison between mature members and new members. However, there was some concern over reliability of the data for per capita income, though in fact the main purpose of using the data was to develop client entry and monitoring forms rather than as a test of impact.

The housing index scores, reproduced in Figure 3.1, were also based on recall for mature members, but there was confidence in their reliability in measuring changing quality of housing assets. The results indicated that mature members had managed to improve their housing condition and this is a continuing improvement with membership age. The results also showed the dangers of using new members as a control group because there was a significant difference between scores on the index at entry for mature and new members. CARD shared the widespread *Imp-Act* partner concerns about mission drift and this concern was supported by the better conditions of new client housing at entry. The results suggest that comparisons with new members are likely to underestimate achieved programme impacts on mature members.

The main focus of CARD was on the improving agenda, both in relation to assessment of outreach and in appropriate service delivery through use of a client satisfaction tool. One core concern was the development and pilot implementation of a model for an impact assessment and monitoring information system. Another was its promotion within the MCPI network through helping to build the capacities of MFIs to conduct monitoring and impact assessment. CARD's work was directed at helping MFIs in the Philippines address issues of mission drift by improving knowledge in a systematized way on their poverty outreach. It also sought to demonstrate that financial sustainability could be served effectively through greater attention to client assessment.

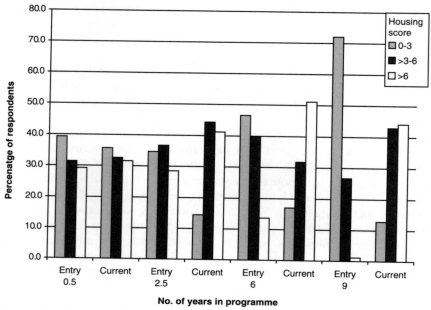

Figure 3.1 CARD housing index results

One example of this was the organization's work on exit tracking, which showed that the majority of the 25 per cent of clients who had left had done so because of the lack of access to compulsory savings and because of the mutual guarantees on loan repayment among group members. Given the costs involved in new member recruitment and group formation, as well as the slowdown in growth of loan size associated with replacing dropouts, the high level of dropouts was undermining financial performance. Like Grameen itself,[14] CARD is now revisiting those operating principles that contribute to high dropout and looking at alternative approaches in the light of these findings.

FINCA

FINCA has some 250,000 current clients in 17,000 village banks in 24 country programmes on four continents. FINCA's international network has focused on financial sustainability and has achieved operational self-sufficiency, but the measurement of FINCA's compliance with its *social* mission of poverty alleviation has been largely neglected. Its results on outreach showed that, 'using the US$1-a-day definition of poverty, among 981 new clients in 11 countries, only 4 per cent are severely poor (<US$1 a day), 12 per cent are moderately poor (US$1–2 a day), and 84 per cent are non-poor (>US$2 a day). By this standard not a single FINCA programme is even close to minimum social mission compliance' (Hatch and Crompton, 2003).

FINCA's involvement in *Imp-Act* was primarily directed towards an improving agenda and most specifically towards improving their outreach by developing client entry data that assessed poverty status. The approach it adopted, described in Chapter 2, was the most ambitious within the *Imp-Act* programme, involving the estimation of poverty outreach for 11 country partners. It also included an assessment of economic and social impacts. The report is strongest on social impacts but also includes an assessment of household expenditure.

Based on results across 11 countries, the average daily per capita expenditure for new clients was US$2.10, that of current clients US$2.27, that of ex-clients US$2.23, and that of non-clients US$2.12.[15] The report concludes that outreach was not segmented but spread across the community proportionately and that membership of FINCA did result in modest income improvements. The study also looked at gross income earnings from enterprises supported through loans and found that FINCA clients earned an average of US$10.73 per day, 130 per cent more than non-clients (US$4.65), 36 per cent more than new clients (US$7.91), and 21 per cent more than ex-clients (US$8.86). This was further support for the welfare benefits from programme participation.

The analysis included an assessment of housing assets and the study found that income increases had resulted in better housing, where the average score (in an inverse ranking) was 1.8 among clients versus 2.2 for non-clients, indicating that overall the former saw themselves as 18 per cent better off than the latter. This difference was established for 10 of the 11 countries surveyed, Kyrgyzstan being the exception.

The FINCA research established some significant impacts but also raised concerns about the scope of these impacts, the poverty status of beneficiaries and missed opportunities for new products. It led to a set of recommendations designed to help FINCA focus more effectively on its social performance agenda, as set out in Box 3.1. The FINCA recommendations are a good example of the positive responses on social performance that have arisen directly as a consequence of the learning associated with the *Imp-Act* research.

CMF

CMF is a service organization promoting and supporting the microfinance industry in Nepal through research, training, advisory and advocacy activities. In *Imp-Act*, it worked especially with savings and credit organizations (SACCOs) in the hill regions of Nepal. These SACCOs are partners of special interest since they are the only legally constituted cooperative MFIs in the action-research programme. CMF, as one of its research activities, assessed impact in four SACCOs through a carefully designed and implemented cross-sectional survey. A key finding was that of differential performance between the programme-initiated SACCOs and those that were self-started by members of the community without any external catalyst. Specifically, the programme-promoted SACCOs were better on poverty reduction performance. This is a potentially important finding, particularly if it applies to other models where

Box 3.1

First, at the level of senior management and regional directors, establish consensus regarding FINCA's mission and vision, supplemented by a policy document that describes how poverty will be defined, what performance expectations will be implemented, and how exceptions to these norms will be handled, based on special regional or country conditions.

Second, where market saturation and scarce populations of unserved poor and very poor families can be documented, shift client selection criteria from 'poor and poorest' to 'least well-served', then mount an aggressive marketing/publicity campaign to entice clients away from other financial service providers.

Third, entrust the FINCA International Research Department with the responsibility of monitoring compliance with FINCA International's social mission. This will include: 1) four monthly reports to the board of directors on FINCA mission compliance; 2) continuation of poverty assessment research; 3) developing tools for mapping poverty niches; and 4) training regional directors and field staff in their use.

Fourth, in at least three FINCA country programmes – preferably one per region – institutionalize the client assessment methodology, training field staff to routinely conduct poverty assessments of new clients and monitor social performance metrics over time.

Fifth, to help ensure compliance with its social mission, FINCA will encourage its field programmes to implement – at the national and (where applicable) sub-national levels – a new position to be known as 'social performance manager'. This officer will supervise poverty mapping, poverty assessment, impact evaluations and market research activities. She or he will assist in the development of new products and services that capture opportunities identified in the monthly reports, and also promote, supervise and evaluate efforts to re-energize village banks as support groups.

Source: FINCA (2004)

both self-started and programme-supported MFIs exist; it could be relevant, for example, to the adoption of different approaches to SHG development in India and elsewhere in South Asia.

CMF used purposive sampling of clusters and then random sampling to select 400 member and 200 non-member households in the area of four SACCOs. Preparation of village profiles and conduct of institutional audits was followed by a survey on impact. Well-being ranking was used to identify poverty categories locally and results were used to draw the sample proportionately from among the categories (probability proportional to size sampling). The results showed that members had higher incomes and more livestock and jewellery assets than non-members. As Table 3.1 illustrates, members also used their higher incomes to spend more on education and food than non-members. The proportion of members who had made a profit using their last loan varied from over 98 per cent in one SACCO to less than 23 per cent in the worst performing. Differences in profits are explained through

Table 3.1 CMF expenditure patterns from four hill-region SACCOs

	Expenditure pattern			
	Per-capita expense on household food consumption (NRs*)	Ratio of health to total expense	Ratio of main asset purchase to total expense	Ratio of education to total expense
Member	10,488	6.44	10.58	8.40
Non-member	9,702	6.84	4.22	5.60
Member vs. non-member (t-value)	2.48**	–0.52	3.66**	3.36**

Source: CMF (2003)
Notes: *US$1 = NRs78; **significant at 5% level.

household links to the wider economy and the difference in availability of livelihood opportunities in agriculture and petty trade.

The results of the *Imp-Act* research were useful in promoting learning because CMF paid attention to working with board members and managers of the SACCOs so that there was a clear sense of ownership of findings. In particular, better training, better market research and a need to improve poverty outreach were implications that the board members drew from the results and CMF is now working with them to respond to these needs.

CERUDEB

CERUDEB is a fully licensed bank in Uganda with over 200,000 depositors and 46,000 borrowers. It is of particular interest because it is a formal financial sector institution and, like CMF partners in Nepal, represents a different model of financial service delivery to other *Imp-Act* partners. CERUDEB, as a private bank responsible to shareholders, has to focus on profitability but it also has a social mission to provide financial services to low-income clients and farmers. This distinguishes it from other formal sector financial institutions in Uganda that have very limited outreach to low-income borrowers or outside of Kampala.

Based on conclusions from earlier studies recommending more attention to monitoring impact, CERUDEB became an *Imp-Act* partner on an improving agenda. Its goal is to try to improve the effectiveness and efficiency of their services to clients, especially smallholders, through social mission compliance and new product development, including crop insurance. Prior to *Imp-Act* participation, the organization only collected data on numbers of clients and portfolio at risk; its strategy through *Imp-Act* was to develop a more substantial management information system to provide rapid access to current data by product and client. This information will be used for monitoring and allow the organization to expand its microfinance programme in ways that are consistent with its financial and social objectives.

As a part of these activities CERUDEB undertook an initial impact survey. It used random sampling techniques to select a sample of borrowers: 191 farmer members from six branches spread across four agro-climatic zones. The final report provides detailed findings by branch, followed by a cross-comparison. In all branches except one there was a significant increase in asset holdings. In the one branch, Kasese, where performance was poor, agricultural output was particularly badly affected by low prices, poor storage and drought; these conditions resulted in an average fall in agricultural sales income of 25 per cent. Non-farm income from side businesses also fell by 22 per cent. As a consequence, farmers were unable to service loans from income and sold assets instead. Sample clients from that branch 'registered reductions in expenses on food, entertainment, education, healthcare, agricultural inputs and salaries to labourers. This was generally caused by reductions in the free cash flows of farming businesses' (Centenary Rural Development Bank, 2004).

The contrast between the branches is evident from Table 3.2. In five of the branches it is clear that direct material impacts were substantial.[16] Better quality agricultural lands, more benign growing conditions and ability to store output to wait for favourable prices all contributed to the impacts achieved.

As expected, the five branches that performed well on assets also performed well on income, as shown in Table 3.3. 'Salary' in this table refers mainly to payments to labourers, some of whom are permanent, and the increases are evidence that multiplier effects are operating through this employment, as

Table 3.2 CERUDEB changes in average value of assets during loan period

Branch	Tororo	Mbale	Kyotera	Kasese	Mityana	Hoima
(1) Mean asset value before loan (Ush thousands)						
Residence land (no title)	2,923	3,662	7,815	4,450	1,850	7,333
Other land (no title)	1,880	2,036	1,045	459	400	2,113
Bicycle	42	45	34	65	13	38
Radio	57	99	61	96	34	30
Cattle	820	972	1,785	2,081	3,122	876
Sheep, goats and pigs	110	106	248	99	36	149
(2) Change in value of stated asset (%)						
Residence land (no title)	+53	+41	+31	−9	+36.2	0
Other land (no title)	+5	+16	+85	+61	+20	+59
Bicycle	+74	+7	+265	−4.6	+134	+23
Radio	+50	+6	+8	−40	+30	+20
Cattle	+30	+30	+116	−42	+43	+22
Sheep, goats and pigs	+19	+11	+6	+51	+95	−30.8

Source: Centenary Rural Development Bank (2004)

Table 3.3 CERUDEB – changes in average monthly incomes and expenses

Branch	Tororo	Mbale	Kyotera	Kasese	Mityana	Hoima
(1) Mean value of income/expenditure item before loan						
Side income	248,000	291,700	229,700	292,000	54,900	268,000
Food	48,400	110,713	17,100	66,000	49,100	50,600
Entertainment	9,300	46,100	2,900	25,194	8,400	11,300
School fees	46,100	75,500	34,300	140,000	31,000	51,513
Healthcare	22,300	97,700	12,200	20,600	14,400	20,000
Sales	308,900	1,148,700	218,600	758,000	572,900	809,000
Ag. inputs	166,800	219,000	46,800	272,900	133,000	208,400
Salary	65,300	56,300	18,100	111,600	36,395	128,600
(2) Change in value of stated item of income/expenditure after loan (%)						
Side income	+51	+36	+43	−22	+206	+6
Food	+27.4	+37	+44	−15	+18	+29
Entertainment	+147	+5.6	+63	−26	+37	+35
School fees	+3	+20	+115	−1.4	+48	+57
Healthcare	+8	+4	47	−11	+22	+6
Sales	+26	+44	+5	−25	+64	+14
Ag. inputs	+33	+265	+124	−18	+34	+14
Salary	+44	+90	+48	−16	−2	+46

Source: Centenary Rural Development Bank (2004)

well as through the increased value of transactions in agricultural input and output markets.

Similar changes to those reported in the Tables 3.2 and 3.3 were also reported for asset ownership and savings. In the five branches that performed well, average savings with CERUDEB increased by 46 per cent to 220 per cent, depending on branch. By contrast, in Kasese, savings decreased by 24 per cent. CERUDEB learnt from cross-branch analysis about product performance and suitability of products given the cash-flow patterns of their target clients. It is also incorporating key questions from the impact form into the loan application form for clients and is utilizing software that will allow impact to be an integral part of its management information system. One specific response to the differences in performance across branches, and in particular the agriculture-related problems in Kasese, is that CERUDEB is actively developing a crop insurance product.

SHARE

SHARE is a Grameen replicant operating since 1993 in Andhra Pradesh, India, and had over 130,000 clients in 2003 with a 100 per cent repayment rate. SHARE is operationally self-sufficient and has a strong financial record that has enabled it to borrow funds commercially. In 2001, a study, led by Helen Todd, used the five AIMS tools to undertake an assessment of impact (Todd, 2001).

The report is one of the most comprehensive under the *Imp-Act* programme; one of its strengths is the case studies (see Chapter 4) describing the pathways out of poverty for 25 clients and the wide range of impacts identified.

The report also gives a detailed account of the direct material gains achieved. It is based on data collected from 125 clients and 104 new clients. SHARE has a good record-keeping system and collects poverty status data on entry. This made it possible to compare the status of mature clients at the time of the survey with programme entry status (all but two of the sample were on their third or fourth loan cycle). Poverty status was based on four equally weighted indicators: sources of income, productive assets, quality of housing and the dependency ratio.[17] Scores on these indicators were grouped into three poverty categories, as reported in Table 3.4. The table shows that over three-quarters of client households had seen a reduction in their poverty, with only two cases recorded of a worsening of client poverty status.

The widespread reduction of household poverty is confirmed through the comparison of mature and new clients, as shown in Table 3.5. This result, unlike the case of several other *Imp-Act* partners, does not suffer from potential selection bias because the entry-level data of the two groups were tested and found to be essentially similar. The analysis of results showed that the number of income earners in a household and income diversification were key reasons for change in poverty status.

SHARE started as a pilot action-research project exploring models of micro-finance service delivery and they remain committed to a learning agenda; they

Table 3.4 SHARE sample estimates of poverty reduction

Poverty movement	Mature clients	%	Cumulative
Very poor to moderately poor	48	38.4	38.4
Very poor to non poor	22	17.6	56
Moderately poor to non poor	26	20.8	76.8
No change	27	21.6	
Non poor to moderately poor	1	0.8	
Moderately poor to very poor	1	0.8	
Totals	**125**	**100**	

Source: Todd (2001)

Table 3.5 SHARE overall poverty status of mature and new clients

Sample group	Very poor	Moderately poor	Not poor
Mature clients	6%	58%	37%
New clients	58%	39%	4%

Source: Todd (2001)

are aware of the experiences with the Grameen model elsewhere, including Grameen itself, and have been ready to make changes to avoid the problems identified. Two such changes are greater flexibility in access to savings and a greater diversity of savings products. Members reported that these were important features of SHARE and allowed them to avoid going to other loan providers, even moneylenders. Indeed, 71 per cent of the mature clients reported that they had not borrowed outside of SHARE during the previous year. Of those (29 per cent) that had borrowed externally most (64 per cent) said that they had borrowed from moneylenders or relatives charging interest. More than half used these loans for business development (to buy inputs or to expand their activities) and the rest borrowed for consumption needs: weddings and funerals, household needs or house repair, school fees or the health needs of their children.

SHARE has an enviable reputation amongst MFIs for being effective in poverty outreach and impact and achieving commercial viability at the same time. Its social performance management is embedded within its programme, including staff training, client selection and entry data recording, loan use monitoring and management commitment to a sustainable poverty reduction agenda. The *Imp-Act* results confirm that this commitment is reflected in performance and their reputation is well deserved.

SAT

SAT is the leading provider of microenterprise and small-business loans and business support services in Ghana and works in over 100 communities. SAT's objectives in the *Imp-Act* programme were the development of 'holistic client transformation indicators' and their integration into management information systems. They applied the AIMS tools using a sample of mature (>two years in the programme), former and new clients, as detailed in Table 3.6. This sample was selected from a client base of over 40,000 people from six branches distributed across four regions. The analysis of results showed that there was significant economic progress. Mature clients had on average been in the programme for two to three years and received five loans with an average current loan amount of US$238. More than half (52 per cent) of the clients had used their last loan solely for business purposes, including

Table 3.6 SAT sample selection and instruments used

Client type	Impact survey	Exit survey	Loans and savings use	Empowerment	Client satisfaction
Mature clients	312		56	49	171 (19 groups)
New clients	259				
Former clients		178			
Total	571	178	56	49	171

Source: Sinapi Aba Trust (2004)

vegetable selling (29 per cent), petty trading (15 per cent) and clothing (11 per cent). Main non-business uses were for food, school fees, minor household assets and utilities. Most (92 per cent) of the clients had financed their microenterprises with SAT loans, while 4 per cent had borrowed from family members and 1 per cent from moneylenders. None of the respondents had borrowed from commercial banks, other loans programmes or other group members.

The results showed that 78 per cent of the mature clients increased their business income during the 12 months prior to the survey and this was a statistically significant increase compared to that reported by the comparison group of new clients who had not yet received any loan. Moreover, four-fifths of new clients had to seek additional working capital during the 12 months prior to the survey, but this was true for less than half of SAT's mature clients. As Table 3.7 shows, there was also a significant increase in savings by mature members.

The increase in business income resulted in a greater number of mature clients who reported contributing significantly to their household budget (63.6 per cent), leading to increasing ability to provide sufficiently for their families in terms of food (67 per cent), payment of school fees (40.7 per cent), medical bills (44.7 per cent) and family funerals (36 per cent). About half of the mature clients (49 per cent) invested in their housing. For nearly all the mature clients, their microenterprise was the largest source of income to support the household. The results also showed that mature clients were less likely to have experienced hungry times than new clients. The results on former clients showed 'a relatively high degree of satisfaction' (Hishigsuren, 2003), with a majority wanting to rejoin even though most had originally left voluntarily. The reasons for exit were largely to do with delays in loan disbursements, group conflict and discomfort with the lending methodology.

The economic impacts for SAT clients were positive, though there were some negative findings in other domains (such as less involvement in community affairs). SAT did not use this research as a one-off exercise in impact assessment but as the basis for the development of a client impact monitoring system (CIMS).[18] It adapted the AIMS tools to ensure coverage in the research of eight domains that it identified as important for assessing client poverty on entry and for subsequent assessment of progress. These were: business employment,

Table 3.7 SAT members' improvement in savings volume

Average amount saved per month	Mean (cedis)	Mean (US$)	P value
Mature clients	196,468	28	
New clients	127,867	18	0.00*

Source: Sinapi Aba Trust (2004)

Note: *Statistically significant difference at 95% confidence level using Chi-square test.

personal cash savings, housing, children's education, decision-making, community involvement, religious involvement and health. SAT developed indicators and a points system for performance in these domains. It then categorized the scores into three levels of poverty and compared the scores of mature and new clients, as shown in Table 3.8.

The results showed that, according to the CIMS aggregate, SAT was reaching poor and very poor households in most cases. The use of client entry data also showed that mature clients had moved up from an average score of 16.8 upon programme entry to an average score at the time of the survey of 18.7. This compared to an average of 18 for the new clients and, as Table 3.8 shows, 17 per cent of these new clients were from the non-poor category. These scores for poverty have not yet been tested against national poverty measures but SAT is reasonably confident that they reflect the distribution of poverty nationally. SAT is now integrating its CIMS with its computerized MIS to provide information for management decision making on meeting the needs of clients.

LAPO

LAPO was established in 1987 and currently operates in six states of Nigeria, using a group lending methodology and with a membership of over 25,000. LAPO was one of the most active *Imp-Act* partners in developing a client monitoring system, which is based on its participation form. This is a form that has been designed to capture client poverty status on entry and then to monitor client status at the beginning of each new loan cycle. LAPO has invested heavily in developing the form and refining ways that allow both ease of data collection and comparability with national-level poverty estimates. The organization has also invested in integrating the instrument into its management information system and in training staff on the appropriate use of the form.

The importance of staff training is documented in the final report: 'Another major influence of the *Imp-Act* programme for LAPO is the change in staff attitudes and behaviour. The process of implementation of the *Imp-Act* project has cushioned the practice of field staff to deliberately admit the least poor into the programme while excluding the poorest from programme' (Garuba,

Table 3.8 SAT results on their client impact monitoring system

Levels	Definition	Points	Mature clients	New clients
Level 1	Very poor	Up to 15 points	32%	38%
Level 2	Poor	16–25 points	52%	45%
Level 3	Not poor	Above 25 points	16%	17%

Source: Sinapi Aba Trust (2004)

2004). This statement reflects both a high level of integrity with respect to reporting problems faced, an integrity reflected throughout its reporting, and the way in which the introduction of the participation (poverty monitoring) data collection has influenced staff attitudes positively. During the *Imp-Act* programme LAPO became one of the most important examples of progress on social performance and this was driven, above all, by a senior management committed to social goals. LAPO used its participation in the programme to promote far-reaching changes in products, staff training and management information to achieve effective poverty outreach and impact.

Summarizing the results

These results on impact demonstrate that *Imp-Act* MFIs are providing services through which their clients are achieving significant direct material gains. There are examples of negative impacts, the Kasese branch of CERUDEB being a serious case. These are usually related to the wider economy and underline the importance of context in evaluating impact findings. They are also valuable for organizational learning; the CERUDEB response of seeking to develop a crop insurance scheme is a good example. The results also demonstrate that these gains were achieved regardless of the specific MFI service delivery model. Results from other *Imp-Act* partners are also available, but the case studies reported here are those for which the information base is most complete and reliable. There are no cases for which this overall picture of generally positive results is not true.

In some cases, such as BRAC, the MFIs' objectives within the *Imp-Act* programme did not focus on measuring direct material impact because existing knowledge was already strong. These MFIs had other research priorities, such as micro insurance and wider social and financial market effects in the case of BRAC. In Central and Eastern Europe and the Newly Independent States, *Imp-Act* partners focused on the improving agenda and other aspects of impact – wider impacts and client exit – rather than direct material impact. CYSD and PRADAN, working in poor and excluded communities in rural India, have not been discussed here because their programmes are best understood in a more holistic context: microfinance is only one of several services they provide in their models of community-level intervention. Nevertheless, with regard to direct material impacts of microfinance, their results were also positive.

The key feature of the action research was the use of the impact assessment process to promote organizational learning on social performance. We have briefly described this for each partner but their reports provide further detailed evidence both on lessons learnt and actions taken in response. In several cases, actions included the integration of outreach and impact assessment into client entry, loan application and renewal forms, together with the computer storage of such data and the use of appropriate software to utilize it effectively.

Conclusion

Imp-Act partners are able to demonstrate that their services are directly improving the material assets of client households. This has been achieved through three main routes: enterprise development, loan use for household asset acquisition and enhanced savings. The impacts of microfinance interact most obviously in the case of asset acquisition and income generation, but also in less tangible ways. Group membership, for example, has sometimes boosted earnings opportunities and the courage to exploit them. Also length of membership and the total value of loans received have been significant in several cases in the attribution of impact by MFI researchers. At least two MFIs, however, reported a slowdown in earnings growth eventually. This is important to various notions of 'graduation' (out of poverty, from MFI membership to formal finance, to self-sustainability of livelihood). Nevertheless, the research demonstrated that one of the sector weaknesses is insufficient knowledge about the progress MFI clients make over time. A more widespread adoption of institutionalized systems of poverty monitoring could provide important and more comprehensive evidence on the progress out of poverty achieved through the provision of microfinance services.

Imp-Act partners usually handled the key problem of attribution by using comparison groups (non-members or new members) and this has been a valuable source of insight into impact pathways, allowing different characteristics of households, families and enterprises to be compared. This is a rich vein for analysis of impact that has only been partially mined to date. Despite the immense value of the research, the *Imp-Act* partners faced the full range of difficulties in implementing their studies. Sampling procedures, identifying and interviewing comparison groups, design of instruments, staff training, data analysis and report write-up were all problems of varying seriousness. Organizational capacity and commitment were challenged and, sometimes, managing partnerships with consultants was taxing. The support and networking available as a result of the *Imp-Act* programme helped to address, if not resolve, some of these problems.[19]

Despite the problems, most *Imp-Act* partners welcomed the opportunity to engage in impact assessment and to ensure that real and significant organizational changes resulted from the findings. Several *Imp-Act* partners went further and deliberately tried to institutionalize social performance assessment within their programmes (see Chapter 8). This was a mixed experience but resulted in important examples of progress that can inform further development within the industry. In several cases change processes were quickly initiated. Products were refined, staff training and incentives modified, and areas of operation changed as a result of impact assessment activities. The *Imp-Act* partner reports demonstrate clearly that learning has begun, but there is a need for further promotion of a social performance agenda building on knowledge about clients and on product impacts on client welfare.

CHAPTER FOUR
Direct social impacts for the Millennium Development Goals

Naila Kabeer

Introduction[1]

A great deal of the analysis relating to microfinance has focused on two core drivers: outreach to poor households and the financial sustainability of the microfinance organization. Where attention has been paid to impact, it has increasingly fallen on economic impacts in terms of household income, savings and assets, as seen in the previous chapter. While social concerns were very much alive when microfinance and microenterprise development began in the 1980s; they soon drifted into the background as concerns with financial sustainability came to the forefront. Yet, as the Millennium Development Goals (MDGs) (displayed in Box 4.1) remind us, poverty is only partly encompassed by economic concerns. Microfinance has the potential to impact on the wider dimensions of poverty as well and hence to contribute to the achievement of the MDGs (Kabeer, 2003b; Littlefield *et al*, 2003).

Box 4.1

Goal 1 Eradicate extreme poverty and hunger

Goal 2 Achieve universal primary education

Goal 3 Promote gender equality and empower women

Goal 4 Reduce child mortality

Goal 5 Improve maternal health

Goal 6 Combat HIV/AIDS, malaria and other diseases

Goal 7 Ensure environmental sustainability

Goal 8 Develop a Global Partnership for Development

Given that different organizations operate in very different contexts, face different kinds of challenges and address them through different kinds of strategies, not all forms of microfinance provision give equal importance to the achievement of social impacts. This chapter seeks to synthesize the evidence from the *Imp-Act* programme of 'direct social impacts'.[2] However, before we move to a discussion of the findings, we elaborate on what is meant by social impacts, as well as the distinction between direct and indirect social impacts. This will help to provide the analytical framework for the subsequent discussion.

Integrating the 'social' into impact assessment

The concept of 'the social' has been used to make a variety of distinctions within different disciplines (Kabeer, 2004). Economists generally use it in distinction to 'the economic', by which they imply the domain of the market and the profit-maximizing forms of behaviour that characterize this domain. Money-metric measures of poverty, with their focus on household income or expenditure, reflect this 'economic' understanding of poverty. The 'social' dimensions of poverty, from this perspective, reflect the recognition that poverty is a multidimensional phenomenon. The poor are characterized not only by low levels of income and assets, but also by other tangible and intangible forms of disadvantage, such as illiteracy, poor health, isolation, material dependency, sense of powerlessness and fatalism, all of which add to their vulnerability (Chambers, 1992; Appudarai, 1989). A social understanding of poverty takes account of these other deficits that matter to people, sometimes more than money.

The concept of 'capability', put forward by Amartya Sen (1987) to challenge money-metric approaches to poverty, represents the other end of spectrum to that of 'vulnerability'. It refers to the potential that people have to achieve valued ways of 'being and doing'. Such potential is embodied in the resources that people have at their disposal, together with their capacity to utilize these resources in ways that achieve valued outcomes, in other words, their agency. The resources in question might include various economic resources, including the financial services that MFIs provide, the human resources (nutrition, health, education, skills, knowledge) that people bring to their efforts, as well as the various affiliations and networks that they draw on in their search for survival, security and prosperity.

A second meaning of 'the social', the sense in which sociologists use the term, is defined in relation to 'the individual'. This notion of the social is used to challenge the idea that human beings are atomized individuals, driven by self-interest, competing with each other in the market place. Instead it argues that all individuals are part of, and influenced by, networks of social relations that shape their identity and provide an institutionalized framework of beliefs and values, claims and obligations, within which they act.

This interpretation also recognizes that these social relations are not necessarily egalitarian. In fact, they are often deeply hierarchical, giving rise to inequalities of resources, status and capabilities, some of which cut across economic strata. As a result, while the poor in general may be economically deprived relative to less poor sections of the population, they are also differentiated by gender, caste, religion, race and ethnicity, giving rise to socially excluded groups among the poor. A focus on the individual as the unit of analysis obscures the heterogeneity of poor people and the inequalities that divide them.

A social analysis of poverty has important implications for impact assessment methodology. In the first place, it broadens our understanding of the *substance* of change, in other words, of what it is that has changed. It suggests that, along with economic impacts of the kind dealt with in the previous chapter, we also need to explore other kinds of change that are likely to impact on the processes by which economic deprivation and social discrimination are reproduced within a society. Here we adapt the typology suggested by Chen and Mahmud (1995) to capture these other kinds of change. This includes:

- *Cognitive* change,[3] or change in how people think and what they know, about themselves and the world around them.
- *Behavioural* change, or change in how people choose to meet their needs and achieve their goals.
- *Material* change, or change in the resources available to individuals and groups to meet these needs and achieve these goals.
- *Relational* change, or change in how individuals perceive and interact with others and in how others perceive and interact with them.

A social analysis of poverty also widens our understanding of the *location* of change, that is, where change is likely to occur. It extends the search for impacts beyond the level of the individual and her enterprise to the different institutional domains of family, community, markets and state, whose rules, norms and practices combine to explain the societal patterns of economic deprivation and social discrimination that prevail in a society. In this chapter, we confine our analysis to impacts that occur within the family-based household, while in Chapter 5 we examine impacts in the wider society.

The household is the domain in which many decisions about household needs, priorities and goals are taken, including those that bear directly on the achievement of the MDGs. It is particularly important in relation to the MDG on gender equality and women's empowerment. Like most spheres of society, relations within the household tend to be organized along hierarchical lines, giving rise to inequalities between different members in their ability to participate in making critical decisions and setting priorities and goals. Gender, along with age, seniority and stage of life course are examples of the key forms of inequality that prevail within the household. The language of 'clients' and 'members' in the microfinance literature obscures the fact that the majority of the clients or members in question are women, and women from poor households. In so far as familial gender ideologies and practices play an important role in reproducing and legitimizing gender inequality within as well as beyond the household domain, intra-household relations are clearly important for assessing the gender-related impacts of microfinance and its potential to promote women's capabilities.

The organizations that are discussed in this chapter are those that included a concern with the direct social impacts in their assessment studies: CYSD, PRADAN and SHARE (India), CARD (Philippines), SAT (Ghana), LAPO (Nigeria) and PROMUC (Peru). Their missions and organizational strategies are summarized in Table 4.1. It is evident that the organizations in question vary considerably from each other. They vary in the contexts in which they operate, in their analysis of the problems they were seeking to address and in the organizational missions and strategies they adopted.

Consequently their reasons for including a concern with the social impacts of their work in their assessment studies also varied, as did the methodologies they used. Some, like CYSD and PRADAN, whose organizational strategies were explicitly geared to the achievement of social goals along with the promotion of livelihood strategies, had designed their own assessment methodologies to explore the extent to which these goals had been achieved. Others, like CARD, which had a more minimalist strategy, nevertheless believed that economic improvements in the lives of its clients would be translated into social impacts. It therefore used its study to identify key social indicators that could be included in its monitoring system. Still others included social indicators as part of the AIMS-SEEP methodological framework that they were testing. Table 4.2 reports on key features of the methodologies used by different organizations.

Given the differences in the contexts in which the organizations work and in their organizational strategies, we would not expect them to achieve uniform social impacts. However, it is not always possible to determine whether the reported variations in impact reflected differences in contexts, in methodologies or in organizational strategies. It is possible that many of the social impacts reported are the result of the linked-service strategy that some organizations provide along with their financial services. However, the provision of financial services may be an important factor in attracting clients so that the microfinance element of organizational strategy plays an indirect role in achieving these impacts.

The findings discussed in this chapter must be regarded as suggestive rather than conclusive, given the problems of attribution in impact assessment generally, together with the fact that most organizations did not have appropriate base-line data to carry out their impact analysis. As a result, they generally relied on comparisons of 'mature' members with either new or non-members. Greater reliance can be placed on the findings when some attempt was made to triangulate them through different methods or studies, or when the data collected allowed the pathways through which changes are likely to have occurred to be made explicit. For instance, access to microfinance services represents one set of the 'pathways' through which household-level changes, particularly the material changes documented in this chapter, are likely to have occurred.

Table 4.1 Organizational missions and strategies

MFI	Mission and strategy	Products	Rural	Women	Linkages
SHARE, India, established 1989	Specialized microfinance organization with the mission of alleviating poverty among the poorest of the poor, particularly women	–	Mixed	100%	–
CARD, Philippines, established 1986	Poverty-focused microfinance institution that provides credit and savings services through a solidarity group lending methodology and the Credit with Education programme	Group loans and voluntary savings	Rural	100%	Training and consulting
CYSD, India, established 1982	Development NGO with holistic approach to sustainable livelihoods and institutional development for socially excluded groups	Livelihood promotion, including SHGs	Mixed	100%	Livelihoods and community development promotion
LAPO, Nigeria, established 1993	Microfinance organization working with the poor using solidarity-group lending and savings methodologies along with non-financial services such as training and awareness-raising	Group loans, voluntary and regular savings	Mixed	95%	BDS, health, gender, environ-ment, leadership training
PRADAN, India, established 1983	NGO focusing of building livelihoods systems of poor and socially excluded	Livelihood promotion, including SHGs	Rural	100%	Livelihoods promotion
SAT, Ghana, established 1994	Microfinance organization providing financial services to poor people using Trust Bank and individual lending methodologies	Group/individual loans, voluntary/compulsory savings	Rural	92%	Basic business training
PROMUC, Peru, established 1994	Partnership of 11 NGOs concerned with microenterprise development as a strategy for poverty reduction and the empowerment of women. Operates primarily with village banking programmes	–	Rural	100%	–

Table 4.2 Methods used in *Imp-Act* studies on direct social impacts

Organization and studies	Methods for data collection
CYSD	
Dash and Kabeer (2004)	Household survey based on adaptation of AIMS survey. Sample of 292 mature clients (3 or more years of membership) and 220 new clients (less than 2 years' membership)
Dash and Kabeer (2004)	Focus group discussions and case studies with selected respondents to follow up on quantitative findings
PRADAN	
Kabeer and Noponen (2004)	Socio-economic household survey. Sample of 192 mature PRADAN members (3 plus years or more membership) and 103 non-members
SHARE	
Todd (2001)	AIMS survey of 125 mature clients (3+ years of membership) and 104 new clients (in last 4 months)
Todd (2001)	Survey of 125 ex-clients who left in previous 6 months
Todd (2001)	Qualitative methods: 33 clients using FGD
Cortijo and Kabeer (2004)	Survey of 450 new clients (<6 months) and 450 mature clients (3+ years)
CARD	
Alip et al (2004)	Survey of 591 clients of whom 318 had just joined (control group), 98 had been members for at least 2.5 years, 89 had been members for at least 6 years and 86 for 9 years
LAPO	
Garuba (2004)	AIMS survey of 600 clients from 11 branches: 267 on their fourth loans, 133 on their second loans and 200 pipeline members. Exit survey of 132 ex-clients who had left in first quarter of 2003
Garuba (2004)	In-depth individual interviews for 18 women from 7 different groups from 4 branches all of whom had participated for at least 2 years. Pictorial portraits and case studies
SAT	
Hishigsuren (2004)	AIMS-based impact survey of 312 mature clients (at least 24 months) and 261 pipeline clients. Exit survey of 178 ex-clients
Hishigsuren (2004)	In-depth interviews with 39 mature clients i.e. on fourth loan cycle (some just 13 months) on loan use and savings as well as empowerment. 19 focus groups of 8 clients per group to ascertain satisfaction and dissatisfaction with SAT products
PROMUC	
Wright (2003)	Interviews with 60 clients from 3 MFIs using QUIP protocol

The evidence for material impacts

Food and water

The material impacts of microfinance can be divided into the direct economic impacts discussed in the previous chapter, namely changes in the means by which poor people meet their basic needs, and the indirect ones discussed here, which relate to the extent to which basic needs are actually met. The basic needs that featured most frequently in the *Imp-Act* studies were food, water and shelter (with the changes in these needs illustrated in Table 4.3).

Table 4.3 Evidence of material change: food, water and housing

Organization	Indicators of change	Positive change	No change	Negative change
CYSD	Increase in months of food self-sufficiency in previous year	✓*		
	Higher value/more nutritious food	✓*		
	Clean source of drinking water	✓*		
	Durable walls	✓*		
	Durable roof	✓*		
PRADAN	Fewer months of food shortage in previous year	✓*		
	Higher value/more nutritious food index measuring household food security	✓*		
	Clean source of drinking water	✓*		
	Durable walls	✓*		
	Durable door	✓*		
	Better quality floor	✓*		
SHARE	Fewer months of food shortage	✓*		
	Higher value/more nutritious food	✓*		
	Index based on size of house and durability of material	✓*		
CARD	Index based household food security/hunger	✓(na)		
	Index based on size/structural condition of housing/quality of roof		✓	
LAPO	Experience food crisis in previous year		✓	
	Ratio of persons to living space		✓	
	Quality of housing		✓	
SAT	Durability of building material		✓	

Notes: *Indicates statistically significant up to 10% level of confidence; (ns) Indicates findings were not significant; (na) Indicates significance tests were not carried out.

Five out of the seven organizations looked at food, the same number examined housing and two studied the satisfaction of water needs.

Some of the differences in the contexts in which MFIs work, and hence the nature of the challenges they face, can be illustrated through a comparison of the severity of basic needs shortfalls they reported. For instance, the extreme poverty of the populations with which both PRADAN and CYSD work is evident from the nature of food deficits reported by the households included in their surveys. In the largely tribal areas of Koraput district in Orissa, India's poorest state, where CYSD is located, 85 per cent of *all* households included in its study (namely new as well as mature members) did not grow enough staple food (rice) to feed themselves for the whole year and around 56 per cent did not grow enough staple food to feed themselves for more than six months of the year. Given the geographical isolation of these households, their distance from markets and their reliance on subsistence agriculture, the capacity to feed oneself was a good proxy for household food security levels. In Jharkhand, another very poor state with a large tribal community, the PRADAN study found that 77 per cent of all households surveyed had experienced food shortages in the previous year, while 38 per cent reported food shortages for more than four months.

Nevertheless, within these contexts of extreme poverty and high levels of food insecurity, duration of membership of a self-help group appeared to make a difference to the quality and quantity of food consumed by households for both organizations. For CYSD, 49 per cent of mature members reported food self-sufficiency for more than six months compared to 38 per cent of newer members. They were also more likely to have recently consumed higher-value foods, such as eggs, meat or chicken than new members, and more likely to report an improvement in their consumption standards over the past year. Moreover, a much higher percentage of new members (24 per cent) relative to mature members (4 per cent) continued to rely on community wells and other open and less safe drinking water sources as opposed to tubewells.

The PRADAN study found that members were less likely to report food shortage than non-members, experienced fewer months of food shortage and were more likely to have consumed higher-value, more nutritious foods in the previous week. In addition, a much higher percentage of PRADAN members had improved their sources of drinking water, with 49 per cent reporting handpumps compared to 29 per cent of non-members. The rest continued to rely on open wells, ponds or streams and other surface-water sources. The greater ability of both PRADAN and CYSD members to meet basic needs can in part be attributed to their membership of an MFI self-help group because of the resulting improvements in their livelihoods (Dash and Kabeer, 2004; Kabeer and Noponen, 2004). It can also be attributed to SHG membership because of the direct relationship that could be drawn between the kinds of improvements reported and the kinds of support the MFIs in question provide to the livelihood activities of their members.

Both PRADAN and CARD experimented with an index that combined measures of hunger and food security. The index classified households into four categories on the basis of severity of hunger and experience of food security:

- Those who ate as much food as they wanted and of all types wanted (fully food secure).
- Those who ate as much food as wanted, but not all types wanted (food insecure without hunger.
- Those who were sometimes hungry (food insecure with moderate hunger).
- Those who were often hungry (food insecure with severe hunger).

The differences in the findings reported from the two contexts are illuminating. None of the households surveyed by PRADAN, which included both members of at least two years and non-members, reported full food security while 63 per cent reported food insecurity with either moderate or severe hunger. However, membership of PRADAN seemed to have made a significant difference: the study reported that 23 per cent of members experienced food insecurity without hunger compared to just 5 per cent of non-members; 74 per cent reported food insecurity with moderate hunger compared to 82 per cent of non-members; and 7 per cent reported food insecurity with severe hunger compared to 13 per cent of non-members.

By contrast, 20 per cent of the population surveyed by CARD, which included members of varying duration, including some who had just joined, reported 'full food security' while only 12 per cent reported food insecurity with either moderate or severe hunger. The study found very little systematic difference in the food security position of its members, regardless of length of membership, suggesting that the index may not have been very sensitive in detecting differences in levels of food insecurity in a context where overall food security levels are relatively high. CARD intends to retain food security in its monitoring system but to use a 10-scale index, which had proved more sensitive in an earlier study.

The SHARE study by Cortijo and Kabeer (2004) found that only 8 per cent of households surveyed had experienced any form of food shortage in the previous year. This varied from 10 per cent in the poorest district to 7 per cent in the most prosperous. However, SHARE membership appeared to have had some impact in that only 6 per cent of mature clients reported food shortage – and for a shorter duration – compared to 10 per cent of new. While patterns of consumption did not vary a great deal between old and new members, older members did report the consumption of higher-value food than new members. Todd's (2001) study of SHARE provides evidence to suggest that these differences in household food security and quality of diet could be attributed to membership of SHARE. Her quantitative findings show an increase in value of asset holding by duration of membership, while her qualitative findings suggest that current members of SHARE valued the more reliable flow of income associated with their membership. Presumably, these economic improvements underpin the findings relating to food security.

The LAPO study found that 19 per cent of all clients included in the survey reported a period of food crisis in the previous year, but this varied between clients with different durations of membership. Around 20 per cent of its new (pipeline) clients and second loan clients reported a period of food crisis compared to only 16 per cent of those on their fourth loans. However, the study did not find appreciable differences between newcomers and fourth-loan clients in the quality of diet.

Housing

Housing was used by a number of MFIs as a targeting indicator to provide the possibility for longitudinal impact assessment in these cases. Once again, while differences in the way that the indicator was defined in different studies make strict comparisons across contexts difficult, the findings still provide important insights both into the adequacy and quality of shelter in different contexts, as well as into the impacts achieved by the MFI in question. The majority of households included in the CYSD study reported housing consisting of mud walls and thatched roofs. However, CYSD members were more significantly more likely to report roofs and walls made with durable materials. Similarly, the PRADAN study found that most of the households included in the survey, members and non-members alike, lived in houses with mud walls and floors, but that PRADAN members were more likely to report durable roofs made of tile, brick or cement rather than tarps, twigs or thatch, as well as the greater security associated with having doors made of tin or wood door rather than twigs or bamboo.

SHARE is one of the organizations that uses a housing index as a first step in identifying the poverty status of a household and hence its eligibility to join, thus allowing it to track progress over time. The index combines the size of the house with the flimsiness or durability of the materials of which it is made. Todd (2001) found that 33 per cent of mature clients could be ranked as non-poor by SHARE's housing index, compared to just 6 per cent of new clients, while 23 per cent of its mature clients remained very poor by this index compared to 40 per cent of its new clients. Using longitudinal data on housing and assets, she found that 38 per cent of its mature clients had moved from being 'very poor' to 'moderately poor' over time, 18 per cent had moved from being 'very poor' to 'non-poor' and 20 per cent from 'moderately poor' to 'non-poor'. The rest (22 per cent) had not experienced any change over time, while 2 per cent had experienced deterioration.

CARD also uses a housing index that combines household size, structural condition and quality of roof to rank its clients at entry and over time. The CARD study showed that new clients were better off at entry in housing terms than its older clients, partly because of a recent tendency on the part of CARD staff to recruit 'second priority clients', as well as a change in eligibility criteria. However, a comparison of the housing index scores of mature clients at entry and at the time of the survey found a discernible and consistent improvement in their housing index scores by duration of membership. This was true for clients who had been members for 2.5–6 years, as well as for those with nine years of membership.

Evidence of 'up-market' drift was also reported by the SAT study. It found that the majority of its members lived in rented accommodation, regardless of duration of membership, but that mature members were more likely to live in mud brick/adobe housing, while newer members were more likely to live in concrete-block housing. As the study points out, this probably reflects the fact that newer members are more likely to be recruited from urban areas than older ones rather than being evidence of SAT's absence of impact on its clients' housing standards. However, it did alert the organization to the 'urban' bias in its new membership. The LAPO study reported an insignificant relationship between number of loans and density of persons in family living spaces as well as quality of housing facilities.

The evidence for cognitive impacts

Reference was made earlier to the concept of 'human capabilities' as a way of capturing the potential that people have to achieve valued goals, or their capacity for agency. A critical precondition for exercising such agency is a cognitive one: the inner 'sense of agency', the belief that one can take some degree of control over one's life. For those who lack this sense of agency, bringing about a change in how they perceive themselves and their place in society will be necessary to change other aspects of their lives. However, cognitive changes can encompass changes in values, beliefs and perceptions as well as changes in knowledge, skills and the capacity for problem solving (as shown in Table 4.4). We start with the last sub-category of cognitive changes.

Skills and knowledge

PRADAN works in a context where 90 per cent of the survey population had no education at all. Only 12 per cent of PRADAN members and 3 per cent of non-members reported some basic level of education. However, relative to the small difference in levels of education between members and non-members, 40 per cent of PRADAN members were able to sign their names compared to 3 per cent of non-members, 47 per cent could count larger currency notes compared to 29 per cent of non-members, and 46 per cent knew how to calculate interest on loans compared to 26 per cent of non-members. PRADAN members also had significantly higher levels of knowledge of family planning and of the government's SDYS (Swama Jayanti Gram Swarozgar) programme than non-members.

Table 4.4 Evidence of cognitive change: knowledge, skills, beliefs and attitudes

Organization	Indicators of impact	Positive change	No change	Negative change
CYSD	Perceive own economic contribution to be very significant	✓*		
	Economic contribution perceived as very significant by rest of family: positive	✓*		
PRADAN	Able to sign names	✓*		
	Able to count large currency notes	✓*		
	Able to calculate interest on loans	✓*		
	Knowledge of family planning	✓*		
	Knowledge of government SGYS programme	✓*		
	Knowledge of government below poverty line list			✓*
SHARE	Knowledge of reading and/or writing	✓*		
	Knowledge of family planning	✓*		
CARD	Belief that quality of life had improved since joining	✓(na)		
LAPO	Knowledge of causes of HIV/AIDS	✓(na)		
	Knowledge of causes of malaria	✓(na)		
	Knowledge of first aid for diarrhea	✓(na)		
	Confidence that future would be better for themselves and families	✓(na)		
	Felt good about themselves	✓(na)		
	Felt respected by family and community	✓(na)		
	Expressing son preference		✓	
	Approving female circumcision		✓	
SAT	Increased self-confidence	✓(na)		
	Improvement in quality of life			✓(na)
	Improvement in relationship with God			✓(na)

Notes: *Indicates statistically significant up to 10% level of confidence; (ns) Indicates findings were not significant; (na) Indicates significance tests were not carried out.

These are all issues on which PRADAN provides training and so findings can reasonably be attributed to their efforts. However, while PRADAN members were also found to have considerably higher levels of health awareness (the causes of malaria and diarrhoea, and carrying out oral-rehydration therapy), the study points out that this may not have been an organization-wide finding because a series of health camps had been conducted in recent months for members in the areas surveyed.

Todd's (2001) study of SHARE found that 67 per cent of new and 72 per cent of mature clients had no education at all; and 73 per cent of mature and 71 per cent of new members said that they could not read a simple letter. The study by Cortijo and Kabeer (2004) found that 62 per cent of mature clients had no education at all compared to 59 per cent of new clients. However, the study also found that 50 per cent of mature clients said that they could read or write compared to 45 per cent of new, with the difference being statistically significant. Another 46 per cent of mature clients could sign their names compared to 44 per cent of new. Members had testified during qualitative interviews to the importance of this achievement and to the contribution made by SHARE staff. As Todd points out, all of the focus groups she carried out reiterated the patience with which staff had taught them to sign their names: 'They held our hands and taught us to write, otherwise we would never have been able to learn'.

Cortijo and Kabeer also explored knowledge of family planning methods among SHARE members. While there were very high overall levels of awareness about family planning methods among both old and new members (93 per cent and 90 per cent respectively), probably because of the efforts of the Andhra Pradesh government on this matter, the small difference between mature and new members was still statistically significant.

LAPO, which has a strong focus on health issues in its training programmes, focused on possible changes in clients' knowledge of health problems. The study found a discernible difference in knowledge about the causes of malaria and of HIV/AIDS, and about the treatment of diarrhoea, with knowledge increasing consistently with length of membership. The difference was most marked between clients on their fourth loans and those who were either new or only on their second loan. As the study points out, 'In the area of health education, clients are clearly benefiting immensely from their LAPO exposure, and this will go a long way in improving the general health of their families'.

The SAT study used focus group discussions to explore some of the cognitive changes associated with the economic changes its impact survey had revealed. The results suggested that clients believed that there had been improvements in their entrepreneurial skills and confidence as a result of improvements in their financial situation and the business training they had received.

Values, attitudes and perceptions

The other category of cognitive change relates to changes in values, beliefs and perceptions of individuals. However, these are generally harder to quantify than changes in their skills, information and knowledge. They are even more difficult to attribute to a specific intervention, given that they tend to be shaped over an extended period of time by the life experiences of different individuals and the norms and values of the society in which they are located. Nevertheless, they are not immutable and some may lend themselves more easily to change than others. While the studies reviewed used a mixture of methodologies to explore this aspect of impact, there was a considerable emphasis on qualitative and participatory approaches.

CYSD included two questions in its survey that attempted to capture changes in the perceptions SHG members with regard to the value of their economic contribution to the family and changes in the perceptions of other family members with regard to that contribution. It reported that mature CYSD members were more likely to consider their economic contribution to their families to be 'highly significant' (as opposed to 'significant', 'not so significant' and 'insignificant') than newer members. The families of mature members were also more likely to perceive their contribution to be 'highly significant' than the families of newer members.

The CARD survey asked its members if they believed that their quality of life had changed for the better, for worse or remained the same since they had joined CARD. The results suggested that the likelihood of a positive response increased consistently with number of years of membership. The percentages saying that they thought their quality of life had improved rose from 57 per cent of those who had less than a year's membership, to 76 per cent of those who had been members for two to five years, to 81 per cent of those who had six years' membership, and to 86 per cent of those who had joined nine years previously. The most frequent reason given for improvements in quality of life was related to strengthening of business, while the second most common reason was given as being able to afford to send children to school.

LAPO included a number of questions aimed at eliciting changes in how clients felt about themselves and their families: whether they felt confident that the future would be better for themselves and their families; whether they felt good about themselves and whether they felt respected by their spouse, their family and friends. LAPO found that while clients on their fourth loans were consistently more likely to give positive responses than the rest, the relationship between length of membership and responses given was not consistent. Clients on their second loans gave less positive responses than pipeline clients, while the differences between new and fourth loan clients were generally small.

LAPO also sought to examine the effects of its social education programme on the attitudes of its clients with regard to two aspects of gender discrimination in Nigeria: the practice of female circumcision and son preference. Evidence for impact was even weaker here. There was very little difference between clients as far as son preference was concerned, while new clients appeared far more progressive with regard to female circumcision than those on their second or fourth loans. This may be one aspect of people's belief systems that is resistant to change through training and may require longer term and more holistic efforts.

As an organization with strong spiritual values, SAT's training combines business skills, health awareness and religious teaching. The impact survey included a number of questions on possible impacts from the training. It found that 96 per cent of mature clients and 94 per cent of intermediate clients reported an improvement in their self-confidence compared to 83 per cent of new clients. However, there was no evidence of impact as far as their perceptions of their quality of life was concerned or in their relationship with God: indeed newer clients reported a better quality of life and a more positive relationship with God than older ones. The very high levels of new clients reporting an improved relationship with God as a result of training received is particularly puzzling as only 38 per cent had received religious training compared to 62–65 per cent of intermediate and mature clients. The study concluded that quantitative methods might not be the best approach to the assessment of spiritual impact.

Reporting on behavioural change

Behavioural change, changes in the way that people exercise agency, can be assessed by a focus on behavioural outcomes as well as on the behavioural processes. Thus some of the earlier material changes associated with basic needs satisfaction within the household – improved diet, greater durability of shelter – can be seen as the outcome of certain actions taken by the households concerned. In this section, we move beyond immediate satisfaction of basic needs to achievements that signal improvements in human capabilities, such as children's education, health and family planning, as illustrated in Table 4.5.

Children's education

The PRADAN study provides evidence of what an organization can achieve despite the extremely unfavourable context in which it works. We have already noted the extremely low levels of education that prevailed in the locations covered by the study. Although only 91 per cent of PRADAN members lived in villages that had a primary school within a radius of three kilometres compared to 99 per cent of non-members, the study found that PRADAN members were far more likely to send their children to school than non-members: 58 per cent of children aged 5–16 from PRADAN households were at school compared to 18 per cent of non-members. This is a sizeable (and statistically significant) difference. What is *equally* significant is that while gender disparities in schooling continued to persist for both categories, they were considerably lower among PRADAN households than those of non-members: 44 per cent of girls and 67 per cent of boys in the former category went to school compared to 8 per cent and 22 per cent among non-members. This is also a sizeable and significant difference.

The findings from CYSD, which also works in a poor and difficult context, are more mixed. Around 23 per cent of boys and 43 per cent of girls aged 5–15 from older member households could not read or write compared to 35 per cent of boys and 44 per cent of girls from new member households. In other words, while duration of membership of CYSD appears to have had some impact on boys' education, it has had no impact on gender disparities in education. In addition, the survey data also suggested that while older members were more likely than new members to have sent their children to

Table 4.5 Evidence of behavioural change: children's education, health, family planning and other

Organization	Indicators of impact	Positive change	No change	Negative change
CYSD	Boys aged 5–15 who could read or write	✓(na)		
	% of girls aged 5–15 who could read or write		✓	
	% allowing children to miss school to help out with work			✓
	% reporting increase in educational expenditure		✓	
PRADAN	% of boys aged 5–16 currently enrolled in school:	✓*		
	% of girls aged 5–16 currently enrolled in school	✓*		
SHARE	% of boys with some education	✓(ns)		
	% of girls with some education		✓	
	% of boys reporting studying as primary occupation	✓*		
	% of girls reporting agricultural wage labour as primary occupation			✓*
	% taking sick members to clinic for treatment	✓(ns)		
	% going to private provider	✓(ns)		
	% using family planning	✓*		
	% immunizing children	✓*		
CARD	% of children going to school		✓	
LAPO	% of children of school-going age in regular attendance of school	✓(na)		
	% able to provide school necessities	✓(na)		
	% using family planning		✓	
	% immunizing children	✓(na)		
SAT	% of children aged 5–18 attending school		✓	
	% providing their children with information on HIV/AIDS	✓(na)		
	% practicing abstinence as a form of safe sex	✓*		
	% providing food support to HIV/AIDS affected persons	✓*		
	Other forms of support to HIV/AIDS affected persons		✓	
	% observing Christian practices of regular prayer, attending church, sending children to Sunday school		✓	
	% observing Christian practices of organizing prayer groups at home, giving advice based scriptures: negative impact			✓*

Notes: *Indicates statistically significant up to 10% level of confidence; (ns) Indicates findings were not significant; (na) Indicates significance tests were not carried out.

school since joining CYSD, they were also more likely to allow their children to miss school in order to help out on the farm or enterprise.

The two assessments of SHARE that included attention to this aspect report similarly mixed results. While both studies found that membership of SHARE had some impact on children's education, it was largely restricted to boys' education. Gender disparities in children's education remained intact. Todd (2001) found 76 per cent of boys from mature member households had some education compared to 72 per cent from new member households. However, 61 per cent of the former group had completed the grade appropriate to their age compared to 49 per cent of the latter. Among girls, only 53 per cent from mature members' households and 50 per cent from new members had some education, and only 37 per cent of the former category and 39 per cent of the latter had achieved the right grade for their age. As Todd points out, longer membership of SHARE has apparently not affected members' attitudes towards girls' education.

In their study of SHARE, Cortijo and Kabeer (2004) examined education levels attained by children aged 5–14. They found differences in levels attained by duration of membership, but once again restricted to boys. From mature member households, 72 per cent of girls and 78 per cent of boys had some education compared to 70 per cent of girls and 71 per cent of boys from new member households. The study also found a significantly higher percentage of boys than girls from mature member households reported 'studying' as their primary occupation, but a significantly higher percentage of girls than boys from newer member households reported such an occupation. One reason for the lower rates of school attendance by girls among mature households was their higher levels of participation in the paid work force: girls were much more likely to be found in daily waged labour than boys.

CARD also found little evidence of an increased likelihood of children going to school for older members, despite the value it places on this outcome and the various supports it provides. This may reflect the fact that children's education has not been found to be a particularly sensitive indicator of poverty in the Philippines context, as well as the fact that newer members tended to be better educated and hence more likely to send their children to school. CARD has nevertheless decided to retain children's schooling as one of its monitoring indicators because of the significance it attaches to this outcome.

The LAPO study found clients on their fourth loans reported consistently higher percentages of children of school-going age to be in regular school attendance, as well as a generally higher ability to provide schooling necessities such as textbooks, notebooks and school uniforms. A question attempting to explore the benefits 132 clients, who had left LAPO in the first quarter of 2003, felt they had derived from LAPO's services also gave further information on the behavioural changes that lay behind the positive educational and food security impacts of LAPO. The most frequently mentioned benefit of LAPO membership related to contributions to household food

(36 per cent), followed by housing (32 per cent). Other areas of benefit, though less frequently mentioned, included information (17 per cent), education (15 per cent), health (12 per cent) and clothing (11 per cent).

SAT found that over 92 per cent of school-age children (5–18) were attending school among their clients, that gender disparities were insignificant and that school attendance did not vary by duration of membership. The study concludes that 'it is apparent that education is a high priority for all Ghanaians, regardless of socio-economic class. The new clients are just as committed to sending their children to school, and do not wait until a loan helps them to improve their cash flow' (Hishigsuren, 2004). Other information collected by the SAT study confirms this: the most important aspirations expressed by SAT's clients related to improvements in housing and children's education. It was also found that increased contributions by clients to the household budget tended to be translated into increased expenditure on food, followed by payment of medical bills and school bills.

Other forms of behavioural change: health and family planning

Along with evidence on impacts relating to children's education, the impact studies also provide insights into other aspects of behavioural change with implications for social outcomes. The studies of SHARE included a focus on health-related behaviour to explore the impact of its attempts to motivate clients during their weekly meetings. The study by Todd (2001) found that mature clients were more likely to report taking a family member to a clinic to seek treatment for illness, and also more likely to have sought private medical care. While both old and new members preferred private provision, SHARE members were more able to afford it, largely because of higher levels of savings.

Cortijo and Kabeer (2004) found that while the adoption of family planning was very high for both old and new members of SHARE (92 per cent overall), older members were more likely than newer members to have adopted family planning practices. While high percentages of children of both mature and new clients had received polio and BCG vaccinations, mature SHARE clients once again reported significantly higher levels of immunization. They were also more likely to take precautions against malaria than new members. Differences in immunization against hepatitis B and diphtheria were not significant.

LAPO explored various aspects of health-seeking behaviour in its assessment study because it provides training in this field. However, it found that only 32 per cent of all clients practised family planning and that this did not vary systematically by duration of membership. Clearly this reflects contextual factors: fertility decline has been slower in Sub-Saharan Africa than in most parts of the developing world and it has been generally slower still in West Africa. However, LAPO did appear to have an impact in another key area of health-seeking behaviour: while 89 per cent of all clients had immunized their last child, 81 per cent of new, 88 per cent of intermediate and 96 per cent of older members had done so. Such behaviour has extremely important ramifications for the health status of poor families.

The SAT assessment sought information of the possible behavioural impacts of its religious training. However, it found very little difference between mature and new clients with regard to their religious practices (praying with their family on a regular basis, attending church, sending children to Sunday school). One difference did appear to be significant: mature clients generally reported lower levels of religious practice than new ones (organizing prayer groups at home, giving advice based on scriptures). This somewhat paradoxical finding might reflect the fact that as mature clients found their businesses thriving, they may have had less time to engage in such activities.

Reporting on relational change

As pointed out earlier, the primary rationale for exploring relational change within the domain of family and household relates to possible impacts on intra-household inequalities, particularly gender inequalities. Some evidence of impact, or lack of impact, on gender inequalities has already been touched on. Here we consider other evidence, such as that presented in Table 4.6.

A number of *Imp-Act* studies included indicators of women's role in decision-making in various arenas to explore possible impacts in intra-household relationships. The CYSD survey carried a series of questions on their members' roles in intra-household decision-making that allowed for five different responses: decisions were carried out by the woman on her own; by her husband on his own; by husband and wife jointly; by the woman jointly with other family members; and by other family members on their own. Examining the extent to which women participated in decision-making, either on their own or jointly with others, suggested that length of membership of CYSD did have a statistically significant impact on their decision-making role on issues such as the purchase of clothing, improvements to the house, the purchase of non-land assets, agricultural cropping, livestock rearing, sale of non-traditional forest produce, children's education and marriage, risk-coping strategies and decisions related to taking, using and repaying loans and taking part in community activities. However, while mature members participated to a greater extent than newer members in decisions about daily consumption needs, sale of land, sale of agricultural crops, health and family planning and visiting relatives, the differences were not statistically significant, suggesting an absence of impact in these areas.

In the PRADAN study too, there was evidence of impact on intra-household decision-making processes, but again not across the board. PRADAN members were more likely than non-PRADAN members to participate in decision-making on their own or jointly with others making decisions about children's education (suggesting that the higher levels of children at school and lower levels of gender disparity in member households may partly reflect women's

Table 4.6 Evidence of relational change

Organization	Indicators of impact	Positive change	No change	Negative change
CYSD	% participating in household decision-making regarding:			
	a) purchase of clothing	✓*		
	b) improvement of house	✓*		
	c) purchase of non-land asset	✓*		
	d) agricultural cropping	✓*		
	e) livestock rearing	✓*		
	f) sale of non-traditional forest produce	✓*		
	g) children's education	✓*		
	h) children's marriage	✓*		
	i) coping with risk	✓*		
	j) taking, using and repaying of loans	✓*		
	k) participation in community activities	✓*		
	l) sale of land, sale of agricultural crops		✓	
	m) health and family planning		✓	
	n) visiting relatives		✓	
PRADAN	% participating in household decision-making regarding:			
	a) children's education	✓*		
	b) regarding loans	✓*		
	c) family size			✓*
	d) purchase of assets		✓	
	e) choice of livelihoods		✓	
	f) visit to natal family		✓	
	g) domestic violence	✓(ns)		
	h) % keeping back part of income for own disposal	✓*		
	i) % not under pressure to bear sons	✓*		
SAT	% making decision about savings on their own		✓	
	% making decisions about expenditures on their own		✓	

Notes: *Indicates statistically significant up to 10% level of confidence; (ns) Indicates findings were not significant; (na) Indicates significance tests were not carried out.

greater role in decision-making) and decisions relating to their loans. These differences were statistically significant. However, non-members were significantly more likely to participate in decision-making regarding family size than PRADAN members. Also levels of participation in decision-making regarding purchase of assets, choice of livelihoods and visiting natal family did not vary significantly by membership status.

In addition to shifts in decision-making patterns as indicators of women's changing agency within the household, PRADAN also explored other aspects of intra-household power relations. The study found that while PRADAN members reported lower levels of domestic violence than non-members, the difference was not significant (and it is highly likely that there is considerable under-reporting by both groups). However, PRADAN members were significantly more likely than non-members to keep back part of their earnings to be disposed of by themselves and they were less likely than non-members to report pressure to bear sons.

The survey data on SHARE did not contain any information on intra-household decision-making or other aspects of gender inequalities. However, group discussions involving 33 women from different branch locations carried out by Todd (2001) found that the majority of these women did not have businesses of their own before joining the SHG. They had worked as agricultural wage labourers in the fields, earning less than male labour. Now most had their own businesses and were flourishing. As a result, they felt they had moved from a position of having little economic worth within the family to being active contributors. And while they continue to play a less than active role in household decision-making, they believe that they are treated with more respect by other family members and their views are more likely to be solicited.

The SAT survey suggested that clients either made decisions about the use of their savings by themselves (51 per cent) or jointly with others (40 per cent). The pattern did not vary significantly by duration of membership. Decisions about other expenditures also showed the same dominant pattern of self or joint decision-making with no systematic variation between different categories of membership. It would appear that SAT has not had much impact on decision-making patterns among its members.

As we noted earlier, although longer-standing LAPO clients tended to be more positive about the future and about themselves, the relationship with duration of membership was not consistent. Focus group discussions with 18 women from different LAPO groups suggested that most reported greater feelings of self-confidence as a result of having their own businesses to run. However, this did not appear to have expanded their role in intra-household decision-making except in the area of food: deciding on what the family would eat and purchasing it without consultation. Because this appears to be an area in which women are typically most likely to have a say, including possibly in Nigeria, it is not clear to what extent this constitutes evidence of a change in intra-household asymmetries in decision-making.

Reporting on composite findings

One of the studies under the *Imp-Act* programme investigates the range of impacts reported by clients of PROMUC MFIs in Peru (Wright-Revelledo, 2004) and provides an excellent demonstration of the use of qualitative methodology to go beyond 'anecdotes' and selective listening. An earlier quantitative survey of client households had yielded the result that poor households constituted a smaller percentage of clients than had been assumed by the MFIs in question, but that membership of 'village banks' had a positive impact on the typical clients' income.

The later qualitative study selected 60 of the clients from three MFIs who had been included in the impact survey. Wright-Revelledo used QUIP (Qualitative Impact Assessment Protocol), a tool developed in the course of the programme to systematize the collection and analysis of qualitative information. Interviews with respondents combined open-ended, in-depth discussion on different issues with a number of closed opinion questions on each issue, responses to which were assigned a score. Thus, for instance, discussion of how a member had used her loans would be concluded with a question on how well her enterprise had fared during this period. Those that had experienced an increase in their profits were given a score of +1, those who had experienced a decline were scored as −1, while those who had not experienced any change were assigned a score of 0. Questions on subjective well-being, on generation of new activities and so on could all be similarly scored. As long as all the closed questions are scored consistently to show higher scores for positive responses and lower scores for negative responses, it becomes possible to aggregate the final scores to ascertain whether overall impact was positive, negative, mixed or negligible. This allows investigation of positive, negative and absence of impact and provides a transparent account of how qualitative data is used to arrive at conclusions.

The impacts studied related to changes at the enterprise level along with a range of material, cognitive and relational frameworks outlined earlier in the chapter. The QUIP protocol made it possible to document the fact that the same client might benefit in some areas but lose in others. The study found that improvements in housing and housing conditions were a key area of material impact: 23 out of 60 clients interviewed had been able to improve their houses or furnish them better, while ten had bought utensils and artefacts for the home. Education was a second important area of impact, with nine out of 60 paying for educational costs, sometimes their own, but more often their children or siblings. Around nine clients said they were eating better than they had before.

Out of 60 clients, 40 reported positive cognitive impacts. Most of these related to how people viewed themselves and others: improved self-confidence and higher self-esteem, greater motivation to begin new enterprises and take risks, greater self assurance in the public domain. Far fewer (16 out of 60) mentioned changes that related to their knowledge and skills. Positive relational changes were also reported by 23 out of 60 clients. These changes included: receiving more support for their enterprises from their family members; a greater sense of independence and self-reliance; a greater ability to renegotiate relations with other family members to achieve a fairer sharing of the workload; and an expansion in their circle of friends.

While most of those interviewed reported mixed impacts, around 11 of the 60 clients were classified as 'net losers' from their participation in the programme, reporting far more negative than positive impacts. The group dynamics of the 'village banks' were a key source of dissatisfaction (as discussed in the Chapter 5), but other sources of dissatisfaction included the stress of repaying their loans, having their assets confiscated for non-repayment and being unable to benefit because of robbery, illness and the birth of children. Around 6 had left their organization by the time the study was carried out and another 12 were seriously considering leaving. Analysis of the characteristics of those who were least likely to benefit from their participation in the microfinance activities of the PROMUC network suggested that they were the more vulnerable sections of the community: women with young children and little family support, widows, female household heads and migrant women.

Lessons on impact from the impact assessments

There are a number of general lessons that can be drawn on the basis of the discussions in this chapter. Some of these relate to the methodology of impact assessment, others to the relationship between organizational strategy and social performance, particularly the capacity to contribute to the MDGs.

Attribution

The first point relates to the thorny issue of 'attribution' that hampers all attempts to assess impact. While the problems associated with the selection of a suitable control group have been widely acknowledged, some of the studies discussed in this chapter further illustrate the problem of using 'new' members as a control group. In many cases, where new members appeared to be doing better than old, it was not necessarily because the organization was failing to have impact but because it was recruiting among those who were better off than their older clients had been when the MFI started out.

Sometimes this reflected the problem of mission drift, that the organization was moving intentionally or unintentionally away from the poor. Sometimes it reflected an overall improvement in the standard of living, so that new members were entering a programme with standards of living that had taken older members a number of years of participation in the programme to achieve. In some cases, the very presence of an organization in a particular area could have had impacts on cognition, behaviour and relationships in the wider community, thus affecting the characteristics of new members from that community. And finally, of course, in some cases, the absence of any significant difference between old and new members could simply reflect the fact that the organization was having little or no impact.

Whatever the reason, the findings suggest the need for careful design of the attribution strategy and the collection of information to corroborate or triangulate findings. As already suggested, one way to address this might be to document the 'pathways' through which impacts occur and the extent to which they can be plausibly attributed to the organization in question. Questions on, for instance, possible changes in skills and knowledge could be followed up with questions about how any such new skills and knowledge had actually been acquired. Improvements in food security may be explained in terms of smoother income flows but would require a further follow-up question on why smoothing had occurred.

Time period

The studies discussed in this chapter varied in the ways they defined the time period over which impact was sought, a factor that has to be taken into account in comparing the findings. 'Mature' SHARE members had been with the organization for, at most, five years, while mature CARD members had around nine years of membership. One reason for this difference in how mature and new members were defined is, of course, that the organizations in question had been in operation for varying lengths of time and would be expected to have experienced different degrees of impact as a result. However, the relationship between time frame and impact may also be made more complicated by the fact that over time many more variables can intervene and influence impacts.

Also in relation to the question of the period of time over which impact occurred, the findings suggest that some areas of impact, particularly those related to beliefs and practices that evolve over a lifetime and are reinforced by the context in which she or he lives, are less amenable to change through participation in microfinance activities or training. A preference for sons, religious beliefs and practices, and support for female circumcision are examples of some of the areas that do not appear to respond to MFI attempts to change or strengthen them.

Choice of indicator

The studies make it clear that food security is a key indicator of impact in the lives of the very poor. However, the food security indicator has to be tailored to local context. The Food Security Index, used by both PRADAN and CARD, performed well in capturing variations in the highly food-insecure context in which PRADAN operated, but was too blunt to capture variations in food insecurity in the Philippines. This led to CARD's decision to experiment with a more refined version of the indicator, which allowed for 10 rather than just four values. In other cases, the failure to find impact reflected the fact that the indicator in question sought information on a form of change that had become a society-wide phenomenon. Thus one reason why SAT did not achieve a great deal of impact on children's education was because there had been a society-wide increase in numbers of children in the relevant age groups going to school, partly reflecting Ghana's adoption of a Universal Primary Education policy. In the Philippines too, the absence of impact in relation to children's education can be partly explained by evidence from other studies that children's education is not a particularly sensitive indicator of poverty in the Philippines context.

It is worth noting in relation to this point that an impact study in Peru under the AIMS core impact programme (Dunn, 1999) noted that in a context of already high initial enrolment rates (almost 100 per cent for both boys and girls), changes in enrolment figures were clearly not a meaningful impact indicator. Instead the quality of schooling was more important,[4] that is, whether parents sent their children to more expensive/private schools or invested in some form of supplementary education (for example, tutors) and whether they were more likely to send older children to tertiary education.

It was also evident that certain indicators such as housing may cease to be relevant as indicators of poverty or deprivation after a certain overall standard of living has been achieved in a country. It is worth noting, for instance, the observation made in the PRIZMA study that found that quality of housing was only modestly correlated with poverty among the 'newly poor' in Bosnia-Herzegovina. Poverty here lay in limited and intermittent capacity to earn an income rather than in the adequacy or quality of housing. Yet as Sender (2003) suggests on the basis of a wide reading of the literature on poverty in poor countries, quality of housing is one of the most immediate and consistent indicators of poverty.

Qualitative methodologies

The strength of qualitative methodologies is that they allow an understanding of causalities and meanings that tend to elude quantitative methods. They also help to triangulate findings from quantitative methods and they engage respondents in a more participatory process of interaction that may itself contribute to the kinds of knowledge that are generated. However, qualitative methods do have limitations, some of the technical kind (generalizability, representativeness), but also the problem that the very interactions on which they are based may give rise to certain kinds of bias in the information collected.

In the *Imp-Act* studies, where qualitative methods were used to explore the meaning of findings from survey data or to provide a context to these findings, the information they provided was less likely to contain an in-built bias towards positive findings. However, where focus group discussions were carried out by the staff of the MFI concerned and involved asking existing clients direct questions about the benefits – and costs – associated with their participation in the organization's activities, doubts can be raised about the reliability of the data. Question marks about the quality of the data are also heightened when studies report group consensus from focus group discussions with little indication of whether there had been any dissenting voices.

Qualitative interviews with ex-clients, who are less likely to worry about jeopardizing their relationship with the MFI, may be a more reliable source of information about the positive aspects of participating in microfinance activities – although there is the danger that they are biased in the opposite direction. Consequently, the positive feedback provided by ex-clients of SHARE, SAT and others may be a stronger vindication of organizational impact than that provided by existing clients. In addition, the QUIP protocol utilized by Wright-Revelledo (2004) had the advantage of enumerating different categories of responses, negative as well as positive, and exploring the reasons behind them.

Influence on performance

Participation in the *Imp-Act* programme served as a reminder to a number of organizations that what they choose to monitor can exercise an important influence on how they manage performance and on the motivations of staff. As the LAPO study points out, although it has always had a social concern built into its mission, it has been undergoing a great deal of institutional pressure on its financial performance that had led to mission drift. The work it carried out under the *Imp-Act* programme helped it to refocus on its social mission, while the inclusion of social indicators for the first time in its impact assessment system will ensure this focus is retained at the organizational level. CARD, too, found that its experience of developing a monitoring system as part of its activities in the *Imp-Act* programme helped to clarify what it considers to be its mission, and new indicators will help it to monitor the achievement of its mission.

Contribution to the MDGs

Finally the findings discussed in this chapter suggest that microfinance organizations do have a clear capacity to contribute to the achievement of the Millennium Development Goals, but not to the same extent and not in all contexts. Chapter 3 referred to organizations that are contributing to a goal of halving income poverty in the world. This chapter provided evidence of the kinds of organizations that are contributing to the non-income aspects of poverty such as access to housing and clean water, and to the other MDGs relating to health, education and women's empowerment.

The increasing attention that is being paid to these aspects of poverty by organizations such as PRADAN and CYSD is indicative of their recognition of the multiplicity of the constraints in which they work, resulting in a broader view of poverty built into their missions and mandates. Not surprisingly, PRADAN and CYSD included and reported a wider range of social impacts than many of the other organizations. Their findings tell us that, despite the extreme poverty and social exclusion of particular groups in society and despite the remoteness and isolation of their location, a responsive organizational strategy can make a difference. However, such a strategy is unlikely to be viable in commercial terms.

Operating in contexts of such extreme poverty requires the need for greater attention be paid to achieving the sustainability of the livelihoods of the poor rather than the financial sustainability of the organization. At the same time, the fact that CYSD and PRADAN did not report uniform impacts in relation, for instance, to children's education, suggests that organizational strategy on its own does not deliver results. How these strategies are implemented on the ground and the quality and commitment of staff responsible for implementation are all likely to lead to variations in what they are able to achieve.

Alternatively, the findings from more minimalist programmes like SHARE and CARD suggest that organizations that seek financial sustainability can, nevertheless, achieve impacts that go beyond immediate economic ones, particularly when they operate in a supportive policy environment and a dynamic economy. The SHARE findings included increased levels of child immunization and boys' education, while CARD's clients reported an improvement in the quality of their lives. At the same time, however, the persistence of gender bias in education and of female child labour among mature SHARE members, together with qualitative findings testifying to very limited impacts in terms of personal empowerment, suggest that minimalist approaches may have minimalist implications for the Millennium Development Goal on gender equality and women's empowerment. Given that SHARE's organizational culture has evolved around the achievement of 100 per cent repayment rates, it may not be best equipped to address this goal. Indeed, any attempt to do so could simply undermine its achievements on other fronts. However, SHARE could work in collaboration with other organizations that are better placed to address these more resilient aspects of poverty and social exclusion among its membership.

Conclusion

The findings from this chapter suggest that there need not be a trade-off between financial sustainability and social performance when social performance is confined to direct income-related impacts in economically dynamic contexts, However, the trade-off becomes sharper when the focus is broadened to consider economic and social goals in contexts of extreme deprivation. Even when some difference may be made to income poverty, social goals will not necessarily follow because they reflect constraints that are not purely economic. Organizations can opt to change their strategies to achieve these social impacts but may thereby compromise the goal of financial self-sufficiency. Alternatively, they may rely on other organizations to achieve these impacts because their own comparative advantage lies elsewhere.

However, for those MFIs that are working in contexts where there are few alternative organizations, this is not likely to be an option. In such contexts, it is the concept of sustainability that will have to be broadened to go beyond the focus on organizational sustainability and to address the question of sustainable social change. MFIs' capacity to contribute to the achievement the MDGs will be dependent on this process of sustainable social change.

CHAPTER FIVE

Wider impacts: social exclusion and citizenship

Naila Kabeer

Introduction[1]

Earlier chapters have reviewed the evidence of the direct economic and social impacts associated with MFI activities. This chapter focuses on their wider impacts, more specifically their wider social impacts. It examines changes in the sphere of community, civil society and the polity rather than in the sphere of market and economy. Such impacts have received very little attention in the literature, although for reasons to be explained below, there are grounds to expect at least some organizations to have ramifications that go beyond the individual woman and her household or enterprise. The question of wider impacts was therefore explicitly identified as one of the thematic areas of the *Imp-Act* programme. This chapter reports on the findings of studies that took up this theme.

Conceptualizing wider impacts: social exclusion and citizenship

As has been noted in earlier chapters, an MFI's analysis of why certain individuals or groups in society fail to gain access to existing financial services will clearly influence the strategies it adopts to address such exclusion. For some of the MFIs who participated in the *Imp-Act* programme, the problem was seen as one of *financial exclusion* as a result of market failure and could be addressed through the provision of 'market-like' alternatives to the existing services. For others, however, the problem was symptomatic of more deep-rooted forms of *social exclusion* that not only affected the capacity of the groups in question to gain access to existing sources of financial provision, but also their capacity to participate in other aspects of social life. The mission and organizational strategies of these MFIs was consequently designed to address deeper inequalities.

Regardless of these differences in approach, however, there are reasons to expect that many MFIs have wider social impacts of the kind we are concerned with in this chapter. One reason is that most of them work with women from poor households and, in some cases, from socially excluded groups. To the extent that women generally enjoy less favourable access than men to valued resources and opportunities, financial and otherwise, and socially excluded groups are among the most disadvantaged sections of the poor, the focus on women from such groups has the potential to address both gender-related inequality as well as other forms of social discrimination.

A second reason is that most MFIs operate through group-based strategies. Whether these take the form of Grameen-style groups, solidarity groups, self-help groups, village banks or savings and credit cooperatives, they all rely to a greater or lesser extent on the trust or social capital that exists, or can be built up, between members of a group (Fisher and Sriram, 2002). Group formation strategies hold out the possibility for bringing about social change *for the simple reason that people acting together are often able to achieve what they cannot achieve individually.* This is as true of the privileged sections of a society as it as of the marginalized, the main difference being that the marginalized find it far harder to organize into the kinds of groups, collectives and associations that will help them overcome their marginalization. Consequently, they find themselves either excluded from the social networks that matter or else included on highly asymmetrical terms.

Microfinance organizations offers these sections of the population the possibility of belonging to a group of their choosing in contrast to the socially prescribed or economically imposed relationships that tend to make up the experience of marginalized people, and particularly women, in many parts of the world. It gives them the opportunity to meet on a routine basis with others who share their experience of marginalization and to gain access to knowledge about the world beyond the confines of their immediate experience. These opportunities have the potential to build capacity to act as citizens in ways and at a pace that reflects their particular contexts and constraints.

Two ways of conceptualizing citizenship were evident in the *Imp-Act* studies. The first is closer to the concept of citizenship to be found in the political sciences, traditionally the domain of the study of citizenship, and focused on a state-centred notion of citizenship, defining it in terms of the rights and obligations that govern relationships between the state and the individual. The other interpretation draws on the sociological literature, which has given rise to an alternative society-centred notion, premised on the rights and obligations of citizens to each other (Kabeer, 2002). Sociological approaches have expanded legalistic definitions of citizenship as a formal status, defined by the rights and obligations necessary to exercise voice and agency, to the idea of citizenship as the active exercise of voice and agency, the realization of the potential of citizenship (Lister, 1997).

These are mutually reinforcing, rather than mutually exclusive, approaches to the idea of citizenship. In particular, in contexts where states fail in their duties to uphold the rights of marginalized sections of their citizenship, the efforts of these sections to hold the state to account is likely to represent a more sustainable route to achieving its transformation than others acting on their behalf. Yet it is often part of the condition of marginalization that these groups lack the very capabilities that are necessary for such action to take place. As Lister (ibid.) points out, to act as a citizen requires 'first a sense of agency, the belief that one can act' but, at the same time, it is only by acting as a citizen, and particularly acting collectively, that this sense of agency can be fostered.

MFIs, with their focus on group formation and group training strategies, have the *potential* to overcome this 'agency conundrum', but it is only a potential. There is no *necessary* relationship between membership of an MFI group and the realization of this potential. Given that MFIs have different rationales and approaches to the formation of groups, to the provision and content of training, and to the delivery of services, we would expect them to have varying implications for the agency conundrum. They may promote solidarity and agency on the part of the marginalized or they may promote, or further exacerbate, tensions and inequalities within the community.

The rest of this chapter summarizes the evidence of wider social impacts that emerge out of these various studies and explores their relationship to organizational strategy. Table 5.1 presents the different domains where impacts were assessed and the kinds of evidence that were sought. It suggests that the MFI groups themselves, as a new form of association, attracted special attention in a number of the studies. In addition, evidence was also sought of change in relationships in the wider community and civil society, as well as in participation in the domain of policy and politics.

Linking contexts and strategies

Seven organizations participated in the 'wider social impacts' thematic area of the programme: CYSD (India), PRADAN (India), BRAC (Bangladesh), SHARE (India), FORA Fund (Russia), INTEGRA (Romania) and INTEGRA Foundation (Slovakia). These were mainly organizations whose mission and strategy led them to anticipate such impacts. Table 5.2 summarizes the methodologies used by the different studies, while below is a brief account of the contexts in which these organizations work and the strategies that they use to achieve

Table 5.1 Wider social impacts: domains and substance of change

Domains of impacts	MFI groups	Community/civil society	State, policy and polity
Kinds of impacts	Changes in intra-group relations	Changes in knowledge, agency and relationships within the community	Changes in knowledge, agency and relationships in the domain of policy and politics.

Table 5.2 Methodologies used in *Imp-Act* studies on wider social impacts

Organization/Studies	Methods for data collection
BRAC (Bangladesh) Kabeer and Matin (2004)	Specially designed household survey for wider impacts theme. 203 mature members (5+ years' membership) with 198 new members (<2 years' membership) and 102 individual loanees. Focus group discussions and individual interviews used to follow up on findings
CYSD (India) Dash and Kabeer (2004)	Socio-economic household survey based on adaptation of AIMS survey. Sample of 292 mature clients (3+ years' membership) and 220 new clients (<2 years' membership). Focus group discussions and case studies with selected respondents to follow up on findings
PRADAN (India) Kabeer and Noponen (2004)	Socio-economic household survey. Sample of 192 mature PRADAN members (3+ years or more membership) and 103 non-members
SHARE (India) Todd (2001)	Survey of 125 mature clients (3+ years of membership) and 104 new clients (4 months) using AIMS-SEEP methodology. Quantitative survey of 125 ex-clients who left 6 months prior to survey plus focus group discussion with 33 current clients
SHARE (India) Cortijo and Kabeer (2004)	Specially designed household survey for wider impacts theme. 450 'mature' member households (at least 3 years membership) and 450 'new' client households (6 months or less)
LAPO (Nigeria) Garuba (2004)	Survey based on AIMS-SEEP methodology of 600 clients from 11 branches of which 267 were on their fourth loans, 133 on their second loans and 200 pipeline members. Exit survey of 132 ex-clients who had left in 1st quarter of 2003. In-depth individual interviews for 18 women from 7 different groups from 4 branches of all whom had participated for at least 2 years
SAT (Ghana) Hishigsuren (2004)	AIMS-based impact survey of 312 mature clients (24+ months) and 261 pipeline clients. Exit survey of 178 ex-clients. In-depth interviews with 39 mature clients (i.e. on fourth loan cycle)
PROMUC (Peru) Wright-Revellado (2004)	Interviews with 60 clients from 3 MFIs using QUIP protocol
FORA (Russia) *INTEGRA* (Slovakia) and *INTEGRA* (Romania) Alexeeva *et al* (2004)	Specially designed survey of 141 group loanees (male and female), 19 individual loanees and 40 'control' groups in Russia, 32 group loanees and 14 individual loanees from Slovakia and 50 individual loanees from Romania

their intended objectives. The section provides a background to the rest of the chapter that reports on some of the wider impacts achieved by the organizations in question.

CYSD and PRADAN

Context

Both PRADAN and CYSD work in the poorest states of India and use geo-graphical targeting to identify pockets of poverty within these states. PRADAN used to use wealth ranking to then further identify the poorest households but now both organizations aim at saturation coverage of the areas in which they work. The membership of both organizations is drawn not only from some of the poorest households in India but also from socially excluded groups. Around 97 per cent of the PRADAN membership covered by the survey belonged to the 'untouchable' or *dalit* castes (officially known as scheduled castes), *adivasis* or tribal groups (officially known as scheduled tribes), along with others drawn from what are officially known as 'other backward castes'. Of this figure, around 21 per cent came from scheduled tribes. Approximately 86 per cent of CYSD's membership included in the survey was from these groups, with over 60 per cent of that figure being from the scheduled tribes.

These percentages show that both organizations work with a membership that is economically disadvantaged because, as we saw in previous chapters, their households lack the means to assure even their minimum basic needs. They are also socially disadvantaged on the basis of gender, as well as caste and ethnicity. The tribal population in India reports the highest levels of poverty followed by scheduled caste groups. In addition, tribal groups in particular are often geographically disadvantaged because they are located in remote forest areas, poorly connected by transport and communications and poorly served by government and non-government services. And finally, both *dalit* and *adivasi* groups are politically disadvantaged because they are excluded from processes by which critical decisions are made at the national, state and local level.

Strategies

Both CYSD and PRADAN promote the organic formation of self-help groups (SHGs) as a strategy for addressing these disadvantages. They view micro-finance not only as a means to promote sustainable livelihood systems for the poor and marginalized, but also as a means to promote 'people's organizations' that are owned, controlled and managed by their members (Fisher and Sriram, 2002). They recognize that poor people are more likely to organize around concrete activities in which they have a direct stake and that microfinance provides such a concrete activity. They do not see themselves as MFIs, but as organizations that promote MFIs. Each SHG can be regarded as a micro-finance organization writ small but that, through federation with other SHGs in a locality, takes on a larger presence within the community. Both organizations carried out a comprehensive household survey into direct and wider impacts.

SHARE

Context

SHARE works primarily in Andhra Pradesh in the south of India, a state that has experienced a marked decline in poverty levels and is considered to be one of the more economically dynamic in India. SHARE not only has been successful in targeting some of the poorest households in the areas in which it works, but also targets socially excluded groups, with around 83 per cent of its members belonged to *dalit, adivasi* and other 'other backward castes'. The populist politics of the chief minister of Andhra Pradesh for much of the 1990s led to a proliferation of programmes for the poor, including the government's version of the self-help group approach embodied in the DWCRA (Development of Women and Children in Rural Areas) programme, so that Andhra now accounts for around 40 per cent of the country's DWCRA groups.

Strategies

SHARE began with a Grameen-type approach but has modified it to local needs. Screening of clients takes place through a means-based client profile, and pre-lending training is followed by a group recognition test to ensure that members have understood the programme's rules and regulations. Clients are organized into groups of eight at most. Groups come together into centres of 35 to 40 members. SHARE has its own version of 'the 16 promises' that are used to motivate behavioural change among its membership. Meetings take place weekly but, in addition, SHARE has bi-annual cultural programmes, as well as annual workshops to listen to its clients' views.

BRAC

Context

BRAC was established in 1972 in Bangladesh and is less concerned with hard-core exclusions of the kind that PRADAN and CYSD focus on, and more with the poor in general, and poor women in particular. In Bangladesh, as in other parts of South Asia, women are incorporated into family and kinship groups on highly unequal terms, and their access to resources and relationships in the wider community is mediated by male members of the family. In addition, poor women, along with the rest of their family members, play little or no role in the informal structures of decision-making and conflict resolution within the community, while high levels of fear, suspicion and mistrust characterize their relationships with the state and its various representatives.

Bangladesh has been described as a society in which relationships take the form of concentric circles of 'moral proximity' (Wood, 2000). The inner circle is constituted by the immediate family, which, despite its internal inequalities, remains the primary moral economy in people's lives and their primary source of security. As interactions move towards ever wider circles of increasingly impersonal relationships, levels of trust decline and more instrumental forms of behaviour become evident. A number of studies of people's attitudes towards the state and its various representatives confirm their high levels of mistrust and also document levels of corruption and other unruly practices on the part of state officials, which help to explain why (World Bank, 2000; Transparency International, 1997).

Strategies

BRAC organizes women from poor households for microfinance services using a Grameen-style group approach. However, its multidimensional analysis of poverty and its recognition of the structural nature of the constraints that its members face in the wider society, have led it to provide a range of different services to its group members, along with its financial services. Within a village, seven or eight BRAC groups of five are organized into village organizations (VOs), representatives from which make up the *palli samaj* (ward-level federations intended to complement the government's initiative to set up local government bodies). Weekly group meetings focus on credit operations, while monthly meetings are issue-based meetings where education is provided on a variety of issues. BRAC provides various kinds of training to its members, including human rights and legal awareness and since 1998, legal aid services. It also provides health education and basic forms of health care. There are different officers responsible for these different activities.

In recent years, BRAC has reached out to two categories of households who were overlooked by existing forms of financial service provision, including its own. The first were the 'ultra-poor' who could not participate on the terms on which BRAC and most MFIs offered their services. A special programme has begun for these sections. The second were households above the poverty line whose enterprises had considerable growth potential but who were still too poor in assets to access the formal banking system. The MELA (Microfinance Lending and Assistance) programme was begun in 1996 for this section of the population; loans are made on an individual basis and are larger than those typically lent to the poor. The BRAC study on wider impacts focused on a comparison based on years of group membership in its Rural Development Programme (RDP), but was also able to add a comparison with those of its members who were given individual loans. As the latter were clearly better off, education levels, food security and land ownership were used to control for socio-economic differences between individual and group members.

FORA Fund, INTEGRA Foundation Slovakia and INTEGRA Romania

Context

The three MFIs included in the study by Alexeeva *et al* (2004) are located in Russia, Slovakia and Romania. These are all contexts where the historical experience of a highly centralized and totalitarian state has led to a huge gulf between state and citizen and left behind a dual legacy of high levels of trust by individual citizens in their immediate informal social networks (family, friends) and high levels of mistrust in the formal political and civic institutions of the state, which are in any case characterized by widespread corruption. MFIs are still relatively new in these contexts, but it is anticipated by the international financial institutions that they will help to construct new forms of social capital. They can play an important 'bonding' function within the community, complementing and extending existing networks and reaching out to those who are socially isolated and have no friends or relatives to fall back upon. They can also play a 'bridging' function by helping to close the distance between individuals and the various institutions of the state.

Strategies

The organizations in question have somewhat different approaches to financial provision. FORA Fund in Russia and INTEGRA Foundation in Slovakia provide a mixture of individual and group credit mainly to women. INTEGRA Romania provides only individual credit. FORA Fund puts its emphasis on quick and easily accessible credit to the micro-business sector. The two INTEGRA organizations both belong to the INTEGRA Ventura network of organizations operating in a number of post-communist countries. The rhetoric of the network, as Alexeeva *et al* (ibid.) point out, is 'redolent of a social capital-building mission', committing it to 'help people build their businesses so that they can become "islands of integrity" [such that] they can participate in the transformation of their communities'. Both members of the INTEGRA network put an emphasis on the social objectives of reducing corruption and extending credit to the socially excluded, along with its business objectives. INTEGRA Foundation's group lending is largely aimed at 'women at risk', lone mothers and other marginalized social groups. It also offers training and carries out research to develop tools to assist small businesses struggling to survive in 'the corrupt and corrupting environment of Central and Eastern Europe'. The approach taken to assess the wider social impacts of these organizations compared the impacts associated with individual and group lending in the three different countries and also included a control group of non-client entrepreneurs and newly accepted clients.

Clearly the organizations with an explicit mandate to promote wider social impacts were the main MFIs to include a concern with this category of impact in their assessment studies. However, a number of organizations that did not have such a mandate also agreed to participate in the 'wider impacts' thematic group. One was FORA Fund, which focuses on providing quick and easy credit to the microenterprise sector. The other was SHARE, which styles itself as a minimalist microfinance programme whose Grameen-style group strategy has been primarily concerned with reducing the poverty of its members. Both SHARE and FORA Fund were included in the study of wider impacts to explore the extent to which they might generate such impacts as unintended effects.

Others

In addition to studies explicitly aimed at exploring wider social impacts, this chapter also reports on findings from impact assessments of SAT and LAPO, neither of which participated in the thematic research but both of which included a concern with building participation in the wider community into their organizational strategy.

SAT is based in Ghana and works with poorer clients, mainly female, but also some male. It describes its Trust Bank methodology as similar to the Grameen model. It focuses on poor but economically active individuals who form themselves into groups of between five and eight members. Between three and five groups make up a Trust Bank whose members agree to co-guarantee each other's loans. Trust Banks have an average of around 25 members. Groups meet weekly, while Trust Banks usually require bi-weekly or monthly meetings. The meetings serve multiple purposes: they are essential for building the relationships between the group members, as well as building the relationship between the members and the institution. They are used for the collection of loan repayments, but also as vehicles to provide clients with useful information in areas such as business management, family and community relationship building, interpersonal skills and health. SAT also seeks to promote its members' participation in various religious activities within the community, as well as in leadership roles in the civic life of the community.

LAPO is one of the leading MFIs in Nigeria with a clientele that is 95 per cent female. It follows a Grameen model, based on groups who agree to guarantee one another's loans. Five members are required to form a group, and a larger group, known as a union, is formed from 8 to 10 groups. Each union is under the jurisdiction of a branch office and receives regular visits by a credit officer from that office. In addition, a union leader and secretary elected by the union members report periodically to the branch manager. LADEC, the social development section of LAPO, organizes training and awareness raising for members and potential members on various aspects of community and home life. In order to qualify for a loan, members must first attend sessions in social development. Courses are offered in hygiene, health and nutrition, as well as in gender awareness and leadership skills. Working in the newly democratized context of Nigeria, LAPO places a great deal of emphasis on raising political consciousness among its members.

We also touch on findings from organizations associated with PROMUC in Peru. This was founded in 1994 as a partnership of NGOs concerned with microenterprise development as a strategy for poverty reduction and the empowerment of women. By the end of 2003, 12 NGOs were active members and 11 of them operated village or communal banking programmes under a common brand, *La Chanchita* (the piggy-bank). It also provides training of various kinds.

Group dynamics and the construction of social capital

Of all the studies reviewed (the evidence from some of which is presented in Table 5.3), the CYSD research (Dash and Kabeer, 2004) contains the most comprehensive coverage of group dynamics. It provides useful insights into what can be achieved when attention is given to the process of group formation as a route to changes in attitudes and behaviour. One important finding from the study was that, although the SHGs were made up of people who lived in close proximity to each other, they nevertheless brought together individuals who may not have had a great deal of routine interaction in the past. Of those interviewed, 91 per cent said that their group did not include close relatives, while 51 per cent said that their groups included members of other caste or tribal groups.

It was also evident from the CYSD study that interactions within mature groups differed in important ways from those within newer groups. First, older members were more likely to report arriving at group decisions through

Table 5.3 Evidence of impact: indicators of group dynamics

Organization	Indicators of change	Positive change	No change	Negative change
CYSD	% taking group decisions through discussion/consensus rather than through group leaders/CYSD staff	✓*		
	% reporting regular and active involvement in group activities	✓*		
	% reporting different kinds of group responsibilities	✓*		
	% preferring persuasion to peer pressure to ensure loan repayment	✓*		
	% considering group leadership to be effective in group solidarity/group action	✓*		
BRAC	% reporting independent management of loans	✓*		
	% expressing trust in group members	✓*		
	% expressing trust in other members of federated BRAC societies	✓*		
	% reporting exclusionary practices by group members			✓*
SHARE	% reporting improvement in relationship with other group members	✓*		
SAT	Received help from other group members		✓	

Note: * Indicates statistically significant up to 10% level of confidence.

discussion and consensus, while new members were more likely to rely on their office-bearing members or CYSD staff to take decisions on their behalf. Second, older members reported much higher levels of involvement in most group activities, with statistically significant differences in participation in monthly meetings, making decisions about credit, selecting group leaders and deciding group involvement in social activities, although not in executing them.

While the majority of all members agreed that their responsibilities as group members included attending group meetings and saving on a regular basis, older members were significantly more likely to consider getting members together for meetings and to take on involvement in credit-related and wider development activities as part of their group responsibilities. Interestingly, while neither old nor new members viewed sharing the training they had received with other members of their SHG as a group responsibility, 92 per cent of both categories that had received such training had in fact shared it with their group members. This suggests that sharing information between group members was regarded as a taken-for-granted aspect of group member-ship rather than an explicit responsibility.

While over 95 per cent of all members reported that loan disbursal decisions were based on group consensus,[2] a significantly higher percentage of mature members preferred to use persuasion by other SHG members to encourage repayment, while a significantly higher percentage of new members preferred to exert peer pressure. However there was very little support in either group for the use of penalties and even lower support for other tactics, such as per-suasion by SHG office bearers, pressure to leave the group or reconsideration of loan terms.

Mature members were also significantly more likely than new members to consider the group leadership to have been effective in promoting group solidarity and group initiatives. Lower percentages of both mature and new members considered group leadership to have been effective in building networks with other organizations and even lower percentages considered group leadership to have proved effective in book-keeping.

On balance, therefore, it would appear that CYSD has played an important role in extremely adverse circumstances. Their success relates not so much to building social capital, since strong social ties already existed between members of these isolated communities, but to diversifying associational life within the community. It has achieved this by building routine interactions between those who would not necessarily have met on such a regular basis and by shaping the nature of these interactions in order to promote new forms of solidarity and social relationships among its members.

The BRAC study (Kabeer and Matin, 2005) also included a component exploring intra-group relationships and interactions in its analysis of wider social impacts. It argues that 'The formation of women into groups that they can choose to belong to in a society in which they are normally secluded within the home and where social interactions tend to be restricted to family and kinship domain can itself be seen as a form of wider social impact. However, the significance of this impact will depend on the resilience of these groups and the extent to which they promote forms of change that might not otherwise have occurred'. The study found that most RDP group members, old as well as new, were made up of family members or people from the same neighbourhood. Given that groups tend to come together on the basis of physical proximity, this was not surprising. However, because a significant minority of group members did not come from the same neighbourhood, it could be said that participation in BRAC groups was serving to widen the social networks of its membership.

The BRAC findings suggest little difference between mature and new members in terms of attendance at group meetings: 68 per cent of new and 65 per cent of mature members had attended the last meeting. There was also very little difference in levels of dispute over loan size or repayment with other members, but significantly higher percentages of older members reported disputes with BRAC staff over size of loans and savings withdrawal. This could reflect greater assertiveness on their part or the fact that they had a different set of needs regarding loans and savings to newer members. Older group members were more likely to report independent management of their loans (that is, without help from BRAC staff in filling in forms and so forth) than new members, but this is to be expected since they have had longer experience in managing loans. Significantly, from a social capital perspective, older members were more likely than new members to express trust in other members of their group as well as in other members of the *palli samaj* that represented BRAC village group members at the ward level.

The study also found, however, that a higher percentage of older group members reported knowing of women who had wanted to join a BRAC group but could not. While this may once again reflect differences in duration of membership rather than a greater exclusionary tendency on the part of older groups, the finding does highlight the point made in some other studies that microfinance organizations have the potential for exacerbating inequality within the community by excluding the very poor.[3] As noted earlier, it is findings such as these that led BRAC to develop a programme aimed at the extremely poor.

Focus group and individual interviews with BRAC members provided other insights into their perceptions of their group identities and activities. They suggested that group meetings were an important forum through which they acquired information about various government programmes and provisions. They also provided an opportunity to exchange views about various social issues. However, older members felt that there had been a decline in the quality of group meetings over time as well as a decline in attendance. This was partly because of what they perceived as the increased amount of time devoted to borrowing and lending processes as BRAC accelerated the pace at which it expanded its microcredit activities in the 1990s. It was also because women themselves had become busier; some because of the success of their enterprises, others because more paid work had become available for women as a result of NGO activities of various kinds in their localities.

Analysing data on group dynamics reported by 450 mature and 450 new SHARE members, Cortijo and Kabeer (2004) found that 85 per cent of mature members and 61 per cent of new reported an improvement in relationships with other members since joining SHARE, while 9 per cent of mature members and 30 per cent of new reported no change. For those who reported a positive change, a sense of group unity was the main reason given by both mature and new members. Other less frequently given reasons included better understanding between group members and mutual assistance in times of difficulty. There was also evidence that mature group members were more likely to have given and received assistance in times of trouble than new members, a statistically significant difference.

However, the study suggests caution in interpreting this last finding for two reasons. First, duration of membership is positively related to the incidence of crises in the life of group members so that part of the difference may be reflecting this. Second, it is SHARE practice to require members to take responsibility for loan repayments of all group members. To some extent, therefore, there is an in-built mechanism to ensure that group members help each other in times of difficulty.

Insights into intra-group dynamics were also provided in Todd (2001) who asked 125 mature clients what they liked most about SHARE. While the most frequent response related to possibilities for saving (67 per cent), 32 per cent said that they liked group unity, responsibility and discipline. This partly supports the finding reported above by Cortijo and Kabeer. However, her analysis of why clients left SHARE offered a different, perspective on group dynamics. She randomly selected 125 ex-clients from among those who had left three branches in the six months prior to the study. The study found that the rate of exit of clients had grown over the past three years from an average of 7 per cent per year to 17 per cent and that 80 per cent of those interviewed had left within two years of joining SHARE.

The most frequently given reasons for leaving related to SHARE's group-lending methodology. As Todd points out, SHARE achieves its near-100 per cent repayment rate through the exercise of extremely strict discipline. All group members are jointly liable for the weekly repayments of all other members so that strong group pressure is exerted on those who do not come up with their weekly repayments. Moreover, field staff do not close the weekly centre meeting until all payments have been made; negotiations and house visits often make meetings extremely long. In addition, the obligation to cover the arrears of other members has led to considerable resentment, either on the part of the women themselves or their husbands. Various personal and business factors made up the other reasons for leaving.

While a study of ex-clients, made up as it is of those who have chosen to leave an organization or been expelled from it, might be expected to be biased towards extremely negative views of the organization, Todd's study revealed otherwise. Of the ex-clients she interviewed, 30 per cent were willing to return to SHARE, without condition, while another 40 per cent would have been willing to return if certain changes were made in organizational practices, including changing the weekly repayment system, shortening the length of meetings and allowing for individual lending, so that clients do not have to be responsible for each other's loans. An overwhelming majority of ex-clients said that their families had benefited from their loans, with improvements in food security the main category of benefit mentioned. Although group pressure had been the most frequently given reason for leaving, 91 per cent felt that they had benefited from their group membership. While the benefits they listed were largely instrumental (help in repayment of loans, access to new information and knowledge, new business contacts), 27 per cent felt that it had helped them make new friends, while 9 per cent felt it had improved their leadership skills.

The LAPO study (Garuba, 2004) did not include any specific question on group dynamics in its assessment of its impacts on existing clients, but a component of 132 ex-clients' views about their experience with LAPO provided some insights into this aspect. While most of the ex-clients put forward practical needs such as food and housing as the main benefits to their families of LAPO membership, only 11 per cent of them mentioned being able to join social groups. However, when asked more specifically about the benefits of being a member of a LAPO union, 46 per cent of the total sample cited the chance to form new friendships. To that extent, it would appear that participating in LAPO had strengthened social ties between group members. At the same time, however, among the problems associated with union membership, 30 per cent mentioned the burden of shouldering responsibility for others' loans and 26 per cent had been expelled from their union.

The study of SAT (Hishigsuren, 2004) found little evidence of internal solidarity between group members. It reported that 54 per cent of members stated that they did not share knowledge and skills with members in their group, while 52 per cent mentioned that they did not share ideas. However, if this implies that over 40 per cent of members *do* share knowledge, skills, and ideas – the study does not report on this – it would seem to be a positive impact. Nevertheless, only 9.7 per cent of the mature clients responded that they had received any support from other group members. As the study points out, these findings have implications for the attempts by SAT to promote social solidarity among its group members and suggests that greater efforts should be made to achieve this goal. Also, a survey of 178 ex-clients revealed that about 40 per cent had left for reasons related to group-lending methodology, the most common being the length of group meetings and exclusion by group members, presumably because of problems in repaying their loans.

A study of 60 clients from three PROMUC-related MFIs by Wright-Revelledo (2004) used the QUIP protocol (see Chapter 4) to carry out a qualitative investigation into various impacts. These were drawn from a sample of clients who had previously been included in an *Imp-Act* survey. In terms of group dynamics, the study reported that 41 clients expressed either enthusiasm or at least satisfaction with intra-group relationships. In explaining why, many stressed the democratic nature of group relations, the camaraderie, the ability to make new friends and the feelings of solidarity.

The emotional value of group membership was evident in the metaphors used by members to describe their attachment. One described the village bank (VB) 'as like a child who has helped me'; she had devoted her time in developing it and now that it had matured, it could protect her financially. Familial metaphors also cropped up in other interviews: 'the bank is like a family; we always say we are going to leave it but as we know each other we stick with it'. Another likened the VB to 'a friend . . . if you get ill, it helps you out'. One client, who also likened the bank to a family, added that she felt more 'looked after' in the village bank than in her own household, while another felt the VB represented a system of banking that she could trust.

The dissatisfaction expressed by 19 of the 60 members interviewed reflected a variety of reasons. Members of one MFI stressed conflicts and divisions within their VB. Although the MFI in question stipulated only two members of an immediate family could join the VB, there were many members who were related and who tended to dominate the group. In the other two MFIs, reasons for dissatisfaction ranged from mistrust of the leadership to non-repayment of loans by particular individuals. However, only 6 of these 19 were dissatisfied enough to have left the organization since the baseline survey on which the sample had been drawn. A further 12 were seriously considering leaving. In all of these cases, the main reason was group dynamics and in particular, dissatisfaction with the 'authoritarian and repressive' way the group was run, or personal conflicts with individual members who are often related by family networks.

The study of FORA Fund, INTEGRA (Romania) and INTEGRA Foundation (Slovakia) (Alexeeva *et al*, 2004) also used qualitative methods to explore aspects of group dynamics. It found that, in general, it was mutual interactions prior to joining the MFI group that helped to explain the social cohesiveness of a group, rather than the experience of MFI group membership. However, the quality of group leadership may have been important in holding a group together: 'There are tensions in any solidarity group. But if anyone oversteps the line, aggravating these tensions, this is dealt with collectively. Each of the group members has a confidential relationship with the group organizer, and the fact of these confidences not being broken strengthens the group's cohesion'.

To sum up, even this limited number of studies highlights that groups organized for microfinance purposes embody varying social relationships and represent very different potentials in their members' lives. Greater attention to the actual process of group formation can serve to construct new kinds of social relationships within a community, to provide alternative models of social interaction, as well as to act as a source of emotional support for group members. However, in some cases, it appears that the MFIs relied on the existing social capital among its members, depending on their prior knowledge of each other to ensure that its lending operations went smoothly. Group membership may represent a source of conflict and tension in the lives of members if procedures are not put in place to manage such conflicts and to build a sense of solidarity. The consistency with which ex-clients, who had left within a short period of joining, gave their reason for leaving as the demands of the group-lending methodology suggests that group solidarity cannot be taken for granted.

Building citizenship: participation in the community

A second set of impacts included in the wider impacts studies related to inter-actions between MFI group members and the community in which they were located. Such impacts can be analysed in terms of the 'concentric circles' of relationships referred to earlier, starting with the immediate circle of family, neighbours and sections of the community with whom MFI members had frequent inter-personal encounters, and moving gradually outwards to those with whom their interactions were based on institutionalized rather than personal ties. Finally, there is an outer ring in which there are more general categories of people: the élite, the state, people from other religions and so on. In this section and in Table 5.4, we report on changes in the domain of

Table 5.4 Evidence of impact: indicators of community participation

Organization	Indicators of change	Positive change	No change	Negative change
BRAC	% expressing trust in 'other villagers'	✓*		
	% expressing trust in people from 'other religions'	✓*		
	% expressing trust in informal village justice	✓*		
	% expressing trust in money lenders	✓*		
	% expressing trust in village elites	✓		
	% expressing trust in members of other NGOs		✓	
PRADAN	% expressing trust in people from other religions	✓*		
CYSD	% invited to community gatherings	✓*		
SHARE	% expressing improvement in relations with customers	✓*		
	% expressing improvement in relations with suppliers	✓		
SAT	Increased partipation in voluntary community activities		✓	
FORA Fund	% expressing trust towards customers	✓*		

Note: * Indicates statistically significant up to 10% level of confidence.

community and civil society, while in the next section, we consider changes in relation to policies and politics – the domain of the state.

The BRAC study on wider social impacts was carried out using the 'concentric circles' approach. A comparison based on descriptive statistics showed that the number of years of membership of a BRAC group made little difference to whether or not they were consulted by neighbours for advice, whether or not they were members of other informal committees and associations within their villages, or whether or not they had participated in a *gram shalish* (village tribunal). In fact, individual loanees were generally more likely than group members to respond positively to all three of these questions, possibly a reflection of their higher socio-economic status compared to group members.

However, the study also found that around 15 per cent of both mature and newer members, and 8 per cent of individual loanees, were members of at least one other NGO. Clearly, it was possible that any findings of impact could be attributed to either dual membership or to membership of another NGO rather than to membership of a BRAC group. Consequently all results were re-analysed using multiple regression analysis to control for dual NGO membership for both group and MELA (Micro Enterprise Lending and Assistance) members. Regression analysis did not alter the findings for group members but interestingly, revealed that length of involvement with BRAC increased the likelihood of MELA members participating in a *gram shalish* (often organized by BRAC members), independently of their age, education and household wealth. Since women have not traditionally participated in *gram shalish*, this represents an organizational innovation in the informal justice system of the community.

Given the importance of the concept of trust in both the older literature on social solidarity as well as in more recent work on social capital, a series of questions on trust relating to closer and more distant relationships was asked as part of the BRAC study and explored in greater detail through qualitative interviews. The results appeared at first to confirm the belief of those who describe Bangladesh as having a culture characterized by high levels of distrust. The vast majority of BRAC members, regardless of years of membership agreed with the statement 'you always have to be careful in dealing with people', while only 6 per cent of new groups members, 4 per cent of MELA loanees and none of the mature members agreed with the statement 'most people can be trusted'. It was only in relation to immediate family members that all BRAC group members, both old and new as well as individual loanees, expressed high levels of trust (99 per cent).

However, responses to other questions suggest that this lack of trust is not an immutable aspect of social life in Bangladesh and that participation in the kinds of activities associated with group membership had helped to increase levels of trust in different categories of actors and institutions within the community. Years of membership did not make much difference to levels of trust expressed towards neighbours – both old and new members expressed high levels of trust. However, years of group membership did increase to a statistically significant extent the levels of trust expressed with regard to other villagers, to members of other religions and, as we noted earlier, to other members of BRAC groups and to members of BRAC's *palli samaj*. The findings relating to trust in relation to people from other religions are worth noting: in a part of the world where religious divisions have been a source of intense, often murderous, conflict, any form of intervention that serves to increase religious tolerance deserves strong support.

Years of membership did not, however, make a great deal of difference to whether or not BRAC members trusted members of other NGOs – unless they were themselves members of another NGO – and nor did it make much difference to attitudes towards BRAC's legal centres. It also did not affect levels of trust expressed towards actors and institutions that represented local power structures: the *gram shalish*, the village élites and moneylenders. Levels of trust expressed towards moneylenders were particularly low. Finally, simultaneous membership of another NGO had very little independent effect on most of these findings, with some exceptions. Dual NGO membership was strongly associated with higher levels of participation in various informal associations within the community and in the *gram shalish*.

Regression analysis was also carried out on the sample of individual MELA loanees. It suggested that here too, years of participation in BRAC's lending programme made a difference to certain outcomes. As we noted, longer-standing participants were more likely to have participated in *gram shalish*. They were also more likely to express trust in *gram shalish* as an institution, in the BRAC legal centre and in the local village leaders. However, land owner-ship also played an important role in explaining some of the variation in expressed levels of trust: MELA members who had more land were more likely to be consulted for advice and conflict resolution by neighbours, to have participated in *gram shalish* and to have trust in other villagers.

In general MELA loanees, the better-off group in the sample, expressed higher levels of trust in actors and institutions representing the local power structure than did the poorer BRAC group members. This suggests that the findings on trust may tell us more about the social hierarchy in Bangladesh than they do about public confidence in the integrity of the actors and institutions concerned. The qualitative interviews supported this interpretation. They suggested that trust was generally related to a better understanding of who the actors were or how the institutions worked and hence a greater degree of comfort in dealing with them. Thus, older group members and wealthier MELA members trusted other villagers, not necessarily because they were more trusting or that they had experienced other villagers as more trustworthy, but because they were more self-confident in their dealings with them. As we will see, this is similar to the interpretation of trust that emerged from the study in Eastern Europe and Russia, though not from the PRADAN study.

The PRADAN survey included a series of questions on levels of trust, both generally and towards specific actors and institutions within the community.

However, it became clear from preliminary results that the large presence of tribal groups within the sample (34 per cent of total sample) was complicating the results because tribal people as a group appeared to express higher levels of trust than the rest of the population, regardless of whether or not they were members of PRADAN. Thus, 47 per cent of tribal people in the survey population agreed with the statement 'you can generally trust people', compared to 25 per cent of the rest of the population; whereas 45 per cent agreed that 'you have to be careful dealing with people', compared to 73 per cent of the rest of the population. Tribal communities clearly have high-trust cultures, based on strong ties of cooperation among their members. This culture does not seem to reflect how they are treated by the rest of society, which, as we have noted, is generally very harshly.

Because of this, the analysis explored levels of trust among PRADAN members and non-members separately for tribal groups and for the rest of the population. It found high levels of trust expressed towards members of the immediate family for all sections of the population. It also found uniformly high levels of trust towards PRADAN field staff by all PRADAN SHG members. For the rest of the results, while membership of PRADAN was usually associated with higher levels of trust, for both tribal and non-tribal groups, differences between members and non-members were generally not significant. The only significant results related to trust in people from other religions: members of PRADAN, whether tribal or not, were more likely to trust people from other religions than non-members.

The assessment of FORA Fund, INTEGRA (Romania) and INTEGRA Foundation (Slovakia) compared participation in a variety of formal associations by group members, individual loanees and the control group of non-members. Its findings suggest that the people most likely to receive individual loans were those who were already members of formal associations prior to their involvement with the MFI in question. By contrast, those receiving loans through groups may have had active informal networks but reported much lower membership of formal associations. This is consistent with the point noted earlier that group membership was generally aimed at the more socially excluded groups.

Access to MFIs did not have any consistent effect with regard to improving clients' relationships with other business organizations. Positive responses this issue were low for both mature and new or non-clients of FORA Fund clients, although mature clients were more likely to report some improvement. Higher positive responses were reported in Slovakia but new or non-clients were more likely to report improvements than mature clients. In Romania, however, there were higher levels of improved links with business organizations, and INTEGRA Romania's mature clients reported much higher levels of improvement than new or non-clients.

The study also included a number of questions on trust in relation to different categories of actors and institutions. As in the other contexts studied, the highest levels of trust were expressed in relation to family members (although interestingly, in Russia, group loanees appeared to trust their customers more than their families!). High levels of trust were also expressed in relation to customers and commercial banks in Slovakia and Romania, but differences between group and individual borrowers were not significant. In Russia, group borrowers expressed significantly higher levels of trust towards their customers than did individual borrowers. Both groups expressed high levels of mistrust towards commercial banks.

The SHARE study on wider social impacts explored the extent to which duration of membership of SHARE had affected relationships within the community (Cortijo and Kabeer, 2004). However, in exploring membership of different kinds of associations and committees within the community, it was found 40 per cent of mature and 31 per cent of new SHARE members were also members of DWCRA, a government-sponsored SHG programme that promoted the practice of savings among group members before linking them up to a variety of government services, including the banking system. As noted earlier, the government, under the previous chief minister of Andhra Pradesh, had been extremely active in promoting such self-help groups so that Andhra accounted for around 40 per cent of all DWCRA self-help groups in the country. Some overlap between DWCRA and SHARE group membership was inevitable. Membership of other formally constituted associations was low, while other NGOs were almost non-existent.

However, participation in an alternative form of microfinance organization, and one closely related to government, was clearly likely to have an influence on the kind of wider social impacts the study was investigating. Consequently, multiple regression analysis was used to separate out the effects of membership of a SHARE group from the effects of DWCRA membership. The results showed that years of membership of SHARE had led to an improvement in business relationships within the community (with suppliers and customers), but had had no effects on other relationships within the local community. DWCRA membership, on the other hand, did not lead to any significant improvements in business relationships, but did improve relationships with the rest of the community.

The single most frequently given reason for improvements in relationships was greater personal discipline. Other frequently given reasons were increased respect from others and, particularly among new members, the perception that they were credit worthy. This finding corroborates findings from the qualitative interviews carried out by Todd (2001). The clients she interviewed said that they were easily recognized by others within the community, that they 'cherished' this recognition and that they no longer feared anybody but God: 'What is there to fear now? We are grateful to God and may we have His blessings'.

While Todd's qualitative interviews suggested that others in their villages often came to SHARE members for advice, partly because they were seen as more literate than others, the quantitative results reported by Cortijo and Kabeer suggest that this did not translate into higher levels of participation in various traditional forums. This was true for both those who were only members of SHARE groups and for those who were also members of DWCRA. Instead, it was the age of member that was most strongly associated with participation in traditional forums.

Regarding improvements in relationships within the community, the SAT study mainly reported evidence of improvement in business relationships. Of members questioned, 85 per cent reported improvements in relationships with customers and suppliers as a result of the training received on customer care and retention, planning and good pricing as well as payment of suppliers upfront. In contrast, in the past they vented their frustrations on their customers and charged higher prices because they had to credit their goods at a higher price from middlemen. Suppliers also used to refuse them supplies because they could not pay them in the past. Suppliers also had greater confidence in them and therefore were more willing to give their goods on credit without fearing that the clients would not pay.

The study also included the type, frequency and kind of role played by its members in community activities as indicators of their social empowerment. Regular participation in community activities varied from high in the case of worship services (79 per cent), funerals (54 per cent), social activities (41 per cent) and other religious activities (35 per cent), to the lowest levels of participation for civic activities (25 per cent). There was no clear pattern in participation by duration of membership, but some differences were observed in terms of frequency of participation. Mature clients were far more likely to attend funerals than newer clients, a statistically significant difference. They were also more likely to have contributed to funeral expenses. This appears to be partly a function of their older age composition. New clients participated far more frequently than both intermediate and mature clients in civic activities: 43 per cent participated on a weekly basis compared to 23 per cent of intermediate clients and 20 per cent of mature. There was little variation by duration of membership in terms of the leadership roles played in various kinds of community activities, with lowest levels of leadership reported for civic activities.

SAT had anticipated that participation in its programme would 'empower the clients and increase the frequency with which they participated in civic activities'. This was clearly not borne out by the findings. The study suggested differences in participation might reflect the more youthful composition of newer clients, or else the demands on the time of older clients who might have more successful businesses to run.

Taken together, the findings in this section suggest that the quality of relationship between group members and other sections of the community was very unevenly associated with group membership, partly because other factors may have been more important. In the BRAC study, for instance, it was to the relatively better-off MELA clients that other villagers went to for advice rather than to longer-standing BRAC group members. At the same time, however, duration of group membership did serve to promote greater trust on the part of group members towards others in their village community, as well as towards members of other religions.

Both the SHARE studies as well as the studies of FORA Fund and the two INTEGRA organizations suggest some improvements in business relationships, but less in wider community relationships. The findings in terms of wider relationships within the community were weak for PRADAN and SAT, although the finding that PRADAN members were more likely to trust members of other religions is worth noting. One conclusion to draw from this is that the hierarchies embedded in the informal relationships of the community appear to be much harder to transform through group membership than relationships within the groups themselves.

Building citizenship: participation in policy and politics

Finally, we turn to the evidence provided by the *Imp-Act* studies for impacts that come closer to state-centred notions of citizenship and relate to changes in the domain of policy and politics (as illustrated in Table 5.5). The starting point for a number of studies on this aspect of impact is change in knowledge. As Galston (2003, in Alexeeva *et al*, 2004) points out, 'basic civic knowledge is central to democratic citizenship'. One route through which knowledge trans-

Table 5.5 Evidence of impact: participation in policy and politics

Organization	Evidence of impact	Positive change	No change	Negative change
CYSD	% knowing bank rules and procedures	✓*		
	% attending CYSD-related meetings	✓*		
	% interacting with forest officers	✓*		
	% interacting with bank officials	✓*		
	% interacting with government health officials	✓*		
	% interacting with teachers	✓*		
	% participating in *gram/palli sabha* meetings	✓*		
	% voting in ward elections	✓*		
	% voting in *sarpanch* elections	✓*		
	% voting in *samity* elections	✓*		
	% voting in *zilla* elections	✓*		
	% campaigning in ward elections	✓*		
	% campaigning in *sarpanch* elections	✓*		
	% expressing desire to contest elections	✓*		
	% participating in public protest against alcoholism	✓*		
	% participating in public demand for schools	✓*		
	other political protests		✓	

Table 5.5—*continued*

Organization	Evidence of impact	Positive change	No change	Negative change
PRADAN	% knowing legal age of marriage	✓*		
	% knowing of SGYS programme for the poor	✓*		
	% attended *gram sabha* meeting in previous year	✓*		
	% approached bank for individual loan	✓*		
BRAC	% knowing name of elected woman member	✓*		
	% accessing government programs	✓*		
	% voting in national elections	✓*		
	% voting in local elections	✓*		
	% participating in protest/campaign		✓	
	% not paying bribe in past year	✓*		
	% expressing trust in locally elected officials	✓*		
SHARE	% accessing government programs	✓*		
	% interacting with elected and local officials	✓*		
	% attending a *gram sabha* meeting	✓*		
	% able to name *mandal* president	✓*		
	% voting at local *gram panchyat* elections			
SAT	Membership of district assembly		✓	
FORA Fund, Russia	Trust in customers	✓*		
	Trust in government officials	✓*		
	Commercial bank	✓		
	Police			✓
	Overall levels of trust	✓*		
	Political participation (as member or financial contribution)	✓*		
INTEGRA Foundation Romania	Trust in customers			✓
	Trust in local government officials	✓*		
	Commercial banks	✓		
	Police	✓		
INTEGRA, Slovakia	Trust in customers		✓	
	Trust in local government officials	✓*		
	Commercial banks		✓	
	Police	✓		

Note: * Indicates statistically significant up to 10% level of confidence.

lates into citizenship is through its effect on levels of trust in the public domain: 'The more knowledge citizens have of civic affairs, the less likely they are to experience a generalized mistrust of, or alienation from, public life. Ignorance is the father of fear, and knowledge is the mother of trust' (ibid.). The other route is through its effects on the willingness of citizens to participate in both formal and informal political activity.

CYSD and PRADAN work in poor and illiterate communities in extremely isolated areas so that their members have very limited access to the means by which new knowledge can be acquired. For instance, less than 1 per cent of the entire sample covered by the CYSD study mentioned newspapers as a source of information, around 10 per cent mentioned the radio and only one person mentioned the television. In the PRADAN study, only 15 per cent of the entire sample owned a radio, 2 per cent owned an electrical bulb and less than 1 per cent owned a television or a telephone. Not surprisingly, both organizations placed a great deal of emphasis on providing their group members with information and skills that would equip them to operate with greater assurance in their relationships in the wider world. Both organizations sought to explore the effects of their efforts.

The PRADAN study attempted to ascertain the extent to which SHG group membership had promoted greater awareness about official entitlements and obligations on the part of its members. The findings showed that PRADAN members were significantly more likely than non-members to know the legal age of marriage and about the government's main poverty alleviation programme. However, a higher percentage of non-members knew about the 'Below Poverty Line' list that entitles certificate holders to eligibility for poverty programmes and other subsidies. There were no significant differences between the two groups in the numbers who knew about the minimum wage (19.3 per cent of the overall sample) and insurance programmes for the poor (3 per cent of the sample).

The CYSD study included a number of questions on 'civic knowledge', including rules and procedures for applying for a bank loan, opening a bank pass book, filing a complaint with the police, where to file complaints about harassment, how to put demands to the local *panchayat* and so on. However, levels of knowledge were generally low and did not vary significantly between mature and new members, with one exception: mature CYSD members had significantly higher levels of knowledge about bank rules and procedures.

CYSD also explored the extent to which membership of its groups had helped to diversify the channels of communication through which members obtained information relevant to their needs. It found very little difference between new and mature groups in terms of the number of different channels they mentioned. There was also scant difference in their reliance on other villagers, on their SHG and on village elders for information. However, mature members were significantly more likely to rely on field workers from CYSD, while newer members were significantly more likely to mention government officials. While both categories mentioned the importance of such information for improving their livelihoods, for helping them to cope with crisis and, to a lesser extent, for gaining access to government services, newer members were much more likely than mature members to consider that access to information had enhanced their sense of self-esteem and social status within the community. It may be that this latter effect wears off once access to such information comes to be taken for granted.

Along with knowledge about rights and entitlements, impacts on citizenship practice included in the PRADAN and CYSD studies related to participation in community life. Levels of participation in the formal public domain were found to be extremely low for members as well as non-members in both the study locations, partly an indication of the absence of formal public institutions and partly of low overall levels of public participation that characterize these contexts. Only 7 per cent of the entire PRADAN sample had approached a government official in the past year to obtain services, solve a problem or obtain eligibility for a programme. Similarly, only 8 per cent had attended a community meeting in the previous year. One reason for this is that that the traditional *panchayat* system was not functioning in Jharkhand, so village-level *gram sabha* meetings were not being held regularly. However, 11 per cent of PRADAN members had attended such a meeting compared to just 1 per cent of non-members, a statistically significant difference. Only 3 per cent of PRADAN members, and none of the non-members, were members of a village committee. 15 per cent of members had approached a bank for an individual loan, indicative of the exercise of individual initiative, while only 2.3 per cent of non-members had done the same, again a statistically significant difference.

The CYSD study found that mature CYSD members were more likely to be invited to social gatherings, to have attended group-related meetings and to have gained recognition from government officials and other local bodies in their community. The percentage of CYSD members who had visited a government official in order to address some problem, while also extremely low among both mature and new members, was generally higher among mature members. The categories of officials with whom interactions were highest, and for whom differences between mature and new groups were statistically significant, tended to be those with responsibilities for services that impinged most directly on the section of the population concerned: forest officers, bank officials, government health officials and teachers (with whom the highest levels of interaction were reported). A significantly higher percentage of mature members than new members participated in the *palli sabh* and *gram sabha* meetings (these are the lowest tier of the local governance structure in India), but, as in the PRADAN study, overall levels of participation were low.

The study also explored various forms of political agency on the part of CYSD members. It found that the percentages voting in elections were highest at local level (ward level, for the *sarpanch*, for the *samity* member and *zilla* elections), with mature members reporting significantly higher levels of participation than new members: generally between 80–90 per cent. Percentages voting declined at higher levels (legislative assembly and national elections) and differences between mature and new members disappeared. Much lower percentages of both mature and new members campaigned in these elections, but mature members generally reported significantly higher percentages of participation in election campaigns for ward members and the *sarpanch*. Around 14 per cent of mature members expressed a desire to contest a local election compared to 9 per cent of new members (a statistically significant difference).

Finally, the study investigated various instances of protests and campaigns by CYSD group members. Once again, levels of such action were extremely low for most issues but considerably higher for those issues that had most direct impact on members' lives. The highest levels of involvement were reported in relation to fighting male alcoholism within the community: 43 per cent of mature members and 37 per cent of new members had taken part in protests against the making and selling of liquor, while 55 per cent of mature and 30 per cent of new members had participated in anti-liquor campaigns within their community. The differences were statistically significant. Such action has to be interpreted in terms of the strong relationship between male alcoholism and violence against women noted in various studies, as well as the drain that alcohol consumption represents on family resources. Education was the other main issue around which members were active, with mature members reporting higher levels of activity than new. Such action generally took the form of demands for schools under the education guarantee scheme in areas that lacked schools, as well as protests against teacher irresponsibility.

The study of BRAC found that individual MELA loanees, who were better off and more educated, generally reported higher levels of political knowledge than RDP group members. Among RDP group members, most were able to correctly name the prime minister and the union chairman, regardless of duration of group membership, while somewhat lower percentages knew the name of the party in power, the name of an opposition party and the name of the leader of another party. Far fewer were aware of their main constitutional rights.

The regression analysis of the sample of RDP group members allowed comparison on the basis of actual years of group membership, rather than between 'mature' and 'new' categories, and also controlled for dual NGO membership. It suggested that duration of membership did have some statistically significant impacts in the domain of policy and politics. The likelihood of access to government programmes increased with number of years of membership, as did the likelihood of voting in national and local elections, and knowledge of the name of the elected woman representative at the local level. Years of membership reduced the likelihood of having paid a bribe during the previous year (although not the likelihood of ever having paid a bribe). It also increased the likelihood of trust in locally elected representatives: male and female members of the union *parishad*, as well as the chairman of the union *parishad*. However, it had little effect on levels of trust expressed towards the police or government health providers or private doctors, although it increased trust in BRAC health workers.

With regard to individual MELA loanees, number of years of participation in BRAC's lending programme increased the likelihood that they knew the name of the woman member of their local union *parishad*, but it was their ownership of land, rather than participation in BRAC, that determined the likelihood that they expressed trust in the locally elected male and female members of the union *parishad* and in the union *parishad* chairman. The study concluded, on the basis of its findings, that while material forms of capital, such as land, clearly increased the likelihood of various kinds of participation and recognition within the village community and polity among the better-off, for the poor, group membership did act as a form of social capital, achieving some of the effects associated with wealth, and thus partially compensating for their material deficits. It was also clear that type of group membership mattered. Separating out the effects of BRAC membership from membership of another NGO showed that much of the impact could be attributed to years of membership of BRAC. Since these other NGOs (most frequently ASA and Grameen) tended to be more minimalist in approach than BRAC, this is not surprising.

As noted above, while SHARE does not have any explicit programmes to promote wider social impacts, it participated in a wider impacts study in order to examine the extent to which its group methodology might bring about social changes of an unanticipated kind. Regression analysis allowed the effects of DWCRA membership to be separated from the duration of membership of a SHARE group. The results suggested that membership of DWCRA had an independent, positive and statistically significant effect on the following outcomes: the likelihood of access to government programmes for the poor, the likelihood of meeting with various elected and government officials (the *sarpanch*, the district collector and the revenue officer), the likelihood of attendance of various public meetings (*gram sabha, Janma Bhumi* and collector's grievance day), the likelihood of participation in political protests and campaigns, and the ability to name the *mandal* president and the prime minister of the country.

Controlling for DWCRA membership, SHARE membership also had certain impacts that generally reinforced the 'DWCRA effect'. Thus, years of SHARE membership reinforced the positive and significant effect of DWCRA on the likelihood of having met with the *sarpanch*, the likelihood of attending a *gram sabha* meeting and the likelihood of naming the *mandal* president. In addition, membership of SHARE increased the likelihood of voting at the local *gram panchayat* elections, an effect that DWCRA did not have.

Qualitative findings reported by Todd (2001) on the basis of interviews with 33 SHARE clients support the view that SHARE had weak social impacts in the wider community. While participation in SHARE had increased clients' self-confidence and entrepreneurial activities and brought them greater respect from extended family and neighbours, the majority had no involvement with community activities outside their attendance of SHARE centre meetings and also had no desire to get involved. The only four clients who were active had been active before joining SHARE, although two said that the training they had received from SHARE had strengthened them. Todd concludes that 'The general perception of most of these women is that anything to do with community should be taken up either by elected representatives or by government officials. They do not feel that they are equipped to play any role. The majority refused to acknowledge that there are any problems in their community'.

The importance of controlling for alternative routes through which observed impacts might occur is clearly demonstrated through the study of SHARE. Indeed, it may be that some of the positive wider impacts associated with SHARE members represent 'externalities' of DWCRA membership, in that members of SHARE groups that also included DWCRA members are likely to be influenced in their knowledge and behaviour by their indirect association with DWCRA.

The possible externalities of DWCRA membership were noted, though not controlled for, in the Todd study of SHARE's poverty impacts. Todd noted, first of all, that most of the SHARE clients in her study were members of DWCRA before SHARE began operations. Second, SHARE clients were saving twice as much with organizations outside SHARE, mainly with DWCRA. As Todd points out, as a government programme, DWCRA had a high confidence rating among rural women and was accessible in even the more remote rural areas. This raises the question as to whether some of the poverty impacts that her study documents might have partly reflected the DWCRA effect. However this is made less likely by the subsequent study by Cortijo and Kabeer (2004), which did control for DWCRA membership, and that found that in fact SHARE membership had a much stronger effect on economic impacts (household food security and business relations within the community) than did membership of DWCRA.

The political impacts sought in the Nigerian context by the LAPO study reflected the country's long history of military dictatorship and the significance attached by LAPO to its political education programme to promote democratic values. The study found that clients on their second and fourth loans were generally more likely to register to vote than new entrants, while clients on their fourth loans were more likely to vote than both new entrants and those on their second loans. Percentages registering and voting were, however, extremely high and differences between groups at different stages of membership were not large. The reasons given by respondents for voting for a particular candidate emphasized the perceived ability of the candidate (67 per cent), while party affiliation came very low down (9 per cent). In terms of preferred form of government, 56 per cent expressed a preference for elected government, while 18 per cent expressed a preference for 'any good one'. Worryingly, 23 per cent preferred a military government. Length of participation in LAPO did not appear to make any consistent difference to these expressions of preference.

The study of FORA Fund and the INTEGRA organizations explored policies and politics from a number of different perspectives. One proposition explored was that higher levels of exposure to the media might lead to higher levels of political knowledge and trust, but the evidence collected did not support this proposition. However, the data reported provides a picture of very literate and 'media-connected' societies: for instance, 70–80 per cent of the sample in Russia read a local paper, while 50–60 per cent read a national paper; 47–62 per cent heard the news on the radio, over 90 per cent heard it on TV and 6–17 per cent were connected to the internet. Access to media was as high, and even higher in some cases, in Slovakia and Romania. In Slovakia, for instance, 42–50 per cent of the sample had internet access. The contrast could not be more striking between the communication channels used in Russia, Slovakia and Romania and those utilized in the contexts in which PRADAN and CYSD work.

The study also investigated whether involvement with an MFI was associated with an improvement in access to government services for entrepreneurs. A positive but small effect was found in both Romania and Russia. None of the new or non-clients reported an improvement. In Slovakia, however, 13 per cent of clients reported an improvement, but an even higher percentage (54 per cent) of new or non-clients gave a positive response. Experience of corruption appeared to be highest in Romania among both clients and non-clients (52 per cent and 54 per cent); it was higher among clients than non-clients in Russia (23 per cent and 17 per cent), but lower among clients than non-clients in Slovakia (13 per cent and 29 per cent). In general, problems of corruption grew with the size of the enterprise because there were only 'small pickings' to be had from microenterprises.

While there were no systematic differences between clients and non/new clients in terms of their experience of corruption or exposure to the media, some significant differences were found in relation to levels of trust expressed towards representatives of the state. In all three countries, microfinance clients were significantly more likely than new or non-clients to express trust towards government officials. While they were also more likely to express trust towards the police, differences were not significant. Alexeeva *et al* (2004), like the Bangladesh study reviewed above, argue that a lack of trust stems from ignorance and fear of the unknown: 'The more we know about the world, the less intimidating and opaque it seems'.

Finally, the study by Alexeeva *et al* also explored political activity. We have already noted that it found that mature microfinance clients in all three countries were less likely to participate in various formal associations than new or non-clients. The Slovakia component of the study reported a somewhat different finding for membership of political associations. Here clients generally reported higher levels of political association than non-members. However, this was mainly restricted to individual clients, 29 per cent of whom reported such an association compared to only 3 per cent of group clients. In addition, findings from all three countries suggest low levels of formal political participation everywhere but somewhat higher levels among clients. By and large participation also tended to be of a passive kind: membership of a party or providing a financial contribution. Less well captured by the survey data was the kind of informal political activity that was reported during the qualitative interviews. In many cases this took place outside of the MFI groups but sometimes though them, such as the transfer of a federation of entrepreneurs into a political entity to negotiate with government, or taking a collective stand against corruption on the part of local authorities.

Comparing the findings in this section to those in the previous sections seems to suggest that MFI group membership may be more effective in promoting participation in the political process than in transforming the informal social hierarchies of the community. It is an effective means of disseminating information about policy entitlements and political rights. It is more consistent in promoting trust in elected officials and government service providers than in promoting trust in local élites. Such changes can be a starting pointing for bringing about other changes.

It is also evident that organizational mission and the question of 'intent' do appear to make a difference to what is achieved. Both CYSD and PRADAN reported small but significant achievements in promoting knowledge and practice in the domain of policy and politics, despite the challenging conditions under which they work and the virtual absence of other complementary organizations. BRAC, which supplements its Grameen-style group methodology with a variety of social inputs, reported a range of wider impacts in this domain than appeared to be associated with the kinds of NGOs that its members belong to. Alternatively, SHARE, which follows a more minimalist version of the Grameen approach, benefited from the widespread presence of DWCRA groups, membership of which either interacted with or acted independently of SHARE membership in achieving a range of wider social impacts.

Conclusion

This chapter deals with an area of impact that has not received a great deal of attention in the microfinance literature: impacts in the wider community and policy arena in which microfinance clients and members are located. The findings reported highlight the importance of context and the nature of the challenges the MFIs face in determining which impacts to look for and where. An understanding of context also helps to explain the impacts that they were able to achieve. For instance, the MFI role of providing its members with the knowledge and skills they need to operate in the wider community is clearly likely to be extremely different in Jharkhand, where a sample of 800 households reported four electric bulbs between them, compared to Romania where over 40 per cent of those interviewed had access to the Internet.

The findings also provide a reminder of the differences in the length of time that the organizations have had to achieve certain kinds of impacts. Many of the mature clients included in the BRAC study had been with the organization for ten years or so, while those included in the SHARE study had joined a maximum of five years ago. It is not surprising that the organizations reported very different degrees of impact.

Bearing in mind these differences in contexts and duration, it is nevertheless worth noting the extent to which the impacts achieved appear to partly reflect differences in organizational strategy. Organizations that invest a great deal of effort in the promotion of social change were also most likely to report social impacts. The process approach to building self-help groups taken by both CYSD and PRADAN resulted in significant impacts in relation to community, to policy and to politics in extremely challenging circumstances. However, while CYSD was more likely than PRADAN to explore and to report political action on the part of its members, PRADAN was more likely to report changes in practical knowledge and livelihood practices at the level of the community. BRAC also reported some important changes in the political behaviour and trust relationships within the community, including greater likelihood of voting at both local and national elections. Such behaviour appeared to be more strongly associated with years of membership of BRAC, rather than to membership of other more minimalist microfinance programmes to which some of its members also belonged.

The SHARE studies also illustrate the relationship between organizational strategy and impact. Many SHARE members also belonged to government-promoted DWCRA self-help groups. The findings showed that SHARE membership tended to be associated with changes in business relations with clients and with members' economic standing within the community, while DWCRA membership was more strongly associated with improved access to government programmes and government officials, reflecting its status as a government programme. It is important, however, to emphasize the finding that membership of SHARE was more strongly associated with the likelihood of voting at village level elections than membership of DWCRA. Neither organization appeared to affect voting at state or national elections. The process by which MFI membership translates into behavioural change in the political arena has not been well researched, but it is clear that there is an important research agenda here.

The study of FORA Fund and the INTEGRA organizations found that while it was prior participation in the formal associational life of the community that explained which sections of the community obtained individual loans, the more socially-oriented INTEGRA organizations had a much strong effect in terms of building trust among socially excluded groups than did the more business-oriented FORA Fund. They also had a greater effect in strengthening political participation.

Another important point, illustrated by the BRAC study, is that under some circumstances, the social capital or group relationships promoted by the MFIs appeared to substitute for their lack of material capital. In other words, certain attitudinal and behavioural outcomes that were associated with land ownership among the better-off and more recently enrolled individual loanees, were also associated with years of RDP group membership among poorer group members.

A number of studies also point to the possibility that not only is microfinance provision failing to reach the very poor (see Chapter 3), but it might also be having the effect of widening inequalities among the poor (Copestake, 2001a; Hulme, 2000b; Buckley, 1997). We see some evidence for this in Wright-Revelledo's (2004) finding that it was the most vulnerable sections of the community who benefited least from their participation in microfinance activities of the PROMUC network in Peru. Evidence also comes from the BRAC study that showed that women who wanted to join BRAC groups were actively excluded by group members (presumably because they were seen as credit risks). Further support is provided by various *Imp-Act* studies in which ex-clients report their expulsion. BRAC, as we have noted, is now aware of this and has begun a separate programme aimed at the 'ultra-poor' within the communities in which it works.

Finally, it is also clear that findings such as these have implications for calculating the trade-offs between poverty impacts and financial sustainability, as discussed in earlier chapters. Certain forms of microfinance provision are successful in particular contexts in going beyond a narrow range of economic impacts, important as these undoubtedly are, to achieve a wider range of impacts that address the multidimensional nature of the causes and consequences of poverty and social exclusion, including the capacity of poor and excluded groups to think and act as citizens. This should be factored into attempts to compare the value of impacts relative to the costs of achieving these impacts. To limit the calculation to immediate and tangible costs and benefits is to lose sight of the underlying structures of poverty and social exclusion and to concentrate only on their immediate manifestations.

CHAPTER SIX
Impact in local financial markets

Susan Johnson

Introduction[1]

Impact assessment studies of microfinance programmes have mainly examined the direct effects that the provision of small loans has had on the livelihoods and well-being of poor clients. However, when supporting the entry of MFIs into financial markets, donors and academics have also considered the potential impact on the financial market as a whole. They have specifically considered impact on the behaviour of other financial service providers, with the expectation that their entry might precipitate innovation and hence further deepen and expand the supply of services to poor clients. Given the proliferation of these providers over recent years and the emergence of competition among them, it is timely to consider their impact in financial markets more broadly. This research under the *Imp-Act* programme set out to examine whether MFIs have had such effects within financial markets. Moreover, given the huge demand for financial services and the limitations in meeting it through MFIs alone, donor attention is now turning to working with other parts of the financial sector.

This chapter starts by reviewing the rationale for impact at the level of financial markets and sets out the approach used in this study. The second section reports results from three case studies: Kenya, Uganda and India. The third section concludes.

Microfinance institutions in financial markets

The 1990s saw a paradigm shift in approaches to microfinance that moved the rationale for interventions in credit provision from one of subsidized delivery to the need to build healthy financial systems (Otero and Rhyne, 1994). Proponents of financial repression theory argued that measures such as interest-rate controls, high reserve requirements and directed credit policies imposed distortions on financial intermediation and hence that their removal would improve the quality and quantity of saving and investment in the economy. Subsidized lending, both through the state in the form of agricultural credit schemes and through NGOs, was criticized as 'undermining' the market with cheap credit and leading to allocative inefficiency (Adams *et al*, 1984). By contrast, building financial organizations that could cover their costs and be financially self-sustaining would widen the market for financial services in a sustainable way (Von Pischke, 1991). As a result, while subsidized credit to users is seen as distorting the market and no longer good practice, cheap capital for the establishment of MFIs has been the norm.

Using neo-classically based infant industry arguments, Hulme and Mosley (1996) argue that subsidies are valid because the benefits of developing the technology of lending to poor people involve externalities of knowledge that cannot be internalized by the organization itself. However, the case made is a general theoretical one and has not been applied to specific financial markets to demonstrate the legitimacy of subsidies in a particular context. To do so would require the development of criteria to be used in assessing what a 'correct' level of subsidy might be that would avoid undermining already existing financial service providers (Johnson, 1998).

According to Von Pischke *et al* (1983) a well-functioning rural financial market should:

- Mobilize rural savings as well as disburse credit.
- Grow to meet expanding opportunities without the need for subsidies.
- Expand the array of vehicles for attracting savings.
- Offer varied and flexible lending terms and conditions.
- Have institutions that are healthy and expanding.
- Have active competition among formal and informal borrowers and lenders.
- Have financial service cost that fall as a result of innovation.
- Offer expanding access to the economically active population.
- Growing capability of the rural financial market to take part in larger financial markets.

The shifting of the financial 'frontier' (Von Pischke, 1991) is defined as the limit of the activities of formal financial institutions, or alternatively as a 'limit that is pierced by any financial innovation' and, in particular, is expanded when poor people have their first direct and sustainable interactions with the formal financial system. Von Pischke proposes a four-level framework for review that looks at: impact on borrowers; the intermediary itself; financial market development; and the macroeconomy and macrofinancial situation. The first level is the most familiar and the second has been heavily emphasized by the 'intermediary' school (Hulme, 2000a) focusing on the building of sustainable financial intermediaries.

Here we are concerned to examine the third level of impact on financial market development. Von Pischke suggests that this can be established by asking the following questions (Von Pischke, 1991) both at the level of the project or intermediary and at the level of financial market structure:

At the level of the project or intermediary

- Are project instruments innovative?
- Did project instruments promote competition; have they proved catalytic, novel or trivial?

At the level of the structure of the financial market

- What is the relationship of the project to the structure of the financial market and changes in its structure?
- How did the project fare relative to other institutions in terms of market share?
- Have project interventions influenced other players and their pricing?
- What evidence is there that financial instruments have competed with non-financial forms of savings (such as physical assets, jewellery, livestock) and (in-kind) credit?

The analysis of these authors therefore suggests two broad pathways of impact on market development. Hulme and Mosley (1996) indicate that there are externalities of knowledge that will be of wider benefit to the market as a whole. Von Pischke (1991), who suggests that there may be demonstration effects of successful innovations to other players, reinforces this view. However, Von Pischke particularly emphasizes the role of *competition* in creating incentives for innovation and the creation of value through new financial instruments that breach the frontier. High returns to innovation produce incentives to invest and in turn erode those returns, thus fuelling Schumpeter's cycle of 'creative destruction' that carries economic development forward (Von Pischke, 1991). These impact pathways might be expected to result in three types of impact: first, *innovation* in the design and delivery of financial services for poor and socially excluded people; second, a *deepening* of financial markets in a way that benefits poor and socially excluded people; and third, the *expansion* of financial services for them.

The methodology used in this research was innovative. It set out to map the demand and supply side of financial services using the focus of a small town in order to understand the dynamics of the market – in particular the demonstration and competition effects – employing a primarily qualitative approach. On the supply side, data were collected from both formal and informal financial service providers on numbers of clients and values of deposits and loans. Informal provision included groups such as ROSCAs (rotating savings and credit associations) and ASCAs (accumulating savings and credit associations), as well as moneylenders; however, aggregation of informal sector data is particularly problematic and has not been attempted. Providers were also interviewed to understand the range of products and services on offer, how these had been changing and why. On the demand side, data were collected using MicroSave's Market Research for Microfinance tools* to investigate changing use of financial services and explanations for this, use by different wealth groups, and preferences regarding savings and credit sources.

The methodology has, however, been implemented differently across countries. In each case the supply-side work was carried out by an independent researcher, while the demand-side work was carried out in collaboration with a local partner – KDA in Kenya, MicroSave in Uganda and SHARE in India. In Kenya, the study benefited from earlier detailed work on the financial market by the lead researcher and hence gave comparative data over time on the supply side. In Uganda, formal sector providers were not willing to cooperate with data collection but the demand side benefited from a market research survey carried out by MicroSave that provided quantitative data on the use of financial services not available in the other studies. In India, data on the formal banking system were easily available and complemented by specific research on non-formal provision, and the demand-side work was carried out as planned.

Kenya

Background

The research was carried out in Karatina, a small town in Nyeri District in Kenya's Central Province, some 120km from Nairobi. Located on the slopes of Mount Kenya and having fertile volcanic soils and good rainfall, it has an historically strong smallholder cash-crop sector producing tea and coffee, along with a strong tradition of entrepreneurship among both men and women. According to the 1994 Government of Kenya Poverty assessment (Government of Kenya, 1998), there is no absolute poverty in Nyeri when the rains are good. However, economic conditions deteriorated over the late 1990s when GDP growth rates fell from 4.6 per cent in 1996 to minus 0.2 per cent in 2000, recovering to around 1 per cent in 2000–01.

The town possesses a range of financial intermediaries including four banks whose coverage is national, a building society[2] (Equity), parastatals, SACCOs (savings and credit cooperatives) and MFIs. The informal sector abounds with group-based financial arrangements, ROSCAs and ASCAs operating in various ways – with women in particular making extensive use of them.[3] However, moneylending as a commercial operation (that is, not including friends and relatives) operates on a very limited scale.

Four NGO-originated MFI programmes now operate in the area, with Kenya Women Finance Trust being the most established (since 1991). The other three are FAULU, the Small and Micro Enterprise Programme and K-REP, which registered as a bank in 1999 but is treated here as part of the MFI sector. All are now financially self-sustaining. A second microfinance model – the 'managed ASCA' model (Johnson et al, 2002) – operates entirely independent of donor funding. In this model, women form groups and on-lend their own savings to each other in the form of an ASCA. The NGO provides management services to the group by arranging short-term advances (called *gubasho*) at 10 per cent per month and longer-term loans at lower rates. A key feature is that the high interest on the short-term loans accumulates in the women's fund and is used to pay out dividends at the end of the year, which can be very high (up to 60 per cent of savings) if the fund performs well.

Formal sector financial institutions play a dominant role in deposits, savings accounts and loans, but their market share of deposits has declined, primarily to SACCOS, as has the number of savings accounts. MFIs play a small role relative to the formal sector and SACCOS. Their market share of deposits and savings accounts has been stagnant in recent years, while their market share of loans declined to 8 per cent in 2003 (from 14 per cent in 1999). Within the MFI sector, mainstream MFIs have done better than ASCAs in terms of increasing their number of loans. ASCAs have suffered a net loss.

Formal sector banks

Table 6.1 provides data on the performance of formal sector banks over the period 1999–2003. In 1999 the commercial banks offered the usual range of current and deposit accounts, along with loans usually secured against land, shares or cash. These accounted for 73 per cent of deposits by value, 55 per cent of outstanding loans and 24 per cent of the number of savings accounts. By 2003, the number of savings accounts had fallen by 24 per cent, although their proportion of the total deposits remained almost the same. The primary cause of the falling number of savings accounts was increasing minimum deposit levels over the period 1999–2001, when banks decided to move their business towards a high net-worth customer base and even low-level salaried government employees could no longer afford to use them. By early 2003, this had started to change. All the main banks had lowered their minimum deposits significantly, precipitated by the fact that all of them had been chasing high net-worth individuals who were increasingly scarce in the context of recession and retrenchment in both public and private sectors.

On the lending side, in 1999 collateral-based lending – especially against land – was very limited due to the many social and cultural constraints involved that made it a 'silent norm' among bankers to avoid taking agricultural properties as collateral because foreclosure was a 'nightmare of a process' (Johnson, 2004b). However, by 2003 unsecured personal loans (essentially consumer credit products similar to those seen in the high-street banks of developed countries) had emerged as a new product, based on an assessment of cash flow using credit-scoring techniques, with many of the banks deliberately marketing these loans linked to savings accounts.

This move was precipitated by rapidly falling Treasury bill rates that meant that the banks no longer had a risk-free source of income in the face of poor macro-economic performance by lending to the government, and they had to learn how to lend to the middle market of salaried employees. These developments raised the nominal value of lending by 22 per cent when prices rose by

Table 6.1 Savings and loans performance of financial institutions in Karatina, Kenya 1999 and 2003 (Ksh thousands)

		Deposits				Members/savings accounts				Loans				Loan/deposit ratio (%)	
	Note	1999	% of total	2003	% of total	1999	% of total	2003	% of total	1999	% of total	2003	% of total	1999	2003
FORMAL SECTOR															
Banks	1	1,148,593	73	1,093,703	65	24,543	24	17,374	23	429,995	55	537,099	55	37	49
NBFIs	2	113,973	7	160,000	10	25,663	25	21,000	28	70,995	9	82,000	8	62	51
Parastatals	3	0	0	0	0	0	0	0	0	29,961	4	29,961	3		
Sub-total		1,262,566	80	1,253,703	75	50,206	49	38,374	51	530,951	68	649,060	67	42	52
MFI SECTOR															
Mainstream MFIs	4	18,629	1	24,947	1	1,958	2	2,911	4	28,411	4	50,500	5	153	202
Management service MFIs	5	43,184	3	26,628	2	10,329	10	5,790	8	82,050	10	29,919	3	190	112
Sub-total		61,813	4	51,575	3	12,287	12	8,701	12	110,461	14	80,419	8	179	156
SACCOs															
Cash-crop SACCOs	6	168,449	11	235,102	14	37,283	36	25,250	34	53,495	7	112,662	12	32	48
Employee SACCOs	7	90,150	6	147,343	9	2,277	2	2,048	3	80,117	10	114,257	12	89	78
Transport/Business	8	12,560	1	13,373	1	396	0	396	1	11,448	1	12,170	1	91	91
SACCOs Sub-total		271,159	17	395,818	24	39,956	39	27,694	37	145,060	18	239,088	25	53	60
TOTAL		**1,576,909**	**101**	**1,676,149**	**101**	**102,449**	**100**	**74,768**	**100**	**786,471**	**100**	**968,567**	**100**		

Source: (Johnson, 2004)

Notes:

1. Data for one bank in 2003 were not available so its numbers of accounts and volumes have been assumed to have changed comparably to other banks.
2. Data for these institutions are incomplete.
3. Data for Post Office savings were not available as balances are not held at a branch level.
4. Mainstream MFIs' deposits are in the main mobilized by the MFI but deposited in the bank, so are excluded from total deposits.
5. These totals have been estimated based on averages from a sample of groups of one of the organizations.
6. Data for some of these institutions were estimated in 1999.
7. For 2003 data on small SACCOs for which updated information were not collected, deposit growth has been assumed at approximatel 10% per year, with membership unchanged.
8. For 2003 data on transport/business SACCOs were not collected – deposit growth at 5% per year and static membership has been assumed.

17 per cent, suggesting an increase of 5 per cent in real terms, also signalled by a rise in the loan to deposit ratio from 37 per cent to 49 per cent. This is significant given the state of the economy.

Among the commercial banks, the Co-operative Bank in 1999 sought to develop a microfinance product: a small business loan product using stock and household assets as collateral but based on an assessment of cash flows (Bell, Harper and Mandivenga, 2002). It was aimed at clients at the upper end of the microfinance product range at the time, but performance of this product in Karatina was poor.

Demand-side data showed that bank and building society accounts were the second most used type of service after informal ROSCAs. They tended to be used more by those with secondary rather than primary education, those living in Karatina town rather than the rural areas around it, and those in business or employment rather than agriculture (Johnson, 2004b).

The impact of increasing minimum deposit levels in the commercial banks over the period 1999–2001 was that many poorer people whose savings fell below the minimum saw their balances being dramatically eroded through fees and charges – such that within a few months they could disappear completely. It was Equity Building Society (then an NBFI – non-bank financial institution – but a full bank by 2004) that aimed to reach this market and by keeping its minimum deposit low and stable became an attractive alternative to the commercial banks. Equity accounted for a large proportion of the deposit accounts held in NBFIs (which in total rivalled the numbers held in the commercial banks), although these only accounted for some 7 per cent of total deposits, indicating much lower average balances. Moreover, equity offered unsecured loans up to a ceiling of Ksh50,000 (US$666) without the assistance of credit-scoring methods. Collateral needed for loans above this amount was negotiated pragmatically, for example, the deposit of a title deed without it being formally charged. Equity introduced a range of products of this type including medical, education, salary advances, farm input and business loans.

The parastatals were in decline in the late 1990s and this sector was estimated to account for 4 per cent of the value of outstanding loans. Apart from the Post Office, for which deposit data were not available,[4] none of these organizations mobilized deposits.

MFIs

The mainstream MFIs accounted for approximately 1 per cent of deposits by value, 4 per cent of outstanding loans and 2 per cent of savings accounts in 1999.[5] Aggressive expansion over the next four years increased mainstream MFI membership by 49 per cent. Their product offering changed to include school fees, emergency and medical loans, usually at similar interest rates, terms and conditions and repayment frequencies to the working capital loan products. Most of them were also experimenting with individual lending products. This changing product mix reflected a new interest in listening to clients and responding to their needs, partly in response to competition between them, which has also brought a concern to improve service quality and customer care.

At the same time, outstanding loan value increased by 77 per cent, with average balances rising from Ksh20,000 (US$274) to Ksh23,000 (US$303) – a nominal increase of 15 per cent against a prices index of 17 per cent.[6] If this is used as a proxy for depth of outreach, then these data suggest that the expansion has not tended to bring in significantly poorer clients. Moreover this finding can be compared to a country-wide borrower sample of five Kenyan MFIs including KREP, KWFT and FAULU (McGregor et al, 1999) that compared education and income profiles with those reported by the GEMINI survey of a nationally representative sample of small businesses and micro-enterprises. Table 6.2 shows that MFI clients tended to be better educated and a significant proportion had annual incomes above Ksh 200,000 (US$3,577) compared to the national average for microenterprise owners, with a much smaller proportion having incomes under Ksh10,000 (US$179), that is, approximately half the consumption poverty line.

Moreover, results of a countrywide poverty assessment of KWFT clients carried out using the CGAP tool (that assesses the relative poverty status of clients compared to others in an area), supports the view that MFI coverage is skewed towards the better off, with ascending tercile coverage of 16 per cent, 33 per cent and 51 per cent; thus over half of clients are among the richest third of the population (Microfinance Gateway, 2003).

Estimates for the managed ASCAs suggest that their outreach was greater than the MFIs in 1999 and accounted for 3 per cent of deposits by value, 10 per cent of loans outstanding and 10 per cent of the number of savings accounts.

Table 6.2 Comparative indicators for a countrywide sample of clients of five MFIs and a national sample of small business owners and microentrepreneurs, Kenya

Indicator	Five MFIs (%)	Gemini* (%)
EDUCATION		
None	4.2	20.4
Primary	37.9	55.3
Secondary	49.3	23.2
Post-secondary	8.6	1.2
INCOME		
Having annual income less than:		
Ksh10,000 (US$179)	7.9	62.0
Ksh200,000 (US$3,577)	24.6	1.5

Source: McGregor et al (1999)
Note: * Gemini study used slightly different income ranges, so the percentages reported are for amounts less than Ksh12,840 (US$230) and above Ksh240,000 (US$4,296).

This model has significant problems in portfolio performance due to poor economic conditions. Table 6.1 suggests that managed-ASCA membership fell by 44 per cent. However, the 2003 figure reported here is probably a significant underestimate since a number of new organizations had been set up and some took groups from the existing organizations as they did so. A best guess would suggest that membership has remained static or fallen slightly. The proliferation of this model is evidence of the low barriers to entry involved in its replication and its attractiveness to users.

On the demand side, the popularity of the managed ASCAs is due to the small size of savings and loans (as little as US$8), the ease with which loans are accessed at meetings, the periodicity of meetings, and the ability to negotiate repayment. This makes it useful to a wide range of clients, in particular those in rural areas such as farmers, and those with less-steady income streams. The negotiability point is key. When people face livelihood shocks they need to be able either to use their social networks to find funds to repay, to delay repayment or even to negotiate a new loan. User-owned groups offer this possibility and directly contrast with the mainstream MFI model (Johnson, 2004b). In the user-owned model the group can allow delays in repayment or a new loan because it is allowing its own funds to be held for longer. In the mainstream MFI model the group is used to enforce repayment of MFI funds and there is little scope for negotiation.

SACCOs

The third set of financial service providers is the SACCOs, for which regulation was gradually weakened over the 1990s. This has given rise to new SACCOs based on common bonds, such as transport operators or business people, alongside the existing common bonds of cash-crop production and employment. The SACCO sector as a whole accounted for 17 per cent of the value of deposits, 18 per cent of the value of outstanding loans and 39 per cent of the number of savings accounts in 1999. It therefore accounted for a relatively high proportion of the number of savings accounts but a low proportion of deposits by value, suggesting much lower average deposits than the banking sector and reflecting the fact that SACCOs – especially those for cash-crop producers – tend to deal with poorer clients.

By 2003 the SACCO sector as a whole had suffered a fall in the total number of accounts by 31 per cent. However, this decline was almost entirely attributable to the coffee cooperative transforming into a SACCO (requiring farmers to buy shares in the SACCO whereas previously they were automatically given accounts through which to receive their payments) and additional difficulties faced due to low coffee prices.

The cash-crop cooperatives have played a major role in the livelihoods of smallholders in Central Kenya, especially the coffee cooperatives, which date back to the 1970s. Their users are predominantly men (as the controllers of cash-crop income), and survey data suggest that they tend to be older (over

40 years) and have primary rather than secondary education. In the past the cooperatives were a key supplier of credit for inputs, farm development loans and also school fees. Working on the principle of borrowing against future streams of income, they were also popular because they did not put land at risk by using it as collateral (Johnson, 2004b).

Despite this period of difficulty for the coffee SACCO, deposits in all of the SACCOs increased by 46 per cent, mainly as a result of the development of front office services (called FOSAs). These are deposit services for both members and non-members and by 2003 they were offered by three SACCOs, compared to none in 1999. FOSAs offer computerized services, can give their customers chequebooks (that, even though not part of the clearing system, allows payees to come and draw cash and hence gives added convenience), and offer services such as school fees cheques. It is difficult to gauge the number of accounts that might have moved from the banks to the FOSAs. This is because many SACCOs have front office accounts for members through which dividends and loans are paid, but these are accounts that they may not actually use in the way they would a bank savings account, such as having their salaries paid through them. A best estimate suggests that some 5,000 bank accounts (approximately 15 per cent of bank accounts) have shifted to FOSAs since 1999, and this is probably a conservative estimate. This development of FOSA services has been unregulated to date, although supported by the Co-operative Bank, which has also provided technical assistance in many instances.

Interest rates

The main change in rates since 1999 has been in the banking sector where base rates have fallen significantly. All other lending rates in the market have remained virtually unchanged. In 1999, commercial bank base rates were in the range 20–25 per cent but by the end of 2002 these had fallen to 14–18 per cent. Treasury bill rates – that have been the main underlying determinant of bank base rates – underwent further falls in the early part of 2003 to 7–8 per cent and dropping further to 3 per cent by mid–2003.

The MFIs quote annual flat interest rates and in the late 1990s these were (in headline number terms) between 18 and 22 per cent, hence appearing lower than bank base rates. Since few customers are aware of the difference, MFIs were perceived to be cheaper than the banks. This is now changing. Since bank base rates are falling, some clients are now aware that banks are quoting lower lending rates than the MFIs. With this development, MFIs are likely to start coming under much heavier pressure from clients regarding interest rates.

Conclusions

The evidence presented here indicates that the mainstream MFIs have relatively limited market outreach (both in terms of clients and volumes) in comparison to other models. They have expanded outreach in a relatively well-off part of the country by almost 50 per cent in the last four years and at a time when the economy was performing poorly, but this seems to underline the outreach limitations of the model caused by the relatively inflexible design of the loan product on offer (Wright, 2000; Hulme, 1999). By contrast, the SACCOs and the little-known managed-ASCAs have much wider coverage.

In this market it is the salaried employees, such as teachers, government workers and tea farmers, who have regular incomes that are the main focus. It is this market segment that the banks, Equity and SACCO FOSAs are now actively competing over. The key factor driving these developments has been competition among them in the context of changing macroeconomic conditions and SACCO deregulation. For the banks, a rush to target the high net-worth individual retail market led to its saturation. High Treasury bill rates in the late 1990s and the problems of collateral-based landing – particularly against land – led them to neglect lending to rural people. But this is no longer possible with the precipitous fall in these rates over the last three years and now they are again having to learn how to lend, with credit scoring and cash-flow lending beginning to take hold.

Demonstration effects from mainstream MFI group-based approaches are not in evidence. Nevertheless, local people realize that in managed ASCAs that apparently have high interest rates, this comes back to them in the form of dividends. The interest rate in SACCOs has tended to remain relatively low and stable and this also means that they are seen as 'fair'. These price characteristics and the greater ease of borrowing through ASCAs and SACCOs have contributed to people's interest in setting up or joining these types of intermediary, especially during a period of economic difficulty.

The main conclusion is, therefore, that MFIs have reached only a limited segment of the market and have had limited demonstration or competition effects on other providers. In terms of innovation, key developments have been unsecured personal lending from the banks and the establishment of FOSAs by the SACCOs. However, little evidence was available to suggest that these developments have deepened or expanded the market for poor and socially excluded people. The data in Table 6.1 suggest that the overall number of accounts has fallen by 27 per cent and that the movement in accounts has been from the banks to Equity and the FOSAs. This is consistent with a desire to maintain an account that is cheaper to operate in the difficult economic conditions that most Kenyans faced during this period.

This case also shows that there are a number of ways in which the wider dynamics of the financial market are having, and are likely to continue to have, significant impact on the MFIs. The changing macroeconomic environment has put pressure on the formal sector financial intermediaries to change their strategy and to consider how to tailor their products to the middle-income market.

India

Background

The study was carried out in Guntur District of Andhra Pradesh, focusing on Guntur town itself and the smaller nearby town of Sattenpally. Guntur is a prosperous district in one of India's most prosperous states and represents a strongly competitive environment for financial services.

Formal sector banks dominate the financial market in terms of deposits, savings accounts and loans. However, other formal sector institutions – NBFCs (non-bank financial companies), the Post Office and chit funds – play an important role in deposit mobilization and account for a significant number of savings accounts, although the importance of chit funds has been declining. The microfinance sector (including self-help groups) has expanded in recent years and is increasingly important for poor clients compared to the banks, but accounts for only a very small proportion of the overall market.

Formal sector banks

From the point of view of branch coverage, India is one of the most highly banked countries in the world, and Guntur District is no exception with a total of 372 bank branches – one for every 11,800 people. Bank ownership is public, private and cooperative. Table 6.3 indicates that the banking sector in Guntur

Table 6.3 Savings and loans performance of financial institutions in Guntur town, India

	Deposits (value)		Savings accounts		Loans (value)		Loan/
	Rupees (millions)	% of total	No.	% of total	Rupees (millions)	% of total	Deposit ratio
Private sector	3,600	16.4	28,000	6.2	2,010	12.9	55.8
Public sector	13,520	61.6	189,000	41.8	12,330	79.2	91.2
Cooperative banks	330	1.5	6,000	1.3	240	1.5	72.7
Banks – sub-total	17,450	79.6	223,000	49.4	14,580	93.7	83.6
NBFCs	320	1.5	80,000	17.7			
Post Office	3,500	16.0	90,000	19.9			
Chit funds	650	3.0	30,000	6.6	650	4.2	100.0
Other formal – sub-total	4,470	20.4	200,000	44.3	650	4.2	100.0
MFIs	15	0.1	28,000	6.2	130	0.8	866.7
SHGs	0.4	0.0	720	0.2			
Microfinance – sub-total	15.4	0.1	28,720	6.4			
Commission agents/cold storage					200	1.3	
Total	21,935	100	451,720	100	15,560	100	

town accounts for 80 per cent of deposits by value, 50 per cent of savings accounts by number and 94 per cent of loans by value. In Sattenpally the picture changes slightly (as shown in Table 6.4), with the banking sector representing 75 per cent of deposits by value, but 63 per cent of savings accounts by number and 90 per cent of loans by value. These figures reflect the small-town nature of Sattenpally and hence the smaller loans and deposits with which the banks are dealing.

The government's priority sector lending policy is intended to ensure the availability of finance to agriculture, small-scale business, artisans, small-scale transport operators, the self-employed, women and cottage industries. Under this policy, banks are expected to lend 40 per cent of their portfolio in the priority sectors. In practice, in Guntur town this lending complies with the 40 per cent guideline and for the district as a whole, the figure increases to 66 per cent. However, the average outstanding loan size of Rs230,000 (US$4,842) is nine times the small loan definition of Rs25,000 (US$526) (see Table 6.5). Hence while priority sector targets are met, the bias is, perhaps predictably, towards the upper end of this segment.

Despite the dominance of the public sector banks in Guntur town (63 out of 80 branches), they increased their minimum deposit requirements from Rs100 (US$2.1) to Rs1,000 (US$21) between 2002 and 2003. Competition is emerging in part through increased investment in technology (computerization of accounts and introduction of ATMs). This is particularly the case with the private banks whose aggressive marketing strategy is to have a single main branch and ATMs at every corner. ICICI is considered by other bankers as the most aggressive competitor. The private sector banks have 6 per cent of accounts but 16 per cent of deposits, with average deposits 60 per cent higher than the bank average. In the private sector there are two key strategies

Table 6.4 Savings and loans performance of financial institutions in Sattenpally town, India

	Deposits (value)		Savings accounts		Loans (value)		Loan/
	Rupees (millions)	% of total	No.	% of total	Rupees (millions)	% of total	Deposit ratio
Public sector banks	523	72.6	48,400	61.0	430	86.9	82.2
Cooperative Banks	17	2.4	1650	2.1	17	3.4	100.0
Banks – sub-total	540	75.0	50,050	63.1	447	90.3	
NBFCs	15	2.1	5,000	6.3			
Post Office	104	14.4	15,000	18.9			
Chit funds	58	8.1	6,500	8.2	43	8.7	74.1
Other formal – sub-total	177	24.6	26,500	33.4	43	8.7	
MFIs	3	0.4	2750	3.5	5	1.0	171.0
Total	**720**	**100**	**79,300**	**100**	**495**	**100**	

emerging. The first is agents who provide a doorstep service, while the second strategy is technology driven and involves the replacement of branches by ATMs. For the public sector banks, the challenge is to keep up with the race being led by the private banks' investment in technology.

Non-bank financial companies

NBFCs operate a limited banking service that excludes demand deposits and current accounts. Their image is poor, as some large ones have recently failed and regulatory requirements have been tightened. In turn, this has led to significant volumes of deposits moving into the banking sector and increased liquidity in that sector. While a number of NBFCs in Guntur are involved in financing vehicle purchase ('auto-finance'), two organizations are of particular interest: Agri-Gold and Sahara Finance. Agri-Gold collects deposits and invests in its own agricultural enterprises, as well as offering agricultural loans. One such savings product is a doorstep deposit collection system that involves daily deposits in multiples of Rs10 (US$0.21) for 750 days (30 months). At the end of the period, for every Rs10 saved daily, the realization value is Rs8,800 (US$185) representing an interest rate of approximately 15 per cent. Sahara has a similar methodology with a minimum daily deposit of Rs10 for a minimum of one year and a return of approximately 12 per cent. Sahara is a residuary NBFC that invests primarily in government-approved securities.

Registered private chit funds are also a popular mode of savings and loans and operate as bidding ROSCAs[7] in which groups of people (usually 10–50) save a fixed amount every month. The fund is auctioned and the person who bids the *lowest* amount is the winner. The discount represents an interest payment or dividend, which is divided equally among the other participants. The chits are organized and run by private companies, which take security (land and buildings, and guarantees from government staff) when disbursing the bid amount and responsibility for ensuring that the repayments are made. While large chit fund companies such as Sriram and Margadarshi operate in several states, including Andrah Pradesh, informally operated funds were found to be operating all over Guntur town.

Table 6.5 Priority sector lending by banks in Guntur town, India

	Loans (value Rs millions)	% of loans (by value)	Number of loans	Average loan (Rs millions)	Average loan (US$)
Private sector	1,160	58	5,401	214,775	4,773
Public sector	4,680	38	19,751	236,950	5,266
Cooperative banks	2	1	30	70,000	1,556
Regional Rural Bank	10	0	262	38,168	848
Total	**5,852**	**40**	**25,444**	**229,999**	**5,111**

The Post Office is also used by small savers, but offers no loans. It not only benefits from a large number of branches (30), but also employs agents to undertake doorstep savings mobilization, which means that its recurring deposit services compete with those of NBFCs such as Agri-Gold and Sahara.

The outreach of the NBFCs, Post Office and chit funds accounts for some 20 per cent of the value of savings, but 44 per cent of the number of savings accounts (not allowing for multiple use). The NBFCs such as Sahara and Agri-gold rival the Post Office in outreach through their doorstep daily savings product. The Post Office accounts for almost 20 per cent of savings accounts and 16 per cent of deposits, and the average deposit is approximately half that of the banks, suggesting the greater depth of outreach that it achieves. However, when compared to the NBFCs, where the average deposit is only Rs4,000 (US$89), we can see the even greater depth of outreach achieved by these services. These organizations estimated that approximately 15 per cent of their clientele in Guntur town were from the slums and poorest areas, compared to 10 per cent for the Post Office and 5 per cent for Life Insurance Corporation (LIC) and chit fund providers. The incentives for agents operating on a commission basis to move to the poorer areas are twofold. First, the competition for better-off clients is strong and these clients are also more knowledgeable about which services are best for them.[8] Second, the density of population in the slums means that agents can reduce their transaction costs even though the amounts saved may be lower.

MFIs

There are three MFIs operating in Guntur town: SHARE Microfin, SPANDANA and St Ann's Social Services (SASS). All three use Grameen-type models, however, SHARE operates flexible savings accounts through the SHARE Mutually Aided Co-operative Society, which are not linked to loan size or held as collateral. SHARE reduced its range of loan products in 2002 in order to rationalize operations and allow for rapid growth.

SPANDANA has expanded from a similar 50-week core loan product to add a number of related products. Interestingly it has copied the design of loans given by moneylenders and introduced a product for individual borrowers as a 200-day loan in which the borrower pays Rs100 (US$2.1) for Rs1,000 (US$21). While the amounts are the same, the period is twice that of moneylenders, meaning a halving of the interest rate.

Government policy is now strongly behind the expansion of the self-help group sector (Bansal, 2003; Srinivasan, 2002), especially in rural areas. Groups of 15–20 women save together in a bank account and start lending among themselves after six months. After a further six months they are eligible for bank loans. Initially they are entitled to a loan that matches their savings, but this can increase to as much as four times the savings amount. The District Rural Development Authority is the main agency promoting them under the programme called DWCRA (Development of Women and Children in Rural

Areas). By March 2003 it had recorded some 18,815 SHGs in Guntur District with a membership of 228,172. The groups had mobilized Rs356 million (US$7.5 million) in savings and 6,597 were linked to banks to receive loans of Rs180 million (US$3.8 million). In addition, some 2,000 groups with an estimated membership of 20,000 had been formed through four NGOs in the district that are also participating in the programme. The rate of growth of these groups is massive. In 1999–2000 there were 198 SHGs linked to banks but this number had risen to 2,595 in 2000–01 and to 5,072 the following year.

Comparing MFI and SHG performance at the district level (rather than Guntur town because SHGs are a predominantly rural phenomenon), total outreach of MFIs was 100,957 members, while SHGs embraced some 250,000 members. The market share of the MFIs and SHGs is 6 per cent of savings accounts but only 0.1 per cent of deposits by value and 0.8 per cent of loans (see Table 6.3). This illustrates their greater depth of outreach in terms of loan size but demonstrates that there is still a huge market to be served. Indeed, with some 28,000 borrowers, SHARE rivals the number of priority sector loans in the town as a whole, but lending by value is only 2 per cent of the banking sector.

Informal finance

Moneylenders and pawnbrokers operate in both Guntur town and Sattenpally. Their scale of operations varies hugely, with small operators handling some 20–25 clients by themselves and large ones operating through trusted agents, with clients not knowing who the actual moneylender is. In Guntur they exist on almost every other street, as evidenced by the advertising boards. The main product they offer is a loan for 100 days with Rs10 (US$0.21) per Rs100 (US$2.1) lent being deducted up front. This results in an effective interest rate of approximately 73 per cent. Moneylenders interviewed reported that competition had brought the rate down to Rs10 from a previous level of Rs11 (that is, approximately 80 per cent effective).

Life insurance

Life insurance, while not strictly financial intermediation, deserves a mention due to its proliferation and growth in recent years. The government-owned LIC had approximately 300,000 current policies. Although multiple policy holding is common and these policies are mainly bought by salaried employees, they are also important because of their acceptability as collateral for loans up to 75 per cent of the surrender value.

In the main, banks were barely aware of the MFIs, however, they tend to regard them as 'moneylenders in the garb of NGOs'. By contrast, the moneylenders interviewed were very aware of MFIs. First, the introduction by SPANDANA of a product closely mirroring their own loan characteristics, also delivered and collected on the doorstep, meant that they perceived this as direct competition and reported that it was not the number of clients that had declined but the volume of business. This indicates that the MFI year-long loan product did not reduce demand for small and shorter term loans, rather it may have increased it. Indeed the moneylenders reported that borrowers did not wish to antagonize the 'friendly neighbourhood moneylender' and clients still turned to them to fund needs arising during the year. One moneylender also pointed out that co-existence was possible because 'everyone's needs have gone up' (see Box 6.1), and others reported that clients still came to them in the case of emergency. Given the inflexibility of MFI products, such products can also increase the vulnerability of poor borrowers to crises and mean that they have to resort to moneylenders to raise the funds for MFI loan repayments.[9]

Box 6.1

A moneylender had a flourishing business before an MFI started operating in her area in Guntur town. After the MFI started its 'centre', she discovered that her business was in deep trouble. Her regular clients started deserting her. She tried to reach out to other clients but there were not many. She changed her strategy. She became a member of the MFI group and a centre leader, putting her in a position to know the situation of members and to lend to them. She has happily retained all her old clients and gives loans for purposes other than 'what MFI gives'. She has learned how to face the competition.

Interest rates

Interest rates have been falling in the banking sector since deregulation by Reserve Bank of India in 2001 and as a result of rising liquidity resulting from the tightening of NBFC regulations. Competition in the lending market is now strong, however, clients are unaware of the differences in interest rates, apart from products such as SPANDANA's individual loans that are easily compared to those of moneylenders. Although clients reported that interest rates were an important factor in their decisions to invest, it is unclear that they have sufficient information to adequately assess rates in comparable terms.

Changing use

The financial sector trend analysis (see Table 6.6) shows how the use of financial services has been changing over the last decade according to users.[10] Table 6.7 gives an overview of the differential use of these services by wealth categories. Banks and chit funds demonstrate a continued presence over time although more recently facing active competition from other services and especially MFIs. This would appear to reflect their dominant position in the sector as a whole prior to the expansion of alternatives. The trend analysis suggests declining use of moneylenders in Guntur and these do not appear in the list in the last two years. Rather surprisingly, moneylenders do not appear

Table 6.6 Trends in financial service use, India

Town	10 years ago	5 years ago	Last year	Present
Guntur	Friends Moneylenders Chits	Friends Chits Daily doorstep finance	SHGs (DWCRA) SHARE Banks	SHARE SHGs (DWCRA) SPANDANA
	Banks	Banks Moneylenders SHGs (DWCRA)	Chits LIC	Banks LIC Chits
Sattenpally	Chits Banks Finance Daily doorstep	Banks Chits Friends Post Office	Banks SHARE LIC Post Office Chits	SHARE Banks LIC Post Office Societies

Note: consolidated findings from eight financial sector trend analysis exercises in each area held with all wealth groups and clients and non-clients of SHARE.

Table 6.7 Financial service use ranked by wealth group

Wealth Group	Guntur	Sattenpally
Very poor	Sahara SHARE SHGs (DWCRA) SPANDANA Friends and relatives Pawnbrokers	Landlords Friends LIC Pawnbrokers Post Office SHARE
Moderately poor	Chits Banks LIC Post Office Friends and relatives Sahara	Friends LIC Post Office Banks Moneylenders Chits
Non-poor	Banks Chits Friends and relatives LIC Post Office Daily finance	Banks Friends Chits LIC Post Office

Note: data derived from four financial services matrices carried out in each area, one each with poor/rich women/men.

at all in the trend analysis for Sattenpally. The use of chit funds has also declined over time, as has the role of friends. Interestingly life insurance has entered the list in the last two years along with the growth of microfinance through both MFIs and SHGs.

The pattern of use by the very poor in Sattenpally is clearly different to that in Guntur. Sattenpally still relies strongly on landlords, no doubt as a result of the more rural context. The overall relative decline of moneylenders in the trend analysis appears to reflect an increased variety of more formalized services on offer. However, banks do not appear in the list of services used by the very poor and this reflects their ongoing inaccessibility to this group, although the SHG bank-linkage approach is now addressing this (through DWCRA).

In particular, the improved availability of more formalized services is most evident among the very poor group in Guntur; the services provided by MFIs and SHGs do appear to be well targeted towards them. However, this improvement is not solely due to the MFIs but also partly to the LIC and partly to the role of doorstep savings services (such as those provided by Sahara). The evidence suggests that the savings side of the market is one in which the NBFCs, chit funds and the Post Office have a strong position. This yet again underlines the importance of savings services for very poor people, as does the prevalence of doorstep services that reduce transactions costs. Moreover, women are heavy users of doorstep services because they often undertake business while men are out doing agricultural work. Such services offer a discipline in saving as well as a long-term goal, which can be particularly important for poor people.[11]

Conclusions

Banks still dominate the market in terms of deposits and numbers of accounts, and there is evidence that they are used by the moderately poor if not the very poor. There is also evidence of movement down market and deepening of provision in lending and competition for clients in the context of strong liquidity. Bank linkage via SHGs is also enhancing deepening and expansion of provision in a more rural context.[12]

The data – both on the supply and demand side – suggest the importance of savings-led services from NBFCs such as Agri-Gold and Sahara, along with the Post Office. The role of their daily doorstep savings services appears particularly important, and now complemented by life insurance products through LIC. There is evidence that the market is being deepened through these services. MFI provision may have been innovative but still has to make progress in terms of expansion against strong informal sector provision, especially in the more rural area of Sattenpally. This may also suggest the limitations of loans targeted to women and tailored to business rather than agriculture. While banks are starting to lend to new sectors, such as housing and consumer products, and are learning how to undertake cash flow lending in this context, the challenge remains of finding effective methodologies for lending to agriculture.

Uganda

Background

Uganda has experienced significant economic success over the last decade with real GDP growth rates averaging 6.9 per cent over the 1990s and nominal growth rates of 4.8–6.5 per cent between 2000 and 2003. The microfinance industry has been growing and maturing at a rapid rate, with fast developing competition. The government passed the Microfinance Deposit-Taking Institutions Act in 2003, under which a small number of MFI-NGOs are likely to register in the near future. Given that formal financial institutions were unwilling to cooperate with the research to provide detailed supply-side data for specific towns, this section reviews developments in the industry more widely. It uses a range of sources complemented by more detailed research in the towns of Mbale and Masaka.

Developments in the financial sector

The banking sector is now dominated by private banks. The main public sector bank, UCB, was sold in 1988 but by 1999 it was insolvent and taken into statutory management, and then sold to Stanbic, a South African bank. The government sought to control rising inflation in 1998–99 by taking liquidity off the market through treasury bill issues at rates that rose to over 20 per cent in nominal terms. These had the effect of significantly reducing the incentive of the banks to lend. However, these rates fell again from late 2001 to below 5 per cent and, according to Seibel (2003), caused Centenary Bank to start exploring new markets for lending. They rose again by the end of the year to 15–20 per cent, where they remained during 2003.

Estimates suggest that there are some 1,400 MFIs in Uganda with an active loan portfolio of Ush97 billion (US$53.3 million) serving 340,000 borrowers and over 900,000 savers (Nannyonjo and Nsubuga, 2004). The Ministry of Finance classifies them into categories on the basis of their national coverage of borrowers, savers, loan portfolio, financial sustainability, formality of organizational structure, and an assessment of the quality of MIS, business plans and use of industry good practice (as shown in Table 6.8). The majority[13] of these organizations operate as community-based organizations (ROSCAs, ASCAs and small SACCOs) and are 'generally unaware of microfinance best practices, are outside the microfinance "information loop", are focused on rural outreach but have a minimum number of clients' (ibid.).

While there are some 1,000 registered savings and credit cooperatives nationwide, there are few data on them and many are thought to be dormant. The cooperative movement in Uganda suffered as a result of the 1970

Table 6.8 Classification of the microfinance industry in Uganda

Category	Number in category	Characteristics
A	5–8	At or near operational or financial self-sustainability. Well-documented operational procedures. Fairly good MIS, well-qualified management and staff. Applying microfinance best practices. Often registered as companies limited by guarantee. Active clients over 10,000
B	10–15	Mainly NGOs. Also registered as companies limited by guarantee. Charge market interest rates, have adapted a business-oriented approach to poverty alleviation and are moving towards operational self-sufficiency. Fair documentation of procedures and MIS. Good management, operational self-sufficiency at levels between 50 and 85 per cent. Active clients range from 5,000 to 10,000
C	40+	Mainly small local NGOs with limited resources and clientele. Fairly familiar with 'best practices' and are within the industry's information loop. However, most have modestly qualified management and are still far from reaching operational self-sufficiency (35 to 49 per cent)
D	Numerous (i.e. over 1,000)	Small community-based organizations, generally not well known in the sector. Largely outside the national microfinance information loop. Most are generally little aware of microfinance best practices. Focused on rural outreach but have minimal numbers of clients.

Source: Nannyonjo and Nsubuga (2004)

Co-operative Act, which removed their autonomy and resulted in extensive political interference. Although this autonomy was restored in 1992, the marketing cooperatives continue to suffer from a lack of trust and are largely insolvent (Ssemogerere, 2003). An informal indicator of cooperative numbers is the proliferation of signboards for local savings and credit associations in recent years – some of which describe themselves as cooperatives – and this suggests a resurgence of such mechanisms and that many of these organizations are unregistered.

Changing products and services

The development of competition in the market is most immediately evident from an analysis of the changing products and services available from both MFIs and banks. One of the key changes evident over the period 2001–03 is that MFIs have moved to introduce individual lending products, and by the beginning of 2003 almost all the major MFIs had such a product. Their purpose is primarily to retain good clients who MFIs fear might otherwise consider moving to commercial banks because of increasing impatience with the transactions costs of group lending, although group sizes have in most cases dropped from the upper twenties to the upper teens (Kaffu and Mutesasira, 2003). Competition has also reduced processing times for loans.

Competition is also evidenced by the increasing number of products offered by MFIs, such as school-fee loans and loans based on salary (also called personal loans or employer-guaranteed loans). It is this segment of the market that has become the most competitive: the major banks target it and four MFIs had similar products by early 2003. It is unsurprising that the banks are moving into this market because it is the simplest form of cash-flow based lending to manage, with the requirement that salaries are paid through the same institution. The convergence of MFI competition with banks on this market segment does suggest an upmarket drift among MFIs.

Changes in other terms and conditions are also evident. Collateral requirements have reduced, both as the ratio of collateral to loan value and the required compulsory savings amounts. CERUDEB has now recognized *kibanja* (land titles, a certificate of occupancy rather than ownership) as acceptable security for loans up to US$1,000. Length of loan term has also increased with more loans being available for 6–12 months and some extending up to two years. Products are priced in both declining and flat-rate terms, however, no major changes have been observed in nominal interest rates. Meanwhile fees, commissions, insurance and penalties have moved in all directions (Kaffu and Mutesasira, 2003).

Regarding savings, three of the main banks have lowered their opening and minimum balances to open up their services to lower-income people (these were Crane, Nile and Stanbic/UCB). A further development is the offering of chequebooks with savings accounts. Post-dated cheques are a simple form of collateral in Uganda because bouncing a cheque is a criminal offence and hence offering cheques aids contract enforcement. However, Kaffu and Mutesasira (ibid.) further note that many clients still felt that customer service in the MFIs was superior to that of banks, and that clients are becoming increasingly discriminating in favour of quick service. Some of the banks are modernizing quickly through the introduction of ATMs, while others are also undertaking aggressive branding activity (Nile and Crane banks) to attract new customers. Only one bank had adopted a group-based lending product (Orient Bank) targeted at small businesses.

Evidence of financial service use

Data collected by the Uganda National Household Survey in 1999 (Uganda Bureau of Statistics, 2001) from a nationally representative sample of households investigated loans outstanding and fully paid from the formal and informal sectors during the previous 12 months. The results are summarized in Table 6.9. The data suggest that only some 9.2 per cent of the population had borrowed over the previous year, with twice the proportion of men to women doing so. The sources of credit were predominantly informal, with relatives

Table 6.9 Use of loans by source

Source	%	Male	Female
% of population applied for a loan:	9.2	12.8	6.1
Rural	8.8		
Urban	11.5		
% applied by source:			
Relatives and friends	44	46	39
NGO	15	12	21
Government agency	10	11	8
Community funds	9	8	11
Bank	8	8	9
Cooperative credit societies	7	7	6
Moneylender	4	3	5
Commercial firm	1	2	1
Employer	1	2	0
Others	1	1	1
Total	**100**	**100**	**100**

Source: Uganda Bureau of Statistics (2001)

and friends being the most common (44 per cent) source. However, the second most-used source was NGOs (15 per cent). The data include a wide range of NGO programmes and hence also reflect credit from subsidized NGO sources, nevertheless the evidence does suggest that such programmes have achieved an important degree of outreach, though a rate of 15 per cent borrowing from NGOs suggests outreach to only 1.4 per cent of the population as a whole.

Government agencies are still a relatively important (10 per cent)[14] source of loans, followed by community funds (mainly ROSCAs and ASCAs) (9 per cent), with banks representing some 8 per cent of sources or 0.7 per cent of the total population. The data also suggest the importance of savings and credit cooperatives (7 per cent) of the total. The perspective provided by this data suggests still very limited outreach by MFIs and shows the still extensive use of informal sources. The competition that is apparent from the supply-side product review presented above is therefore likely to be meaningful for only a rather limited customer segment.

Further evidence of use is available from a detailed market research survey that was carried out in the major urban centres along the Mbarara–Mbale strip to examine the extent of competition in areas where MFI coverage was strongest. The survey sought to sample the economically active population who are the target market for MFIs. These people were expected typically to be mobile and hence interviews were held in sites of high pedestrian traffic in these urban areas. The survey focused on respondents' use of financial institutions (for both savings and loans) currently or in the previous 12 months.[15]

Table 6.10 shows that 54.2 per cent of the respondents were currently using

Table 6.10 Use of financial institutions, Uganda

% of respondents (within category)	All	Kampala	Other towns
Overall use:			
Has never used	33.7	32.4	34.5
Has used in past	12.1	10.4	13.1
Uses currently or in last 12 months	54.2	57.0	51.8
Of those who currently use or have used in the last 12 months:[1]			
Savings:			
Banks (excl. CERUDEB & PBU)	19.7	23.4	17.2
of which: UCB	9.7	8.3	10.3
CERUDEB	13.2	15.9	12.7
Post Bank Uganda (PBU)	6.9	9.3	5.3
MFIs	12.0	11.1	12.7
Loans:			
Banks (excl. CERUDEB)	1.5	1.1	1.7
of which: UCB	0.6	0.4	0.6
CERUDEB	2.7	1.1	3.8
MFIs:	16.1	15.3	16.5
of which:			
PRIDE Uganda	8.9		
FINCA	2.9		
Uganda Women Finance Trust	1.4		
UWESO	1.3		
Faulu	1.1		
Commercial Microfinance Ltd	0.9		
Ugafode	0.7		
Uganda Microfinance Union	0.4		
FOCCAS	0.4		
MedNet	0.3		

Source: Hudson (2003) and analysis of data collected by *TMS Financial*, South Africa
Note: [1] Figures do not sum to same percentages due to multiple use and use of some smaller institutions.

a financial institution, 12.1 per cent had used one in the past, and 33.7 per cent had never used such an institution. The data are further analysed using four categories: commerical banks, Centenary and Post Bank, CERUDEB, and MFIs. The main commercial sector banks included Barclays, Baroda, Crane, Nile, Orient and Standard Chartered. The figures for Centenary and Post Bank were separated out because they are not conventional banks. CERUDEB was established as a trust fund in 1983 by the Catholic Church and while it developed strong savings mobilization, performed poorly as a financial inter-mediary (Seibel, 2003). It was transformed into a commercial bank in 1993 with foreign and domestic shareholders but the majority share remains with the Catholic Secretariat and the diocese. The key needs for the reform process were management restructuring and the development of the lending technology.

As would be expected, the use of savings accounts is higher than loans, with 19.7 per cent of all those interviewed reporting use of commercial bank accounts. The figure for Uganda Commercial Bank (UCB) alone is 9.7 per cent, showing that this bank also has significant outreach; 13.2 per cent of respondents had a savings account with CERUDEB, which reports having almost 400,000 savings accounts.[16] Post Bank had another 6.9 per cent of reported savings accounts and 12.0 per cent of respondents had a savings account with an MFI. Given the higher proportion reported for loans in Table 6.10 (16.1 per cent), this is likely to be an underestimate, perhaps because many respondents did not regard the compulsory savings required by MFIs in the same way as a voluntary savings account.

The data in Table 6.10 on loans clearly show how MFIs have reached the market for credit, with 16.1 per cent reporting loans from an MFI compared to 1.5 per cent from the banks. While CERUDEB's performance at 2.7 per cent of respondents represents a superior outreach compared to that of the mainstream banks, it also highlights the relatively slow development of its lending capacity in comparison to its savings outreach.[17] At the institutional level, while savers number some 400,000, borrowers totalled only 45,000 by December 2003. CERUDEB itself attributes the relatively low proportion of its assets in loans (40 per cent) to ineffective lending strategies, which in part date back to its poor-quality loan portfolio in the early 1990s, which almost led the institution into bankruptcy (Nalela, 2003).

Among the MFIs, PRIDE has the highest outreach in this sample because overall it is one of the largest programmes and is particularly focused on the town centres surveyed by the research. The data clearly show how microfinance institutions – including Centenary – have extended outreach. Table 6.11 goes further to break this outreach down by the proportion of respondents within a given socio-economic category using a particular service. Although information was not available to undertake a detailed analysis by poverty categories, of the indicators reported here, education most strongly correlates with household income and hence with income measures of poverty (Ministry of Finance and Economic Planning, 2001).

These results establish some expected patterns of access to different services. Access to bank savings is significantly associated with being male rather than female: 23.9 per cent of all men interviewed used these services compared to 15.4 per cent of women, a statistically significant difference. Use of bank savings also rises with levels of education and this correlation is significant: bank savings were used by 5.5 per cent of those with no education; 23.5 per cent of those who had completed secondary education; and 40.6 per cent of those who had undertaken some degree or diploma-level education. Employment status is also significantly associated with access: the percentage of those in full-time employment (33.4 per cent) is more than double the percentage using bank savings services in any other category.

Table 6.11 Use of savings and loans in different institutions by socio-economic category, Uganda

% of respondents (within category)	No.	Savings		Loans		
		Banks	CERUDEB	Banks	CERUDEB	MFIs
TOTAL	1,781	19.7	13.2	1.5	2.7	16.1
GENDER	1,794	**				**
Male	905	23.9	14.9	1.9	2.1	9.8
Female	889	15.4	11.4	1.1	3.3	22.5
AGE	1,788					**
18–25	368	12.2	9.2	0.8	0.8	4.3
26–35	610	20.2	13.8	1.8	3.0	14.1
36–50	661	19.5	14.7	1.8	3.3	25.3
51–65	149	19.7	13.4	0.7	4.0	13.4
EDUCATION	1,793	**	**			**
None	73	5.5	5.5	1.4	1.4	19.2
Primary	436	7.6	5.0	0.9	2.1	18.3
Secondary incomplete	549	12.6	12.0	1.1	2.4	21.3
Secondary complete	302	23.5	15.2	1.3	3.6	15.9
Degree / diploma complete & incomplete	433	40.6	22.6	3.2	3.5	6.9
EMPLOYMENT	1787	**		+		**
Full-time	497	33.4	16.9	2.6	1.8	10.7
Part-time	223	15.2	7.2	0.4	3.3	2.2
Self-employed	983	14.1	13.2	1.3	0	23.4
Unemployed	84	12.9	4.7	0	2.5	1.2

Source: Hudson (2003) and analysis of data collected by *TMS Financial*, South Africa
Notes: ** Significant at 1%; * Significant at 5%; + Significant at 10%.

By contrast, although access to CERUDEB's savings accounts is significantly associated with higher levels of education, it is not associated with gender and employment. For loans, the only mildly significant factor for access to bank loans is employment status, but this is not the case for CERUDEB. In contrast to these institutions, MFIs have clearly established an association with women rather than men, and with respondents who have lower levels of education. However, age appears as a factor associated with MFI borrowing where it does not for other institutions. Cross-checks with survey findings showed the average age of MFI borrowers to be 37 (Barnes *et al*, 2001).

While a greater proportion of the self-employed borrow from MFIs, Table 6.11 also indicates that some 10.7 per cent of those in full-time employment are also borrowing from this source. This in part suggests why MFIs have become more interested in salary-based loan products, but a related point is that livelihood strategies are diverse and many employees also operate businesses. In this context, salary-based loan products are in part responding to the existing client profile of MFIs, rather than necessarily representing an apparent drift up market.

This survey work explored use of formal and semi-formal financial institutions but did not investigate informal service use. Table 6.9 and qualitative research suggest both the continued importance of relatives and friends as a source, along with the importance of SACCOs and community funds. Qualitative research into the supply side of the market in Mbale and Masaka – both medium sized towns with an economy based on agriculture – suggested that the use of ROSCAs and ASCAs was on the rise (Sebageni, 2003), as did similar research in areas remote from formal financial services in Nakasongola and Mubende Districts of Central Uganda (Sebageni *et al*, 2002). In these remoter areas, MFIs and banks are still little used. While use of traditional savings mechanisms was declining (that is, devices such as wooden or metal boxes kept in the home; keeping savings on the person by sewing or tying them into belts or clothing; and moneyguards who are trusted individuals who look after money and who are often shopkeepers) there was a consistent increase in the use of groups. The pattern was similar for credit with a fall in borrowing from friends being matched by increased use of groups and an emerging, though small, use of MFIs.

Reduced borrowing from relatives and friends was explained in a number of ways. In the past borrowing was mainly for emergencies at home but now a wider range of income-generating activities have resulted in rising demand for credit. Also, when borrowing for business, friends were felt to be less trustworthy and people did not therefore wish to risk their good relationships. These factors help explain the increased use of ROSCAs and ASCAs as these offer a structured means of savings and gaining access to larger lump sums of money (for example, above US$25).

Conclusions

Evidence of the changing range of products suggests that MFIs are responding to clients' needs and moving beyond the rigid working capital loan product that most started with. Two sets of survey findings clearly demonstrate that the NGO-MFIs have made a significant contribution in extending access to credit to a segment of the population dominated by women, the self-employed and those with lower levels of education.

The outreach of Centenary alone is significant in responding to the extensive demand for savings services. However, while Centenary does not bias access towards men and full-time employees, as do the mainstream banks, its use still appears to be associated with higher levels of education, which are strongly correlated with wealth. At the same time, the banks are beginning to move down market. The potential is strong for Stanbic to harness the infrastructure of UCB and extend outreach through the use of improved management structures and the use of technology (Wright and Rippey, 2003). The emphasis on innovation in product development among the NGO-MFIs is towards individual and salary-based loan products, with increased competition among MFIs for clients. This suggests a convergence of MFIs and banks as the latter seek market segments that they are best placed to serve (that is, salary-based lending), and raises concerns that competition over customers may lead to over-indebtedness for this narrow segment, as was the case in Bolivia (ibid.).

Overall, product innovation among MFIs in the Ugandan financial market appears to be leading them to move up market rather than to significantly deepen and expand outreach. There is still a huge market of poor and socially excluded people to be reached.

Conclusion

This research set out to investigate the contribution of MFIs to shifting the financial 'frontier' within the overall context of developments in the financial sector. It did this by contextualizing microfinance interventions in particular markets through an exploration of changing provision and use, and qualitative explanations for these. The markets studied were relatively competitive, in part due to their location in better-off towns and districts where the agricultural base is relatively robust: the highlands of Kenya, Guntur district of Andhra Pradesh and the Mbale–Mbrara strip across the south of Uganda.

The findings confirm the importance of this wider market perspective. The changing macro-economic and financial policy environments have produced important dynamics for the financial sector as a whole. In Kenya, poor macro-economic management and high treasury bill rates gave the banks a risk-free source of income in the face of poor economic performance. This changed in 2000 when rates began to fall drastically and led to renewed interest from the banks in lending to the middle market of salaried employees. In India, the rising liquidity of the banking system, due to the closure of some non-bank financial institutions and slowing of the economy, resulted in gently falling interest rates and some banks are responding by seeking to serve a mid-range market of salaried individuals. In Uganda, a dip in treasury rill rates awakened banks to the need to lend, although the fall has not been sustained.

These responses from the banks have also arisen against the backdrop of financial sector liberalization that took place during the 1990s. The new entry of foreign banks, removal of interest-rate controls and in some cases lowering liquidity and reserve requirements have led to increased competition in domestic markets. However, banking sectors in Kenya and India had to be rationalized with the streamlining and closure of NBFIs, and Uganda has also experienced bank failures.

The evidence indicates that in all three cases the private sector banks are investing in technology, developing new products and undertaking more aggressive marketing. On the savings side, minimum deposit or balance levels are a means through which banks have segmented their markets, and the direct receipt of a monthly salary into the account is also a criterion. These savings accounts provide the basis for new loan products characterized by cash-flow lending for a wider range of purposes than in the past, including consumer and housing loans. Some banks have taken on the challenge of more difficult market segments such as business (Co-operative Bank in Kenya, Centenary and Orient Bank in Uganda) and agriculture (Centenary).

The evidence also demonstrates the importance of a range of other financial service providers in serving the middle market and in some cases poorer clients too. In Kenya, the SACCO sector has actively moved into the space that the banks left when they raised their minimum savings balances. The sector has started to develop its savings services to non-members, although this is a regulatory grey area. In India, it is evident that daily doorstep savings services offered by NBFCs and the Post Office are an important means of providing access. India also reveals that commission-based services can provide incentives for agents to reach highly populated slum areas because density can compensate for volume. The numerous small SACCOs in Uganda are a further example.

The studies also demonstrate the enduring importance of informal financial services, especially for poorer people. There is little evidence that MFIs are directly replacing these services. In Kenya and Uganda group-based financial arrangements of ROSCAs and ASCAs are everywhere in evidence and their use is growing. The evidence on moneylenders from Guntur suggests that while ranking exercises show their importance declining, their services still play an important role in responding to people's needs. Indeed, there is plenty of potential for on-lending within groups in the ever-present need to manage liquidity, especially where the rigidity of MFI working-capital loans actually increases the demand for moneylender services (Sinha and Matin, 1998). In Guntur SPANDANA is copying the product design of the moneylenders, an example that other MFIs might usefully learn from if they wish to compete directly with this sector.

Reviewed within this wider context, the outreach of MFIs is still relatively small, although the Ugandan data do suggest that MFIs have deepened and expanded outreach by privileging women and the self-employed and reversing the bias towards higher educational levels for access to bank savings accounts. However, while MFIs have expanded the frontier and the range of financial services available, the needs of poor customers for a variety of savings and loans products have become increasingly clear. Also the limitations of scaling-up provision through MFIs alone have become evident. At the same time there is little interest from the banking sector in adopting the core group-based working capital loan product. Demonstration effects (if occurring at all) are occurring at the very general level of showing to commercial financial institutions the importance of the mass market of poor people waiting to be served. Competition effects are not strongly in evidence either; instead MFIs tend to occupy a small, though important, market segment.

The overall conclusion of these studies is that conditions in the wider economy and financial sector are resulting in more formal financial institutions moving down market. In some cases they are embracing previously unreached customers, while in other cases they may simply be 're-banking' those clients whom macro-economic decline and bank restructuring had led to becoming unbanked. In the main this is leading to greater and more competitive provision for a middle market of less poor, often salaried, people. MFI members are an important source of clients who can be 'creamed-off' by these institutions. This raises the concern that it is these clients who become the focus of new product offerings from MFIs, rather than the vast market of still unserved poor people. Such mission drift is of major concern for the social performance agenda of microfinance.

Implications for the future

The evidence in this chapter supports the emerging view that in order to deepen and expand provision it is necessary to engage with a wider range of providers in the financial sector than NGO-MFIs alone. This conclusion arises, first, from the limitations of MFI approaches: particularly in terms of their ability to provide a wider range of financial services – especially flexible and safe savings – and in terms of regulatory constraints and the cost of overcoming these. Second, it arises out of the growing recognition that a wide range of providers whose physical and institutional infrastructure already produces significant outreach could be effectively harnessed within what is now a more conducive policy environment.

In moving to an approach that engages with a broader range of financial service providers, however, the role of subsidies needs to be carefully considered. The evidence presented here suggests potential dangers in giving subsidies to the private sector to extend provision. First, developments in the macro-economic and financial sector policy environment are creating incentives for financial institutions to move down market. The risk is that subsidy would be used to give incentives to the private sector to do what it is already doing as a result of market forces. This would provide unfair advantage and risk reducing the effectiveness of the market response. Second, existing commercial banks are often operating in the same environments as many MFIs. The risk is that if they were subsidized to develop products and services they would 'cream off' MFI clients rather than expand outreach. Third, there is a risk that the service would only be provided for as long as the subsidy lasted, without the financial institution using it to learn how to serve this market segment profitably. The example of consumer lenders in Bolivia entering a market segment and disrupting it, rather than serving it sustainably, is a cautionary tale in this regard.[18]

Given the scale of the problem, it is clear that a mix of intervention strategies is vital and that contributions to extending outreach from the banks and alternative financial institutions are to be encouraged. However, if subsidy is to be used, then accountability for that subsidy against the overall goal of extending access and use is necessary and should be an area of concern for donors. This requires clarity and transparency in the design of interventions with regard to: first, the market segment to be served in terms of client profiles; second, evidence of existing financial service use, needs of these clients and the justification for improving access; third, how the intervention will improve access; and fourth, how evidence will be produced to demonstrate that the services are used by the intended market segment and are effectively meeting their needs.

While this information is necessary at the level of a particular intervention, it is also necessary to evaluate progress at the sector level to review the changing landscape of access. In this regard, market-level studies of the type experimented with here can play an important role. Supply-side research helps identify the wide range of providers that poor people are already using, the extent and relative importance of different providers in financial inter-mediation, and the characteristics of services provided. Demand-side surveys of access and use, as in the Ugandan example, are particularly helpful as they can offer a detailed profile of use by different socio-economic groups.[19] This information is vital if we are to understand which groups are in fact being reached and how different providers contribute to the deepening and expansion of access. Repeating these surveys over time can then enable a proper evaluation of how interventions are in aggregate contributing to this goal.

CHAPTER SEVEN

Organizational determinants of social performance

James Copestake

Introduction

What protects an organization from mission drift? Does targeting result in deeper poverty outreach? Is individual lending better for clients than group lending? What constitutes an unacceptably high level of staff turnover? Should research and development be carried out in-house or should it be subcontracted? These questions all raise organizational issues that affect what services an MFI offers to whom, for how long, and with what impact (or net benefit) to them. In short, they all concern its social performance.[1] They also illustrate the complex, multi-faceted relationship between structure, operation (conduct or behaviour) and performance of organizations in general, MFIs being no exception.

The central goal of the *Imp-Act* research programme was *not* to research *all* the organizational determinants of the social performance of microfinance. Rather, it was to help MFIs find new and better methods of social performance *assessment* (SPA). However, it would be dangerous to concentrate too much on this narrower task. For SPA to be useful, it must be part of a wider social performance *management* system. It is important for readers to be clear on these distinctions: social performance depends in part upon how effectively (and self-consciously) organizations manage themselves to achieve social performance goals. This in turn depends in part on how systematically they attempt to assess their social performance. In turn, the *social* performance management of an MFI cannot be analysed in isolation from its *financial* performance management, particularly the core functions (or competencies) necessary to sustainably deliver good quality financial services.

The purpose of this chapter is to sketch out the organizational landscape against which a narrower focus on social performance assessment must be viewed. The introductory section explains the limited way in which this ambitious task has been tackled. Middle sections then review four sets of social performance determinants: organizational mission and vision, operating environment, internal operational capability and external relationships. The concluding section lists 14 management dilemmas that MFIs face in seeking to improve social performance.[2]

The 17 MFIs on whose experience (between 2001 and 2004) this chapter is mainly based all had explicit social missions but they were nothing if not diverse. Differences are summarized in Table 7.1. The MFIs are located in 14 countries. They vary in number of clients from less than 20,000 to more than a quarter of a million, but are all at or near financial self-sustainability. Their credit methodology includes individual lending, small group (solidarity) lending, large group (village banking) lending, and sponsorship of autonomous self-help groups and cooperatives. There is also wide variation in the extent to which credit is packaged with other financial and non-financial services, as well as in the nature and extent of rural, poverty and gender targeting. An important caveat to this chapter is that the *Imp-Act* research was not systematically designed to research the multiple determinants of MFI social performance.[3] Rather, we were guided in both MFI selection and the action-research process by the narrower goal of learning (by doing) about innovation in social performance assessment.

The methodology behind the chapter is primarily inductive. First, an archive of data was accumulated for each selected case-study organization. This included quarterly reports on progress with the action research, as well as a final report, incidental working papers and publications. These were supplemented by the report of an independent consultant on a project completion review visit. In addition, one or two key informants with knowledge of the MFI were asked to carry out a SWOT[4] analysis. This asked them to identify the main internal strengths and weaknesses, as well as external opportunities and threats, that affected the social performance of the MFI over the three-year period. We analysed responses by organizing them into themes, which were further consolidated into the section outline for this chapter.[5]

Each section includes one or more boxes of direct quotations from the SWOT analysis. In order to bring fresh empirical data into the chapter in a systematic and inductive way, these quotations have not been culled or classified in any more detailed way. Unfortunately this does result in some repetition, and we are aware that it makes more demands on the reader.

Figure 7.1 summarizes the thematic structure that this process produced. First, we deal with organizational mission, goals, vision and leadership. Second, we juxtapose this with the MFI's external operating environment. Third, we consider how internal organizational factors influence its ability to implement an agreed vision or strategy in a given operating environment. This covers a wide array of management competencies in finance, human resources, marketing and so on. It also includes the key issue addressed by this book: how effectively an MFI learns about its social performance and adapts its behaviour in response to this organizational learning. Finally, we consider how effectively external relationships are managed to facilitate this. In addition, Figure 7.1 illustrates particularly clearly that it is also important to take into account the dynamic feedback effects from performance to goals, operational capabilities and relationships.

Table 7.1 Summary characteristics of selected MFIs for 2003

MFI	Country	Client nos	FSS	Mode	Div	Loan	Rural	Pov	Savings	Wom	NFS	IRC
(See note)		A	B	C	D	E	F	G	H	I	J	K
BRAC	Bangladesh	3,493	n/a	SG	Div	58	Mix.	Strong	Med.	Med.	Yes	Strong*
CAME	Mexico	37	102	VB	Min	1,568	Urban	Med.	Med.	Med.	Weak	Weak
CMF	Nepal	n/a**	n/a	SHG	n/a	n/a	n/a	n/a	n/a	n/a	n/a	Med.*
CARD	Philippines	112	117	SG	Div	111	Rural	Med.	Strong	Strong	Strong	Med.*
CYSD	India	12	n/a	SHG	n/a	n/a	Rural	Strong	Strong	Med.	Strong	Med.
DEMOS	Croatia	n/a	n/a	IND/SG	n/a	n/a	Rural	Med.	Weak	Med.	Med.	Med.
FINCA INT.	USA	256	112	VB	Min	170	Mix.	Med.	Med.	Med.	Weak	Med.
FPC	China	15	n/a	SG	n/a	n/a	n/a	Strong	Weak	Strong		Med.
LAPO	Nigeria	23	72	SG	Div	90	Mix.	Strong	Strong	Strong	Strong	Med.*
ODEF		9	100	IND/VB	Div	34	Mix.	Med.	Med.	Strong	Weak	Med.
PRADAN	India	76	n/a	SHG	n/a	n/a	Rural	Strong	Strong	Med.	Strong	Strong*
PROMUC	Peru	28	97	VB	Min	129	Mix.	Med.	Med.	Strong	Strong	Weak
PRO-MUJER	Peru	18	101	VB	Min	300	Urban	Med.	Med.	Strong	Weak	Med.
PRIZMA	B&H	11	132	IND/SG	Div	624	Mix.	Strong	Weak	Weak	Weak	Med.
SAT	Ghana	42	88	VB	Div	77	Rural	Strong	Weak	Strong	Weak	Med.*
SEF	S. Africa	22	94	SG	Min	102	Rural	Strong	Weak***	Strong	Weak	Med.*
SHARE	India	250	110	SG	Min	92	Rural	Strong	Med.	Strong	Med.	Weak
UMU	Uganda	29	104	IND/SG	Div	220	Mix.	Weak	Strong	Med.	Weak	Weak

Notes: A = Thousands of active clients at the end of 2003; B = Financial self-sustainability rate (per cent), 2003; C = Main lending mode (SG = Solidarity group; VB = Village Bank; SHG = Self-help group; IND = Individual); D = Diversity of lending methodology (Diverse, Minimalist); E = Average loan size (end of 2003); F = Geographic orientation (Rural, Urban, Mixed); G = Pro-poor orientation (Strong, Medium, Weak); H = Savings mobilization orientation (Strong, Medium, Weak); I = Pro-women orientation (Strong, Medium, Weak); J = Strength of linkages with non-financial services (Strong, Medium, Weak); K = Internal research capability (Strong, Medium, Weak); * Indicates an in-house research department; ** CMF is a research and technical assistance outfit rather than an MFI – it works with 30 Savings and Credit Cooperatives, four of whom carried out research under *Imp-Act*; *** SEF does not take savings but requires members to accumulate regular savings using a post office saving account.

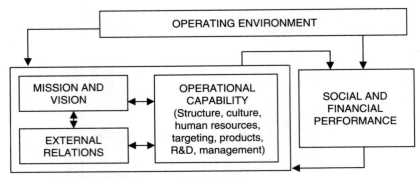

Figure 7.1 Determinants of organizational performance

Of course no piece of empirical work is ever entirely inductive. In this case, selection of themes was not only informed by SWOT responses, but also by our own unavoidably subjective attempt to organize them in a coherent way. An additional influence on this chapter is what may be referred to as a *paradox* view of management that is sceptical of the quest for perfection and emphasizes instead the challenge of maintaining a constructive tension between apparently contradictory forces (Copestake, 2005; Evans, 2000; Handy, 1994). This makes us sceptical of any claim that there is one universal best way of enhancing the social performance of microfinance. Instead, we have sought to identify tensions, dilemmas and contradictions that have to be constructively managed.

Successful organizations (including MFIs) seem to be successful because they strike the right balance between seemingly contradictory pressures.[6] For example, the *potential* for MFIs to achieve greater social performance is greatest if they take on the challenge of operating in the poorest, most unstable and difficult environments. But MFIs would be foolish to do this if they lacked sufficient internal capacity and external support. Paradox management here means simply striking the right balance between challenge and support, or not 'biting off more than you can chew'. A concrete example is K-Rep's decision to operate in remoter parts of Kenya, something it only embarked upon when it identified an appropriate operational model (Financial Services Associations) and could count on external support during a pilot phase.

This example makes clear that getting the balance right is a matter for each organization in its own context, and hence cautions against identifying universal best practices. But this is *not* to say that 'anything goes'. Making right or wrong decisions in each context has huge implications for MFIs, and for the well-being of their current and future clients. Moreover, while rejecting the search for a universal blueprint we do still assume that microfinance managers all face a broadly similar set of dilemmas and can benefit from being more aware of them. At the same time, the relative importance of each dilemma and the right balance that managers find between them will depend upon specific organizational goals and context.

Mission and vision

An almost unanimous observation (indeed almost tautological) is that the greatest power over the social performance of an MFI resides with its leadership. To some extent this power can be divided into two: power to set core values and goals (mission) and power to set long-term strategy (vision). These are not so easily separated in practice, since mission drift is almost inevitable if goals and values cannot be converted into a realistic strategy. Most of the MFIs covered by this review have clear social missions expressed in terms of three dimensions of outreach: breadth (number of clients, particularly in rural or neglected areas), depth (typically poverty status of clients and also gender) and sustainability. Many social mission statements also refer to the range of services that the MFI aspires to provide, and to intended impact on clients' lives – to enable them to rise above the poverty line, for example.[7] Box 7.1

Box 7.1

Strengths

'Visionary founder'. 'Committed and knowledgeable board with strong mission focus'. 'Clearly articulated social mission'. 'Strong board commitment to social mission'. 'Quiet but strong leadership from director based on close relations with staff'. 'Strong social mission, coupled with belief (and evidence) in being able to be financially sustainable and reach the poor'. 'Thoughtful, united leadership'. 'Strong social mission at foundation – recent internal movement to address mission drift'. 'Client-led board'. 'Experienced CEO with central bank experience'. 'Committed leadership on poverty reduction'. 'Well thought-through social mission and strategy to achieve this'. 'Clever incorporation allows cross-subsidy when needed to maintain development agenda'. 'Clear poverty mission and public commitment to it'. 'Holistic understanding of poverty'. 'Sustainability defined in terms of clients'. 'Comprehensive and compelling approach to poor people's development needs – credit, savings, education, insurance'.

Weaknesses

'Leadership in limbo about social mission'. 'Board very strong, but dominated by ex-bankers from one generation'. 'Little top management buy-in to social mission'. 'Leadership in limbo'. 'Risk of mission drift due to transformation'. 'Social mission subordinated to growth'. 'A conflict of interests between social mission and financial sustainability'. 'Internal battle between sticking to mission and being opportunistic to enhance financial performance'. 'Claim to be reaching the poorest, but not true'. 'Bias towards economic dimensions of change, neglecting others – including gender'. 'Assumption that livelihood security automatically empowers women'. 'Cloudy perception of poverty'. 'Charismatic but academic leadership from one board member undermines the position of the director'.

reports on the influence of mission and vision of the MFIs, as reported by key informants.

Few of the MFIs make explicit the relative weight they attach to their different goals, or even their ranking. In an uncertain environment such ambiguity allows leaders to have necessary and important strategic room for manoeuvre. The interesting question is then *who* holds the power to influence such decisions and what guides their thinking. Thus we move to the question of corporate governance. All the MFIs in the sample are private non-profit organizations, formally governed by a self-perpetuating board of trustees or similar. Moreover, few of them are strongly committed to a vision of transformation into a commercial bank; certainly not one that would risk surrendering control to shareholders with purely commercial interests.[8]

The more common model is for the parent NGO to incorporate its micro-finance arm as a separate non-profit entity, while retaining full control of its board.[9] This helps to clarify measurement of the MFI's financial self-sustainability without diluting the influence of the parent NGO on its social mission. However, this generally limits the MFI's legal powers to mobilize deposits and to use them to fund its lending activities.[10] It may also limit growth capacity by reducing its ability to secure equity capital and to leverage loans from other sources. All the MFIs expressed a strong commitment to becoming or remaining financially self-sustainable, but this is a far cry from saying they were out to maximize profits. Rather, financial sustainability was seen as a critical prerequisite for growth and autonomy, and hence as the means to sustain and expand financial services in line with an overriding social mission.[11] They also recognized that sustainable growth created room for manoeuvre with respect to social goals, and was also an indicator of innovation and effective cost control.

The governance structure of most of the MFIs leaves a great deal of scope to individual board members, as well as senior staff, to influence the tension between idealism and pragmatism, mission and vision. The professional experience, orientation and wider social networks of individuals are important. First, there appears to be a common tension between people who have strong commercial business or banking backgrounds (retired central bankers, accountants, business entrepreneurs – generally male dominated) and those with stronger social or voluntary sector backgrounds (NGO managers, activists, academics).[12] Second, there is a tension between the relatively detached view of outsiders and those closer both to the MFI itself and to the microfinance industry.[13] Both tensions have the potential to be constructive or destructive – strength lies perhaps in the balance of interests and the group dynamics that forces context-specific compromise between them. Grand strategic trade-offs and ideological differences are less important than the ability of leadership (often vested in one director or a small nexus of key people) to make an overall judgement on specific problems and opportunities as they arise.[14]

A final point concerns the quality of analysis underpinning social mission.

There is wide variation in this. At one extreme, it is surprising to find how vague an understanding of poverty and its causes persists at senior management and board level. For many, average loan size remains a sufficient indicator of depth of outreach, and it is simply assumed that improved access to microfinance results in improved business income and even the empowerment of women. Other leaders (particularly in South Asia) have a deep and thorough understanding of poverty based on substantial research investments.[15] This gives them a more realistic view of how their financial services can complement other development activities, whether of their own or provided by other agencies.

Operating environment

It is one thing to have a mission and a vision but quite another thing to implement them. Before entering into the details of how MFIs turn goals into practice it is useful to review briefly the challenges presented by their operating environment. The issues identified by the SWOT analysis can be classified into three types: the policy environment, the physical environment and the market environment.

The policy environment

In general, the policy environment for microfinance seems to have improved greatly compared with a decade or two ago, as portrayed in Box 7.2. For example, with fewer controls on interest rates and lower inflation, it has been easier for MFIs to set realistic prices for their services. Donors have more demanding expectations of the MFIs they sponsor, while being more realistic about the potential adverse effects on social performance of pushing too fast for growth and financial self-sustainability. MFI networks have also become

---

Box 7.2

Strengths

'Government generally supportive'. 'Self-help message in tune with public attitudes'. 'Supportive business and social sectors'. 'Supportive policy environment'. 'External donors exert strong challenge to improve performance'. 'Political support'.

Weaknesses

'Unsympathetic government and regulation'. 'Poor people assumed to be unbankable'. 'Hand-out culture and mass default from government programmes'. 'Poverty agenda not valued'. 'Difficult to forge linkages with major financial institutions'. 'Rigid interest rate controls'. 'Some problems of corruption, refusal to bribe resulted in licence for new branch being refused'. 'Delays with legislation restricted development of savings products'. 'Precarious regulatory status, due to being classified as an experiment'.

much stronger (see Chapter 8). Perhaps the greatest exception is China, which has yet to absorb and adapt lessons learned elsewhere in the world. Post-conflict transition (for example, in Bosnia and Herzegovina) also presented particular challenges. The early involvement of specialist MFIs is perhaps one factor that can help to avoid too sharp a break from often wasteful relief to often under-funded long-term reconstruction and development.

The physical environment

It is often part of MFIs' mission and vision to operate in difficult physical environments, yet it is important to recall the implications. Lack of rural infra-structure, sheer remoteness, thin markets and natural calamities all impose costs (as reported in Box 7.3). In Nepal, Peru, Philippines, Bosnia, South Africa, India and Bangladesh these problems were also linked to problems of physical security of staff. Only in the case of SEF in South Africa was good infrastructure and communication noted, but this was offset in part by relatively high salary costs. Operating in remote areas with a dispersed population also reduces client/staff ratios, can make it harder to recruit women and to retain good quality professional staff.

Box 7.3

'Remoteness'. 'Poor infrastructure and corruption'. 'Religious opposition'. 'Safety considerations in Naxalite [Maoist insurgent] areas'. 'Civil conflict'. 'Lack of skilled staff'. 'Low mobility raises costs of hiring managers'.

'Difficulty finding skilled workers as it expands'. 'Impact of HIV/AIDs on client and staff'. 'Recent civil conflicts'. 'Rural poor reside in remote and often difficult to reach locations'.

The market environment

Geographical location also affects the degree of competition that the MFIs face. This has positive and negative aspects, as described in Box 7.4. Operating

---

Box 7.4

Strengths

'Large untapped market'. 'Pioneer in its area of operation'. 'Buoyant local economy'. 'Increasing demand for its services'.

Weaknesses

'Downward pressure on interest rates reinforcing focus on financial performance'. 'Underdeveloped markets for services – communities requesting new branches'. 'Reluctance of banks to downscale – except in more profitable areas'. 'Limited livelihood diversification, hence low growth potential'. 'Increasing competition, over-indebtedness becoming an issue now'.

in relatively remote areas with limited competition allows MFIs to grow more rapidly and establish 'brand recognition' as a pioneer. By contrast, operating in areas where the local economy is weak is a source of frustration because opportunities for new investment and livelihood creation are more limited. The arrival of serious competitors was generally recognized to be a spur to innovation. Hence the deeper problem arises where markets are too thin to accommodate more than one MFI, or where subsidized new entry quickly results in market saturation. Some MFIs made a virtue of a poverty focus not only on social grounds, but also because this enabled them to build up a relatively loyal and resilient core portfolio of clients.[16]

Operations

Agreeing on a broad long-term strategy or vision for an organization is a simple matter in comparison to implementing it. A useful place to start is with the core business activity – sustainable provision of financial services. There are three inter-related sets of choices here: first, targeting (where, who for, how?); second, technical specification of products (what?); and third, delivery mechanisms (how, who by, why?). We consider first the range of options that MFIs face and the implications of different choices for financial and social performance. We then consider the processes by which those choices are made.

Box 7.5 reports on some of the perceived strengths and weaknesses of different targeting and product choices. Perhaps the most obvious choice that MFIs face is over where to operate. To the extent that there is a tendency for richer and poorer people to segregate then geographical targeting is a simple and robust way of prioritizing poorer clients, and most of the MFIs employed this strategy to some extent. This often entailed a trade-off with financial performance because poorer people also live in areas that are more expensive to operate in. However, this is not always the case, as these areas can also be less competitive, allowing MFIs to achieve a higher share of available business and cover higher costs through higher prices. In many cases rich and poor also live close together, so geographical targeting is a weak tool for improving social performance. For this reason some MFIs (notably SEF and PRIZMA) also target poorer clients by using explicit selection criteria.

A more common explicit screening device is gender. Some organizations work exclusively with women, but it is more common for MFIs to work mainly with women. The trade-off with financial performance is weaker here because screening is less costly and women are widely thought to be more reliable as customers. The more intractable question is how far privileged access to services strengthens women's influence over income, expenditure and other matters within household and wider family units. In general, this is a topic that MFIs have been content to leave to academic researchers (see Chapter 4).

In practice, direct targeting through some form of means test was a less common and important influence on the composition of the MFIs' clientele

Box 7.5

Strengths

'Well thought out lending methodology – innovative and diversified'. 'Clear goals, including targeting strategy'. Poverty focused methodology, including targeting and follow-up on loan use'. 'Poverty-focused methodology has been carefully researched'. 'Innovative product development – mobile cash loans, consumer credit, housing loans'. 'Tried and tested products'. 'Strong commitment to geographical targeting'. 'Willingness to start up in difficult zones'. 'Pro-active targeting, including follow-up visit'. 'Deliberate policy of targeting remote and areas'. 'Commitment to health education component, accounting for 5 per cent of operating costs'. 'Commitment to active management of internal accounts of village banks on social grounds, despite high financial cost'. 'Strong shift from village banking to individual loan methodologies'. 'Minimalist methodology in order to maximize depth of outreach and growth potential'. 'Interlinked with non-financial services, but with clear staff/agency division of labour'.

Weaknesses

'Lack of complimentary non-financial services undermines impact'. 'Impact of clients having to cover arrears of others in groups limits growth and outreach'. 'Financial pressures have been a factor behind limited flexibility of products to meet individual client needs'. 'Poverty focus has not been translated into products adapted to client needs'. 'Standardized methodology with little scope to adapt to specific needs of clients'. 'Tendency to charge high interest rates to finance growth limits client loyalty and impact'. 'Poverty focus diluted by decision to go for growth in existing areas of operation'. 'Intensive group formation work being undermined by growth targets'. 'Zero tolerance of arrears has contributed to high drop-out rates'. 'Lending methodology gives too much power to centre leaders, contributing to vulnerability of poorer members'. 'Lending methods increasingly complicated'.

than client self-selection in response to product design. The main aspects of products can be listed as:

- *Range* and degree of bundling of savings, credit and insurance products.
- *Terms* or time restrictions on when funds can be deposited and withdrawn.
- *Collateral*, including group membership requirements and mutual liability.
- *Prices* (and costs), including interest rates, bonuses, fees and fines.
- *Tie-ups* with non-financial services.

Of course these factors affect not only client composition (including depth of outreach) but also the net value of services to clients and cost to MFIs. Indeed product choice is perhaps the single most important arena in which the balance between social and financial performance is struck. Generalizations are particularly difficult given the diversity of the sample of MFIs being reviewed here,[17] however, two general points are important to discuss: the tension between product standardization and diversification, and the relationship between product quality and price.

The general trend has been towards demand-led diversification of products, away from supply-led replication. In turn this has been associated with flexibilization (notably of loan sizes and terms) and simplification (particularly from bundled to unbundled, and from group-mediated to individual services). The influence of these choices on access, sustainability and impact depends critically on the quality of client assessment and product design processes, as discussed at some length later. Certainly there is good evidence that if this is done well, then it is possible to enhance performance along all these three dimensions at once. However, there is also a danger that innovation can be overdone. In particular, diversification and flexibilization of products can confuse clients and staff alike, as well as impose extra operational costs on the MFI.[18] In short, the range of products should broaden in line with the needs of clients and the capacity of the MFI, rather than running ahead of them.

Simplification also presents trade-offs. A particularly important debate here concerns the future of village banking in Latin America.[19] Reducing the burden and rigidity of group activities can lower costs and broaden access. However, it may restrict the range of possible benefits, particularly for poorer clients, and be associated with a general drift upmarket. A similar issue applies to the choice between supporting autonomous self-help groups or more closely controlled solidarity groups in India.[20] MFI income and growth is faster with solidarity groups, but the SHGs can be cheaper and more flexible for users, offer a wider range of services, as well as creating opportunities to gain confidence and leadership skills (Fisher and Sriram, 2002). All MFIs are aware that product design influences both financial and social performance, but very few as yet monitor these effects at the differentiated product level. A rare exception is SEF in South Africa. It has two programmes, only one of which is poverty targeted, and is able to vary the balance between social and performance goals through reallocation of resources between them (Baumann, 2004; Roper, 2003).[21]

Delivery mechanisms

This section takes the goals of the organization as given, as well as the product mix. No matter how well these are developed, much depends on the capacity of an MFI to deliver them. Responses to the SWOT analysis on this issue fell into five categories. First, there were general observations about the cost and quality of staff. Second, MFIs were criticized for being over-centralized. Third, many were criticized for weak internal communication and alienation of staff. But, fourth, many were also praised for maintaining a strong learning culture. Finally, a recurring theme was that success generates success – strong performance is itself a key ingredient of strong capacity. These issues are reviewed in turn here, with particular emphasis on the way they are causally related to each other.

Cost and quality of staff is perhaps the most important issue. The payroll is the largest recurrent cost item and must be carefully controlled, but if average salaries are lowered too much in relation to staff performance targets then staff turnover will increase and cost per client will eventually start to rise. Positive and negative observations are set out in the Box 7.6; they serve as a reminder of the importance of high quality human resources to any organization, especially those in a business as demanding as microfinance. In particular, most MFIs face a tension between recruiting and retaining technically skilled staff, and ensuring a sufficient number of staff also have sufficient insight into the social dimensions of microfinance. Linked to this is the balance between internal promotion of staff with relatively more frontline experience and external recruitment of less experienced but more formally educated staff. The strength of internal culture can be a critical ingredient in helping staff with different backgrounds and perspectives to cohere.[22]

Box 7.6

Strengths

'Very powerful middle management at branch level; a key vehicle behind adherence to social values'. 'Professional leadership, with a strong stress on qualifications and skills in making good use of technology'. 'Highly skilled and committed staff, including some with mainstream banking experience'. 'Strong business ethos, high degree of professionalism'. 'Good profile of field staff – half women'. 'Constant staff training'. 'Well-educated, committed, loyal staff and low turnover'. 'Small, dedicated staff with long experience in the field'. 'Strong field staff'. 'High staff quality'. 'Good level of social commitment among staff'. 'Close-knit staff share a similar vision and experiences'. 'Strong support for social mission from field to boardroom'.

Weaknesses

'High turnover of staff at HQ – low morale'. 'High turnover of senior management staff'. 'Lack of professionalism especially in human resource management'. 'Low morale and rapid turnover of field staff'. 'Excessive staff rotation'. 'Limited ability to take clear, methodical approach to problem solving. Too many activities and variables at play, too many hasty decisions'. 'Much turnover of staff during the last year'. 'Staff and management problems – lack of management skills, staff turnover in development department, industrial action and wage pressure'. 'Low morale and rapid turnover of senior staff – mostly replaced by retired bankers'. 'Technical expertise of staff comes at the expense of appreciation of the social dimensions'. 'Cost of recruitment and training; low new staff retention'. 'Low adherence to the mission among front-line staff'.

The discussion now progresses to overall organizational structure. There are a range of issues here including size, concentration of power, and choice of mechanisms (formal and informal) for coordination and control. Where MFIs are managing large sums of money, and if they are serious about their own sustainability, then an 'iron cage' of management controls and discipline is unavoidable. Nevertheless (and without going into great detail) most key informants criticized MFIs for being excessively centralized, or perhaps more precisely for the rigid and mechanical way in which central control was exercised,[23] as illustrated in Box 7.7. This point becomes clearer when we turn from organizational structure to culture. Here the observations (as reported in Box 7.8) are more divergent.[24] On the negative side, four of the MFIs were roundly criticized for weak internal communication, inflexibility and a lack of willingness to learn from below. On the positive side, several organizations were praised for having established a strong sharing and learning culture.

Box 7.7

'Management highly centralized'. 'Male dominated'. 'Strong leadership offset by limited devolution of power and lack of branch independence'. 'Centralized decision making'. 'Excessive power and control over internal decisions by the president'. 'Centralization has restricted the freedom and initiative of country programmes'.

'Decision making highly centralized to five people in HQ who have been there for 15 or more years'. 'Non-participatory, hierarchical internal culture'. 'Fairly centralized with limited scope for staff initiative'. 'Management highly centralized'.

Box 7.8

Strengths

'Very well thought through mission unpacked into goals and strategy, with strong top and middle management adherence'. 'Strong organizational commitment to social mission apparent at all levels'. 'A learning culture, ability to acknowledge and respond to limitations, emphasis on staff training including human skills'. 'Professionalism includes sharing of tasks'. 'Accountability mechanisms in place'. 'Very good internal communication – even has an intranet'. 'Openness of staff to learning at all levels'. 'Strong culture of learning and willingness to take prudent risks to enhance social and financial performance'. 'Poverty reduction mission strongly communicated throughout the organization'. 'Client-led board with good communication channels'. 'Commitment is instilled in all staff'. 'Participatory internal culture'. 'Recently recognizing the need to appoint staff with an explicit mandate to uphold the social mission'. 'Well managed at county-level'.

Weaknesses

'Lack of good communication from bottom-up and horizontally'. 'Strategic plan is unrealistic compared to capacity of current staff'. 'Board commitment is not translated into action by staff – result is mission drift'. 'Decentralization model reduces cross-organizational learning'. 'Overloaded staff in branches with low support from head office causing demotivation'. 'Limited vertical communication apart from management memos'. 'Weak downward reporting and accountability'. 'Not a strong learning culture in terms of looking out for and admitting problems'. 'Institutional culture seems to emphasize financial over social objectives'. 'Field does not feel supported by HQ'. 'Non-participatory internal culture'. 'Strategic planning is weak – seldom linked to core mission and not implemented'.

This information on organizational culture perhaps suggests a more simplistic picture of good and bad MFIs than is the case. A more accurate view is to link the issues of communication and participation to the profile and motivation of staff at different levels in the hierarchy. At one extreme, there are MFIs with a board and senior staff highly committed to social performance goals, but reliant on staff motivated (by contrast) more by financial incentives, including performance-related pay. At another extreme there are MFIs whose junior staff have a stronger social motivation, but are frustrated by tight controls imposed on them by senior management who are more preoccupied with financial performance and growth. A precondition for effective participation and organizational learning at all levels of the organization is the creation of a shared understanding of the balance of goals (ends) and means. Some internal tension between staff at different levels is inevitable, but some minimum threshold of shared culture is necessary on financial as well as social performance grounds. Otherwise, efforts to hold down overall staff costs will be undermined by poor staff motivation and high staff turnover, which is often associated with wastefully high rates of client exit.

This discussion leads onto the critical role of feedback loops from past to future performance. A minimum level of financial performance seems to be a precondition for improving social performance. The most obvious link is that good financial performance allows faster growth and hence increases strategic room for manoeuvre. An additional positive feedback loop operates between growth, increasing professionalism of staff and staff motivation; however, the relationship is complex. Concerns were also expressed about the adverse effect of too narrow a focus on financial performance and growth, leading to excessive centralization. A narrow preoccupation with growth can be so detrimental to staff motivation and client orientation as to be self-defeating. The dynamic effects of positive and negative performance are shown in Box 7.9.

Box 7.9

Strengths	Weaknesses
'Strong systems and discipline allow for exceptional growth and good financial performance'. 'Able to mobilize resources to encourage innovation and growth'. 'Increasing professionalization leading to improved financial performance, better staff management and growth'. 'Very high rate of growth and depth of outreach'. 'Sustainability and scale'. 'Rapid growth'. 'Strong growth'. 'A big push to improve efficiency'. 'Well-organized delivery channels; national coverage'. 'Breadth of outreach, allowing depth to be examined and steps taken to improve it'. 'Good financial performance'. 'Sound financial performance'.	'Poor growth due to operational problems and external shocks, forcing total preoccupation with financial performance'. 'Incentives all linked to financial not social performance'. 'SPA and monitoring scaled back due to financial pressure'. 'Pressure for operational self-sufficiency'. 'Challenge of scale – how to retain culture'.

Research and development

While much organizational learning within MFIs is embedded within operating practices, most MFIs also invest in specialized research and development capacity. The comments in Box 7.10 emphasize a number of factors that influence the return on such investment. There must be a clear commitment from senior management to such investment, based on recognition of its practical relevance and a willingness to innovate. Specialists are needed for this work, but they must not become isolated from operational staff. The existence of strong monitoring systems as a foundation for R&D is important here. These issues are all explored in more depth in Chapter 8. A willingness and capacity to change in response to its own research was one of six factors emphasized in the concluding chapter of a recent history of K-Rep in Kenya (Fowler and Kinyanjui, 2004). The others were: active management of the environment; a willingness to invest in improving governance; competent, responsive and committed staff; adaptation of organizational structure to suit activities (not vice versa); and gaining an equal partnership relationship with donors.

Box 7.10

Strengths

'Client assessment has brought about changes in practice'. 'Good feedback loop, especially use of information'. 'Organizational culture is conducive to systematic learning'. 'Strong links through board to independent research centre'. 'Staff at the top are keen to develop useful R&D'. 'Strong commitment to pilot testing new practices'. 'Enhanced poverty analysis capacity linked to efforts to institutionalize social mission'. '*Imp-Act* research built understanding of clients'. 'Willingness to experiment and review'. 'Good knowledge of context, including market niche'. 'Lots of progress made with monitoring systems'. 'Flexible products, lots of innovation'. 'Strong monitoring systems'. 'Track record of publications on poverty'. 'Actively sought client feedback on products'. 'Focus via *Imp-Act* on organizational learning, not just research or impact assessment for its own sake'.

Weaknesses

'Feedback is weak, with a focus on formal report writing rather than communication of useful information'. 'Insufficient skills in analysis and research, relative to ambition'. 'Difficult to find money for R&D'. 'R&D is a low priority, so under-resourced'. 'No real monitoring system prior to *Imp-Act*'. 'Patchy monitoring and evaluation systems'. 'Still has no idea how people use loans or of cross-selling of products'. 'Initially very little management buy-in for impact assessment, but this has now changed'. 'Decomputerizing branches has reduced capacity for routine client monitoring'. 'Microfinance and social development units are two voices, lacking a common vision'. 'Overdependence on consultants'. 'Board does not recognize the value of striving for international best practice'.

External relations

Discussion of the internal capacity of MFIs quickly leads to the question of how best they can manage external relationships and through them their wider operating environment. The issues are again complex and inter-connected. MFIs compete with other MFIs and with other financial institutions, but also collaborate with them. They seek flexible financial and technical support from donors and governments, but also risk being coordinated or even coopted by them. Working with other organizations creates new opportunities for resource mobilization, but also exposes MFIs to threats. In this section we briefly review relations with the commercial sector, donors, consultants, other MFIs, wider civil society and governments. Box 7.11 presents the comments of MFI staff on relations between MFIs and regulated financial institutions.

Box 7.11

Strengths	Weaknesses
'Strong contacts with the commercial sector'. 'Ability, through global affiliate, to link up with international capital markets'. 'First MFI to get top rating; transparency and strong financial results make it attractive to investors'. 'Senior staff experience in banking makes them open to collaboration with other financial institutions'.	'Lack of financial support due to poor financial performance'. 'Lacks experience in how to mobilize equity and debt finance for its next phase of growth'. 'Highly dependent on the collection and payment services provided by other financial institutions'. 'Reliance on post office for savings accounts and loan disbursal'.

Strong financial performance and a good understanding of the wider financial system open up new opportunities for MFIs to secure additional funding and hence to grow. Equally important is the dependence on banks for basic financial services (particularly payments and savings), and hence vulnerability to increases in bank charges.[25] While the very existence of MFIs may be a symptom of the regulated financial system's limited outreach, the quality of their relationship with it nevertheless remains critical to their performance.

At their best, donors provide MFIs with finance and technical support to help them innovate, as well as room for manoeuvre within which to find ways of improving social performance, as shown in Box 7.12. The case studies provide many instances where they are successful in doing this, both through direct funding and through donor support channelled through specialist global financial networks.[26] The main challenge here for MFIs is to make good use of such support without at the same time becoming overly dependent on it, or allowing it to undermine their financial discipline and autonomy. For

Box 7.12

Strengths

'Highly diversified support from many international partners'. 'Active engagement with wider policy domain'. 'Strong and loyal financial backing from USAID'. 'Support from Grameen Foundation and UNDP has enhanced professionalism'. 'Support from a mix of local, public sector funders'. 'Strong donor support'. 'Supportive donor community'. 'Capacity to leverage funds and technical assistance from relevant local bodies. Emphasis on local rather than international funds'. 'Ability to make good use of external technical assistance'. 'Effective and strategic use of consultants – for example, activity-based costing, credit scoring'. 'Strong local consultants who are not afraid to be critical'.

Weaknesses

'Donor funding has encouraged it to take on too many projects at once'. 'Little integration of different activities supported by donors'. 'Still highly donor dependent'. 'Push on financial performance by donors has not allowed time for experimentation'. 'Pressure to expand from donors distracts it from its wider livelihood strategy'. 'Donor capacity-building packages not up to date'. 'Excessive external pressure for sustainability'. 'Operations often shaped by funding opportunities, rather than by internal planning or mission'. 'Too dependent on donor support for capacity building'. 'Uncertainty linked to imminent end of donor funding'.

example, while donor-funded consultancy can be timely and effective, it can also distort internal decision-making structures and processes. Perversely, donors' own sensitivity to the charge of being 'soft on subsidies' can also be a problem, prompting excessively optimistic financial self-sustainability targets. Donor funding can also be a factor behind over-rapid and fragmented attempts at innovation.

The potentially double-edged nature of contracts with donors and other financial institutions explains in part the value given to looser networks with other MFIs, both national and international, as reported on in Box 7.13. These provide less constrained opportunities for learning about new practices, as well as for influencing the wider policy and funding environment. Cooperation with national networks involves some tension because other members are also competitors, and this can inhibit information exchange.[27] Partially, for this reason most MFIs find no contradiction in being affiliated vertically to one or more international groups, as well as participating in national networks.[28]

Networking is not just about mutually beneficial joint action, it is also a critical arena within which to build and protect legitimacy. Once a strong reputation is established then there is potential for a virtuous circle: reputation leads to improved funding, to greater professionalism, to improved performance and to further reputation enhancement. However, this spiral can operate downwards as well as upwards. Good public relations are not only a means for improving access to support and for influencing policy, they are also a necessary protection against a hostile press and government attention. One

Box 7.13

'International profile and reputation'. 'Widely perceived leadership role'. 'Leadership role in the microfinance community in Nigeria: well respected as an organization'. 'Innovative leader in the market'. 'One of the most well-known programmes in China: a pioneer in lending methodology'. 'Good interaction with state and centre government'. 'Strong marketing, with high profile sponsors and patrons'. 'Good international profile'. 'Strong network with others – for example, SIPAN'. 'Lots of support from Opportunity'. 'Strong networks with like-minded institutions, affiliates and partners'. 'Strong parallel provision of complementary services – health, education, technology, inputs, product markets and training'. 'Strong international network, with mutual learning. The downside is that country networking is weakened by co-dependence with their global affiliate'. 'Good networks with rest of MFI sector in the country'. 'Good relations with the national microfinance council'. 'Well-established networks built by founders and CECI. A good reputation in the international arena of funders'. 'Strong networks with like-minded organizations'. 'Good links to promote non-financial services'.

role for R&D specialists in an MFI is to ensure that its public relations and marketing activities can be backed up by evidence and do not dangerously distort the reality. This is particularly important given the potential for MFIs to slip into the trap of believing their own marketing literature too readily. Comments by MFI staff on public relations are presented in Box 7.14.

Box 7.14

Strengths	Weaknesses
Very professional promotion (internet, news)'. 'Good relations with the media'. 'Perceived political neutrality'. 'Strong at promoting issues for the industry and communicating the plight of the "very poor" '. 'Reputation for being ethnically impartial'.	'Lack of communication and agreements with institutional partners'. 'The risk is that they do not serve the people they talk about in their marketing materials'. 'Some mud sticks – violence towards members from spouses, tax exemptions, religious opposition'. 'Interference from government and party officials'. 'Growing level of resentment among former clients'. 'Unsympathetic and suspicious local government'.

Conclusion

This chapter has drawn on the *Imp-Act* case studies to survey the many factors that influence the social performance of MFIs. As we move on in Chapter 8 to focus more narrowly on social performance assessment systems, it will be important to keep in mind this broader picture – social performance assessment is important, but the extent of its importance depends on how well it fits into wider organizational systems and contexts. Although a broad range of case studies and issues have been reviewed, a common theme has been the challenge that MFIs face in striking the right balance between apparent opposites. Tensions are unavoidable and can be constructive so long as they do not propel organizations towards pathological extremes.

Table 7.2 provides a summary of 14 dilemmas identified in this chapter.[29] In each case a constructive tension or balance is contrasted with two extreme

Table 7.2 Summary of social performance management dilemmas

Issues	Extreme position	Constructive tension	Opposite extreme position
1. Mission	Dominant financial perspective – neglect of social mission	Social mission constrained by financial realism	Social mission is unsustainable due to lack of financial realism
2. Vision/growth strategy	Growth orientation at the expense of staff motivation and quality of service, leading to high staff and client turnover	Growth subject to minimum standards of service quality for staff and clients	Limited scale of activity, possibly undermining sustainability
3. Board composition relative to MF	Dominant 'generalist' perspective – failure to learn from best-practice within microfinance	Tension between pursuit of best practice within microfinance and wider perspectives	Dominant specialist microfinance perspective – insular view and danger of 'herd effects'
4. Ambition relative to external environment*	Attempt to work in environments that are too difficult relative to the MFI's capacity, or to achieve too much too quickly	Strategy strikes an appropriate balance between challenge and internal capacity	Social performance limited by reluctance to push into new markets. Excessive caution or conservatism in planning
5. Targeting methods	Rigid pro-poor targeting, risks stigmatizing clients and can limit growth	Flexible and low-cost (self-) targeting, especially area based, plus outcome monitoring	No targeting of any kind limits social performance
6. Product design	Highly diversified product range, with and without tie-ups, and with flexible terms	Cautious product diversification informed by careful research	Rigid adherence to one or two standard products
7. Human resources	Bias towards rewarding high qualifications and outside experience	Blend between qualifications and experience; internally promoted and externally recruited staff	Bias towards rewarding practical field experience and loyalty

Table 7.2—*continued*

Issues	Extreme position	Constructive tension	Opposite extreme position
8. Organizational structure	Rigid central control, completely subordinate field staff	Continuous monitoring and review of scope for decentralization of decision-making	Inadequate financial discipline. Low staff productivity and high risk of fraud
9. Organizational culture	Rigid contracts and enforcement. Weak vertical and horizontal communication. High staff turnover	Culture of listening and consultation within a strong framework of work discipline	Weak job specification. Staff overly distracted from core tasks by diverse initiatives
10. Research and development	Specialist staff isolated from operational staff, working mostly for board and donors	Specialist unit integrated with routine monitoring and strong feedback loop	Part-time activity with ad hoc support from consultants
11. Change management	Refusal or inability to contemplate changes to original model and management practices	Culture of organizational learning tempered by careful change management	Proliferation of new innovations and pilot projects often led by funding opportunities
12. Relationships with funders	Stable, open-ended, co-dependent and cosy	Diverse, long-term and focused on enhancing MFI autonomy	Fragmented, uncertain, fashion-driven and insecure
13. Relationships with other MFIs	Fierce competition and mutual suspicion	Flexible mix of collaboration and competition	Complacent and insular closed networks
14. Public relations	Aggressive self-promotion, rhetoric outstripping reality	Public relations effort in line with actual and potential performance	Lack of publicity limits development of external relations

Note: *Includes physical, policy and market aspects of the environment.

positions along a spectrum. No attempt has been made here to relate the spectrum of three responses to each dilemma into a larger theory or typology of organizations: hence the table should be read row by row and not vertically. Neither has any attempt been made to assess the relative importance of each issue, since this is likely to vary between MFIs and contexts. Rather, the more modest purpose of the table is to suggest that, for all their diversity, MFIs share a common set of issues and dilemmas. Systematic reflection and adjustment of these will lead to better social and financial performance.

The purpose of this chapter was to generalize inductively from a set of diverse MFI studies on the many factors that affect their social performance. This has yielded a checklist of 14 issue areas, against which the narrower question of the role of social performance assessment can be viewed. Although not its prime purpose, this checklist could also be developed into a practical diagnostic tool for reviewing the social performance capacity of MFIs. Managers, or even a focus group of different stakeholders in an MFI, could be asked to locate its position with respect to each issue in one of five boxes: first extreme, intermediate, constructive tension, intermediate or second extreme.[30] For each issue they could then indicate: first, where they think the MFI currently lies, and second, where they think it *should* lie. This would then provide raw material with which to suggest how the MFI could improve social performance.

CHAPTER EIGHT

Institutionalizing social performance assessment

James Copestake

Introduction

The previous chapter explored the many factors that influence the social performance of MFIs, whereas in this chapter we focus on just one of them – social performance assessment. This refers to any activity intended to clarify how far an organization is achieving social goals, such as widening access to financial services and strengthening clients' livelihoods. To recap, social performance assessment includes collecting information on breadth and depth of client outreach, as well as impact on clients (net worth). It can also extend beyond clients to cover those who live and work with them or compete with them. It may be routine (continuous monitoring of the poverty status of clients, for example) or it may take the form of discrete studies (of clients' satisfaction, reasons for client exit, direct and indirect impact, for example). Institutionalization refers to work that becomes a routine activity or norm, integral to the way an organization operates: not something that is hidden away behind locked doors in some forgotten corner of the head office. For this to be the case, such work must have a clear and accepted purpose, and be cost-effective. Thus the chapter is ultimately concerned with how data collected are shared among decision-makers and then put to use.

The chapter, like the previous one, attempts to generalize inductively from the experience of a diverse set of organizations that participated in the action-research phase of the *Imp-Act* programme. Table 8.1 lists the organizations and provides a very brief statement of what each was trying to achieve. The chapter again draws on an archive of material collected from each organization, as well as SWOT analyses carried out by external reviewers at the end of the three-year action-research period.[1] However, it is beyond the scope of this one chapter to do full justice to the rich and varied experience of all the organizations. Additional case study material on the process of institutionalization of SPA is also available in other chapters of this book, in special editions of the *IDS Bulletin* and *Small Enterprise Development Journal*, in the companion volume to this book (Brody *et al*, 2005) and in the narrative summaries of each MFI project available on the *Imp-Act* website.

Table 8.1 Action-research goals of participants in the *Imp-Act* programme

Organization	Action-research goals
ASOMIF Nicaragua	To strengthen internal capacity of members in client assessment through country network-based training, following the example of COVELO
BRAC Bangladesh	To complete specific evaluation studies of microinsurance and wider impact – internal research capacity already fully institutionalized
CAME Mexico	To complete a set of in-depth studies to inform strategic decisions about whether to alter its village banking model. To strengthen internal SPA capability through partnership with a local research institution
CARD Philippines	To strengthen internal capability to do client-assessment work. To promote the use of such tools through the Philippines Microfinance Council
CERUDEB Uganda	To incorporate social indicators into its computerized MIS in order to be able to monitor the profile of its clients and improve credit rating
CMF Nepal	To carry out a specific study of the impact of credit unions, comparing those that were self-organized with those externally sponsored
COVELO Honduras	To develop capacity to do client assessment using AIMS-SEEP tools in a way that also allows findings to be consolidated across a national network.
CYSD India	To develop new monitoring tools, including a system for rating the quality of self-help groups. Strengthen wider/indirect impact assessment
DEMOS Croatia	To strengthen internal client-assessment capability
FINCA International	To incorporate social indicators into its computerized MIS. Latterly, to build a robust system for routinely monitoring the poverty status of clients
FINRURAL Bolivia	To develop capacity of the network secretariat to carry out impact assessments for members, to meet both internal and national demand
FOCCAS Uganda	To strengthen internal client-assessment systems, mostly through the use of focus groups
FPC China	To deepen understanding of options for SPA through international networking.
K-Rep Kenya	To evaluate the impact of farmer service associations
LAPO Nigeria	To explore different approaches to measuring progress towards its poverty-reduction mission
MFC Poland	To develop (though learning-by-doing) its own specialist role in the provision of technical support to strengthen SPA among its member MFIs
PRADAN India	To institutionalize self-help group impact monitoring through development of an Internal Learning System based on client diaries and routine reporting
PRIZMA Bosnia-H	To develop a poverty assessment and impact monitoring system using data collected routinely as part of lending cycle
PROMUC Peru	To develop internal capability of the secretariat and member MFIs to do poverty and impact assessment both for internal and external audiences

Table 8.1—*continued*

Organization	Action-research goals
Promujer Peru	To carry out an in-depth study of direct and indirect impact with particular reference to gender. To enhance internal client assessment capability
SAT Ghana	To build internal capability to use AIMS-SEEP tools. To develop a comprehensive impact monitoring and assessment system
SEEP USA	To encourage peer exchange and learning in client assessment among its member MFIs and networks
SEF South Africa	To review and streamline its internal poverty assessment and impact monitoring systems
SHARE India	To carry out an in-depth study of indirect impact. Strengthen internal SPA capability
UMU Uganda	To build up internal capability to do client assessment, including (latterly) through 'data warehousing'

The chapter follows a logic that proved useful in organizing responses to the SWOT. We first review the demand for SPA from both internal and external users. We then turn to the issue of supply of information in response to this demand. The final section addresses the question of the cost-effectiveness of SPA. This chapter is a report on empirical findings, rather than an argument in support of a predetermined position or set of 'conclusions' about how best to do SPA. Chapter Nine presents more detailed recommendations, and some readers may like to glance at these first so as to be able to read the contents of this chapter with the benefit of knowing in advance where they are leading.

While the chapter is structured around a strong distinction between demand and supply for social performance data, Box 8.1 draws on the experience of FINCA International to illustrate the important interaction between them. Lack of demand undermines the quality of supply and this in turn reduces demand. The critical challenge that *Imp-Act* sought to address was how to break out of this trap, replacing it instead with a virtuous cycle: increased demand stimulating better supply, reinforcing increased demand and so on. The chapter argues that the key arena for these dynamics is internal to the MFI. External demand, while important, can indeed inhibit internal ownership of SPA. However, once clear internal ownership is established then external collaboration (of consultants, donors and particularly MFI networks) can be critical to strengthening supply-side capacity.

Box 8.1

FINCA International joined *Imp-Act* with the goal of identifying a small number of social indicators to include in the management information system that it was developing for use by all its affiliate programmes. Staff recognized that clear protocols would be needed for analysing and reporting on changes in the data, but initial pilot work (in Uganda) mostly highlighted the danger of producing too much information without thinking clearly about how it would be routinely used. Discussions across countries about which indicators to adopt also highlighted the complexity of the task, and for nearly two years the project seemed to be going nowhere.

Several factors rescued the situation. Attention narrowed on monitoring the poverty status of clients, partially in response to US legislation signalling that organizations failing to do so in a reliable way could be excluded from future USAID funding. At the same time, the board was becoming more sensitive to the argument that years of dedication to growth through commercialization might be resulting in some mission drift away from relatively poor clients. Rather than relying on an integrated computerized monitoring system (with dangers of 'lock-in'), a small team led by John Hatch and student interns began to experiment with a rapid survey approach using palm pilots. Early rounds demonstrated to the board that useful statistics could be generated quickly, reliably and cost-effectively. This helped to build support for further investments in developing a system that could be institutionalized at country programme level.

Internal demand for SPA

Why do social performance assessment? By far the largest set of comments in the SWOT concerned the nature and extent of internal commitment to social goals within MFIs themselves. Clear and considered formal mission statements are symbolically important, but far more important is the personal commitment of senior staff and board members. In addition to believing in the social mission of their organization, leaders must be willing to allocate time in planning meetings to discussing SPA, to incorporate social goals into strategic plans, and allocate resources to SPA in their operational plans. Clear delegation of responsibility for managing SPA is also important if the task is not to be buried under more pressing concerns.

Participants in the *Imp-Act* programme both selected themselves and were screened for leadership commitment to improving impact on poverty. However, this did not mean that all senior staff in all MFIs were equally convinced of the case for institutionalizing such activities all the time. Box 8.2 provides a summary of positive and negative influences on internal demand for SPA that helps to explain variation in attitudes both between and within MFIs and over time. Perhaps the most common tension was between those who regarded SPA as a core activity and those with an opportunistic view, seeing it as something to be done in an *ad hoc* fashion, especially when others were willing to pay for it or when it was linked to securing external finance on favourable terms.

Box 8.2

Positive	Negative
Good understanding (at senior level) of the nature and causes of poverty, hence awareness of the limitations and potential pitfalls of microfinance.	Preoccupation with rapid growth and a belief that this alone is sufficient evidence of positive social impact.
Experience of shocks (such as high rate of exit or default) that challenged the assumption that growth necessarily means positive impact on clients.[2]	Intuitive and opportunistic management (often by crisis) based mainly on informal sources of information.
Previous experience of benefits arising from past investment in SPA.	Bad experiences in the past of expensive and unhelpful impact assessment often oriented primarily towards external interests.
Peer pressure, particularly if backed up by evidence of other organizations institutionalizing SPA.	Financial pressures and competition diverting attention towards more immediate operational problems.
A general commitment to self-improvement, to giving clients and staff voice, and to constant product development and innovation.	

Internal demand for SPA has also been strengthened by the growing industry-wide perception of its close relationship to more commercially oriented market research. Indeed, SPA can most successfully be institutionalized where it is seen to meet financial and social goals. PRIZMA in Bosnia-Herzegovina, for example, faced the problem of operating in a highly competitive, if not fully saturated market. SPA (in the form of routine poverty monitoring, as well as client satisfaction and exit studies) was consistent with a business strategy of seeking to consolidate a niche market catering for the needs of poorer clients. Likewise, quick studies of the reasons for client exit and client satisfaction surveys can also have a quick financial pay-off, thereby helping to build demand for further and deeper SPA work.

Conversely, large and longer studies of impact can help to reinforce indifference or hostility to SPA among MFI leaders. Several MFIs under the *Imp-Act* programme lost momentum because they missed the opportunity to start with studies that would have yielded operationally useful information more quickly, or because they were overly ambitious. Impact surveys require minimum sample sizes to generate statistically useful information and there tends to be a longer lag between data collection and findings. Hence surveys require more patience and commitment from would-be consumers of the findings. Partially for this reason, there is scope for complementing (and indeed often replacing) impact surveys with qualitative in-depth interviewing, for which *Imp-Act* developed a user-friendly protocol called the QUIP.[3] An added advantage of qualitative work is that it is more likely to generate unexpected findings.

A comparison of the work of COVELO in Honduras and CAME in Mexico illustrates the point. Under *Imp-Act* they both started with the intention of using AIMS-SEEP tools. However, in Honduras the priority was to generate data of direct relevance to operational decisions, such as whether loan sizes were appropriate. In Mexico, CAME's priority was to produce information to inform longer-term decisions about its methodology and growth strategy. COVELO encouraged MFI staff to collect data themselves; CAME subcontracted to an academic institution.

External influences on demand for SPA

The word 'institution' refers not just to legal organizations, such as MFIs, but also to norms or rules of behaviour (North, 1990). Norms or rules may be institutionalized within one organization in isolation. SEF in South Africa, for example, pioneered and institutionalized its targeted and routinely monitored pro-poor approach to microfinance in relative isolation. However, prospects for establishing norms are much greater when the practice is recognized as legitimate within a wider community of organizations. FPC in China, for example, has faced the challenge of working in a context in which understanding of microfinance and how it can be assessed is very limited.

Box 8.3 divides comments from the SWOT analysis on external demand for

---

Box 8.3

Public and politicians

'Positive political environment'. 'Poverty reduction is an important national goal'. 'Political pressure to identify poverty-level impact'. 'Increasing political awareness of potential of microfinance'. 'Dissemination of findings generated great public interest'. 'Local distrust of NGO intentions, accountability and honesty'. 'Political scandal about social performance of NGOs in the country, especially those linked to the president's wife'. 'Meddlesome politicians'. 'Political risks – need for a defensive strategy'. 'Grudging government acquiescence'.

MFI networks

'Network-wide awareness of the need for impact data'. 'Peer organizations look to CARD as leader and example setter'. 'Link with the Microfinance Council has been important in ensuring institutional buy-in and institutionalization'. 'Positive influence of other MFIs with effective impact assessment methodologies'. '*Imp-Act* itself has been key in promoting interest'. 'Minimalist competitors have undermined commitment to SPA'. 'Organization is isolated from peers and international networks'. 'SPA is becoming a hot topic: X doesn't want to be left out'. 'Very weak microfinance sector, dominated by consumer lending'. 'Board does not recognize the value of striving for international best practice'.

Donors

'Support of donors with shared mission'. 'Pressure from USAID prompted a more careful review of its mission'. 'Key role of one highly trusted donor'. 'Donor pressure and patronizing attitudes have undermined commitment to impact assessment'. 'Motivation to institutionalize SPA has been primarily donor driven'. 'Impact assessment conducted primarily to satisfy external demands'. 'Previously seen as a costly extra to be funded by donors'. 'Donor dependence'.

SPA into three: those from the wider public, those from peer organizations and those from donors. An appropriate place to start is with the wider public, as reflected both in the media and through politicians and policy makers. Public attitudes to microfinance can change rapidly, with swings accentuated by political interventions. In much of Latin America, for example, widespread dissatisfaction with access to bank services has prompted some heavyweight presidential political endorsement of microcredit as a means of reducing financial exclusion and poverty. But unrealistic expectations can quickly lead to disillusionment and hostility, particularly where historical norms have erred on the side of low interest rates and relaxed repayment culture at the expense of sustainability. Of course, the primary task of MFIs in such a situation is to concentrate on its 'core competence' of delivering good quality and sustainable financial services. However, the generation of reliable evidence on their social performance can also provide useful material for wider dissemination to build public awareness and ensure more realistic expectations. This can also play an important role in guiding public policy and legislation.

An example from Mexico concerns the extent to which loan funds are directly invested in small businesses and job creation. Within the microfinance industry globally it is well understood that clients are generally the best judge of how to use their funds (whether in business, housing, education, strengthening social networks), and that the protectional impact of microfinance is as important as its potential promotional impact. However, given the strength of the association between microcredit and microenterprise, CAME was rightly cautious about how to share evidence generated by its loan-use survey on the many ways in which clients deployed their credit (CAME, 2004). The example also illustrates the limitations of producing data unilaterally rather than collectively.

Conversely, the case for investing in SPA is stronger where there is already strong public interest in poverty and exclusion, and public demand that development organizations demonstrate how they are contributing to poverty reduction. In post-apartheid South Africa, such pressure extends to profit-oriented as well as non-profit financial institutions. Indeed, an implicit social contract has evolved in which banks have sought to retain autonomy from government in return for a commitment to monitor and to improve social performance at the sector level, as measured primarily by indicators of aggregate outreach (Arora and Leach, 2004).

Generating information about outreach and impact of financial services has 'public good' characteristics, meaning that it is easy to share information with others but hard to force them to share the costs of producing it. If MFIs can 'free-ride' to some extent on information produced by others (as well as the positive effect this has on wider understanding) then there is less incentive for them to collect such data for themselves. For this reason, there is a strong case for sector-wide collaboration or at least coordination of effort. In practice, we have observed under *Imp-Act* that the leadership of one or two MFIs, in alliance with national networks, can play an important role in persuading other MFIs to take the issue of SPA more seriously.[4] In Bolivia, FINRURAL intervened to build understanding of the diverse impact of microfinance when popular dissatisfaction with more aggressive players in the market had already boiled over (Marconi and Mosley, 2004). In Honduras, the COVELO network intervened earlier in the development of the microfinance industry, partially in an attempt to avoid such problems (Copestake, 2004b; Copestake, 2003a).

While these are both examples of national networks, international networks of MFIs and donors continue to play an important role in helping MFIs to make investments in SPA, as well as supporting research and development into how networks can operate more effectively in this and other areas. A recurring theme of the *Imp-Act* programme has been the importance of international links not solely as a means to capacity building, but also for peer support and building legitimacy. In the case of FINCA International, for example, members of the network (as well as those in ACCION) have often warned their affiliates against investing too heavily in impact assessment – regarding it as a potentially expensive and unproductive distraction from the core task of working towards financial self-sufficiency and expanding outreach. Yet, as it has become aware of the need for more realistic and professional social performance management internationally (not least in relation to its own support base in the USA), so it has become a catalyst of SPA (particularly poverty assessment) among its affiliates.[5] This change partially reflects better understanding of how SPA can support, rather than oppose, MFIs' outreach and sustainability goals.

Similar issues arise over the role of donor agencies. The quotations in the third section of Box 8.3 highlight the positive role they can play in sustaining MFI commitment to social goals and performance assessment. For example, donor support was critical in encouraging K-Rep in Kenya to experiment with the 'farmer service association' approach to providing financial services in relatively sparsely populated areas. Likewise donors have helped to raise awareness among MFIs of the pitfalls of relying solely on informal and anecdotal evidence of impact, given the tendency to share stories of successful clients and bury stories of failure. However, the SWOT feedback also alludes to the danger that donors can distract MFIs from their own internal agendas. By colonizing the field for themselves, donors have in the past discouraged MFIs from entering it themselves, or encouraged them to do so in inappropriate ways. Tensions include: emphasis on scientific rigour over sufficient reliability; orientation towards influencing funding rather than operations; written over verbal feedback; *ad hoc* and reactive, rather than systematic and strategic, system development.[6]

Of course donors have their own information and accountability agendas, and in many cases these justify independent impact assessment and research, often focused on the whole financial sector rather than on specific MFIs (see Chapter 5, for example). However, where donors are investing in organizational development of specific MFIs then it is sensible to seek to build their own goals (and mechanisms for assessing performance against them) into the MFI itself, rather than hope they will either be achieved by accident or last only as long as their own aid to the MFI. *Imp-Act* itself represents the Ford Foundation's own enlightened attempt to move on in this regard by breaking the bonds that tend to link support for SPA to its own funding cycles.

MFI internal capability

Given strong and consistent demand for SPA centred within the MFI itself, the next question is how to enhance capability to provide such information. This section focuses on what MFIs can do for themselves, while the next section considers how others can assist them. It has often been said that the foundation for good evaluation is reliable monitoring and Box 8.4 (reporting

---

Box 8.4

Positive

'Procedures in place for institutionalizing SPA and management'. 'The system has now been in use for three years, and has become very effective for monitoring both financial and social performance. Reports are produced regularly for the board. The MIS is also used extensively for data mining'. 'Lots of progress made with monitoring systems'. 'Strong monitoring systems'. 'Relatively good MIS and above all understanding of what you can get out of it'. 'Sophisticated MIS and purposeful data analysis, but some inconsistency in data collection between branches'.

Negative

'No adequate baseline data at the beginning of the process'. 'No real monitoring system prior to *Imp-Act*'. 'Patchy monitoring and evaluation systems'. 'Narrow focus on monitoring'. 'Decomputerizing branches has reduced capacity for routine client monitoring'. 'Failure to computerize client assessment data limits the ways it can be used'. 'Information systems say very little about clients or social performance'. 'Client monitoring is being built into MIS, but so far rigidly linked to income indicators and used only for loan approval'. 'Interest in wide-ranging indicators, so difficult to assess them all'. 'Lack of routine information systems'. 'Weak client monitoring systems'. 'Vision of "data warehousing" is perhaps too ambitious; delayed, yet implications still not fully thought through'. 'Still not mining in-depth data in the MIS'. 'Exit monitoring not institutionalized'. 'MIS not geared

'Effective integration of impact monitoring in programme activities'. 'Good mix of quantitative and qualitative methods'.

to social performance'. 'Weak client monitoring'. 'Still collecting too much unnecessary information'. 'Time lags in delivery of impact assessment results mean no practical lessons have yet been drawn from it'.

Box 8.5

Positive

'Strong central monitoring and evaluation unit'. 'Strong core internal and external team supporting SPA'. 'Demonstrated commitment to seeking out, experimenting with and adapting the most appropriate methodology for the organization – requiring several rounds'. 'Promoting monitoring and evaluation appropriate to PRADAN's culture and mission'. 'Strong, dynamic, young leadership'. 'Good investments in improving tools'. 'Culture of organizational learning'. 'Strong pressure from social development unit to institutionalize social performance management'. 'Client assessment has brought about changes in practice'. 'Good feedback loop, especially use of information'. 'Organizational culture is conducive to systematic learning'. 'Strong links through board to independent research centre'. 'Staff at the top are keen to develop useful research and evaluation'. 'Strong commitment to pilot testing new practices'. 'Enhanced poverty analysis capacity linked to efforts to institutionalize social mission'. '*Imp-Act* research built understanding of clients'. 'Willingness to experiment and review'. 'Good knowledge of context, including market niche'. 'Flexible products, lots of innovation'. 'Track record of publications on poverty'. 'Actively sought client feedback on products'. 'Focus via *Imp-Act* on organizational learning, not just research or impact assessment for its own sake'. 'Small core of committed staff'.

Negative

'Feedback is weak, with a focus on formal report writing rather than communication of useful information'. 'Insufficient skills in analysis and research, relative to ambition'. 'Difficult to find money for R&D'. 'R&D is a low priority, so under-resourced'. 'Still has no idea how people use loans or of cross-selling of products'. 'Initially very little management buy-in for impact assessment, but this has now changed'. 'Lack of R&D Department capacity means not as much regular client assessment as previously'. 'Board of directors prone to micro-manage R&D activities'. 'Not clear about how data would be used in decision making'. 'Weak understanding of poverty and targeting issues'. 'Lack of time for SPA due to preoccupation with other projects'. 'Too much work for a team that was too small'.

on linking SPA to management information systems and monitoring) bears this out, albeit with slightly changed terminology.[7] A small number of MFIs (SEF and PRIZMA being leading examples) have succeeded in integrating collection and use of client level data into routine information and decision-making systems. However, a larger number of organizations are still struggling to do this, despite being clear that it is what they want to do. A common pitfall is to be over ambitious about the amount of data that can be collected and used effectively. Emphasis on impact assessment studies (often for external audiences) has also distracted many MFIs from the simpler and logically prior task of routinely monitoring who their clients are and how this is changing.

A precondition for achieving this level of institutionalization is almost certainly a willingness on the part of MFI leadership to invest in it adequately. Box 8.5 reproduces comments from both SWOTs on investment in specialist SPA. Responsibility for SPA is often lumped together with broader research, marketing and public relations activities. A danger of this is that thinking about the role of SPA becomes confused; specialist staff have less direct involvement with routine operational staff and their work becomes marginal and *ad hoc*.

Box 8.6

Positive

'Willingness to experiment at branch level'. 'Strong cadre of committed long-term employees'. 'Staff enthusiastic and committed to using market-based tools; but little effort to demonstrate relevance of wider impact assessment work to their activities'. 'Bottom-up approach; wide sense of ownership of the poverty scorecard as a critical management system'. 'Involvement of internal control in enforcement of social data collection signalled its seriousness'. 'Strong commitment from staff at all levels to social objective of poverty reduction, and good informal systems for learning from clients. But this does not filter up above branch level'. 'High level of staff awareness of general social performance'. 'Willingness of communities to attend meetings'. 'The internal learning system has involved clients themselves and can empower them'.

Negative

'Involvement of field staff, but undermined by high turnover and weak communication'. 'Staff initially uncooperative, fearing the new assessment efforts were intended to catch them out'. 'Mixed enthusiasm over new entry and monitoring forms; ensuring staff buy-in was an afterthought'. 'Multiple demands on staff time'. 'Limited knowledge of staff'. 'Insufficient integration of SPA with informal organizational systems'. 'Microfinance and social development units are two voices, lacking a common vision'. 'Strong staff induction regarding the primacy of social mission, but lack of follow-up. Client assessment in practice is restricted to the research unit'. 'Lack of general staff capacity'. 'Staff understanding and involvement limited, due to high turnover'. 'Small core of knowledgeable and committed staff, but other staff have a weak grasp of social dimensions and are oriented primarily to financial performance goals'. 'Research fatigue among clients; poor feedback to them'. 'Clients running out of patience'.

It might be concluded from the above that institutionalizing SPA boils down to leadership vision and willingness to invest in the technically difficult issue of integrating selected client-level indicators into its MIS. However, this would be to miss a crucial ingredient: integration with operations. Box 8.6 illustrates the importance of building support among operational staff. It is, of course, particularly important that staff appreciate the value of SPA if they are themselves directly involved in data collection. But even where data is collected completely independently, sharing findings with staff can influence the way they perceive their role, the decisions they make, their motivation and productivity. This was particularly striking in the case of the COVELO project in Honduras, where many of the senior staff who conducted exit interviews and client satisfaction focus groups themselves, reflected on the positive value of reconnecting with clients in this way.

The same applies to clients. To motivate them as respondents it is helpful for them to understand, at the very least, why they are being interviewed and how the information will be used. Feedback, even if it is to explain why suggestions were not taken up, is also important. The Internal Learning System (ILS) used by several organizations in India attempts to go one step further.[8] Self-help group members are encouraged to keep pictorial diaries, and these form the basis for regular dialogue with staff. It is potentially time consuming for both, but the method has the potential not only to inform the sponsoring organization, but also to transform the outlook and attitudes of clients. While PRADAN has persisted with the ILS primarily on the former grounds, ASA in Tamil Nadu found it less effective for its own SPA than a more orthodox system based on quantitative indicators. Scope remains for adapting and rationalizing the kinds of data collected (how often, how long, for which clients) and to find more cost-effective ways of aggregating and summarizing data for operational and strategic purposes.

External support for SPA

We have already explored the role of the public, politicians, networks and donors in generating demand for SPA. Here we consider the experience of external technical support in promoting its supply. Such help takes many forms: nearly all the MFIs hired individual specialist consultants and researchers, as well as receiving technical support through membership of national and international networks.

In turning to consider external support for building SPA capacity it is useful to look back at lessons learnt from strengthening financial performance assessment and management systems. It is interesting to note that this was very much an externally driven process. Specialist consultants, donors and particularly CGAP played a critical role in helping to standardize terminology, systems and training. Of course, there is still considerable variation in internal systems – and competence, but few would question the need to produce, review and act upon routine financial performance data as a core part of doing business.[9] Box 8.7 reproduces relevant observations from the SWOT study.

Some bias should be noted in the sample here, as the participation of MFIs in *Imp-Act* itself revealed a preference for external support de-linked from established donor affiliations.[10] *Imp-Act* was not strictly a technical assistance

Box 8.7

Consultants

'Fragmented relationships with academic advisers'. 'Bringing in academics with a stake in the method being developed may have led to different interests driving the pace of the work'. 'Impact assessment work mostly externally conducted, or half-done internally, leading to poor feedback and organizational learning'. 'Keen support from external research institute, but work is viewed from both sides as a private project of the resource person, with limited internal staff support'. 'Having an outside academic may have contributed to inertia on the part of staff to complete work and draw lessons'. 'Finding an excellent, dedicated, experienced and like-minded academic – earlier choices would not have worked'. 'Over dependence on consultants'.

Networks

'Limited information sharing across the [national] network'. 'As MFIs are transformed into banks, so their international sponsors are taking on technical support roles at the expense of national networks'. 'Long-term support from Ford Foundation has been important both for institutionalization and advocacy'. 'Emerging and dynamic networks are acting as a catalyst for innovation and advocacy'. 'External training from a variety of agencies brings people together usefully across the sector, but in an *ad hoc* way'. 'MFI objectives are compromised by the strong agenda of its sponsoring networks'. 'Strong presence in Washington policy networks'. 'Strong support from its sister organization in Bolivia'. 'Sustained assistance from MFC was critical – especially the quantitative component'.

project, but it is clear from feedback that networking opportunities arising from it (particularly with other MFIs) were an important source of ideas, advice, encouragement and legitimacy in developing SPA systems. But while progress was monitored by a team of UK-based researchers, participants were free to decide for themselves what external support they would need, if any.[11] To think clearly about technical support it is useful to first consider simple bilateral contracts with consultants, funded out of an MFI's own uncommitted income. We then turn to the more common experience of technical support that is tied-up or 'bundled' with finance and long-term partnerships.

External technical support

To what extent should an MFI contract-in technical support for SPA or rely on its own internal staff? This obviously depends in part upon the nature of the work, as well as the experience of the MFI. The previous section argued that the foundation for SPA is routine monitoring of the client portfolio, integrated into the MFI's own management information and decision system. The MFIs who have already developed such systems relied heavily on external technical support to set them up, but on the understanding that the systems would ultimately be managed internally. The SWOT comments reveal a recurring problem with reliance on more academic consultants, in part because they had a greater interest in self-contained studies that could generate potentially publishable findings within a short time period. This is one reason why the impact assessment 'cart' has often ended up in front of the routine monitoring 'horse'.

In sum, MFIs need to make their own decisions on how to design SPA, and a key component of this is routine internal monitoring of client status, which should be fully internalized. But this is not the end of the story. Routinely generated information has to be interpreted; it also generates questions that merit further investigation. Box 8.8 suggests two extreme models for providing such additional assessment: fully integrated and fully contracted-in. Under the first, periodic social performance studies (including quantitative 'mid-range'

Box 8.8

Internal and integrated	*Externally contracted*
Reliance on operational staff with limited external technical advice.	Reliance on external consultants or partners in liaison with management.

Strengths	**Strengths**
Total control over work done.	Specialized skills.
Work fully reflects internal criteria (timing, cost, utility, reliability).	Opportunity to carry out the work intensively, without other distractions.
Easy to control distribution of findings.	Formalized process of defining scope (and cost) of work.
Easier to monitor the work and sanction failures within organizational hierarchy.	Opportunities for transfer of knowledge and skills to staff.
Chance to learn by doing and to build a pervasive learning culture.	Greater potential credibility to external audiences.
Easier to adapt and change work as it evolves.	Avoids cost of employing specialized staff full-time.
Avoids expensive consultancy bills.	

Weaknesses	**Weaknesses**
Staff may lack necessary skills, and MFI may not be able to keep specialized staff busy full time.	Consultants have their own goals and agenda.
Staff distracted from other tasks.	Consultants fail to understand fully the context and priorities of the MFI.
Staff distracted by other tasks.	Consultants distracted by other activities.
Staff prone to biases or elicit biased responses.	More costly to set up and monitor.
Reduced credibility to external audiences.	Harder to enforce contracts through legal and/or social sanctions.
Danger of weak cost control, especially taking into account opportunity cost of time.	Harder to adapt and change as work evolves.
	Harder to control dissemination of findings.

impact surveys and/or qualitative studies on the QUIP model) are regarded as core to operations and activities that periodically involve selected internal members of staff. A leading example is ODEF in Honduras. Annual studies involve fieldworkers doing interviews in other branches. Analysis is carried out internally and results are discussed at all levels of the organization. In addition to generating client-level data, the exercise is valued as an internal learning process, as a way of giving staff voice and thereby hopefully reducing staff, as well as client, turnover (Cohen and Wright-Revolledo, 2003).

This contrasts strongly with the second model, under which performance assessment is largely contracted out to specialist experts so as not to distract operational staff and management from 'core' operational tasks. An example of this approach is CAME in Mexico, which contracted in specialist researchers to carry out a series of impact studies. As already noted, CAME and ODEF (as part of the COVELO Network) both started off using the AIMS-SEEP toolkit for client assessment, but while the latter adapted these to fit its integrated model and to generate internal findings within a few weeks, CAME adapted them for more rigorous research, for external as well as internal use. The main drawback of CAME's approach is that it is too expensive to repeat such studies regularly. Internal staff involvement was limited and so any future studies would still need to be contracted in and probably require external funding.

An intermediate model is to invest in a permanent internal unit of one or more specialist researchers under the direction of a senior manager. Such units often combine social performance assessment with other responsibilities, including market research, marketing, donor liaison and public relations.[12] SEF, in South Africa, is an example. Operational staff carry out most of the data collection as part of routine operations, but specialist staff in the monitoring and evaluation (M&E) unit are responsible for aggregating the data and generating routine programme-wide reports (Roper, 2003).

The diversity of organizational models for SPA adopted by MFIs participating in the *Imp-Act* programme reflects variation in their size, experience, goals and many other characteristics. It is not surprising that they could not agree on a single model. In general those with the strongest commitment to social performance management also argued most strongly for full internalization of SPA. In contrast, those for whom external audiences were more important argued more strongly for external involvement on the grounds that it enhances credibility.[13]

A subsidiary issue concerned the relative merits of different kinds of researchers. Again generalization is hard because individual differences (of personality, interests, values, motivation, experience) within each group are so large. However, some important general differences can be linked to differences in the governance and incentive structures of those working in universities or private consultancy firms, for example. These are summarized in Table 8.2.[14] Again, it is not possible to say that one stereotype is preferable to the other because much depends upon the nature of the information required and by whom. However, awareness of such differences within contracting

Table 8.2 Stereotypical differences in the characteristics of external consultants

Primarily research oriented	Primarily business oriented
More likely to be university-based	More likely to be in a private firm
Stronger commitment to academic rigour in deriving conclusions (often discipline-specific)	More willing to adopt 'quick and dirty' and eclectic multi-disciplinary methods
More familiar with pure social science methods	More familiar with applied and market research methods
Greater interest in writing-up material in detail for external consumption (potentially publishable). Reluctance to make intuitive judgements	More willing to present findings verbally or through 'bullet point' briefings, leaving internal staff to draw their own conclusions from findings
More jealous of intellectual autonomy, therefore more likely to say uncomfortable or surprising things, but also harder to keep to terms of contract	Stronger commitment to providing the client with what they want within specified time period
More value attached to the quality of findings than keeping the client happy in order to get paid quickly	More likely to restrict quality standards and expenditure to that required to comply with contract requirements

MFIs is important, as is the need to augment the supply of consultants with the vision and experience to transcend them.

Networks

Much of the external technical support that MFIs receive for SPA is linked to longer-term inter-organizational relationships. In discussing the role of networks in generating demand for SPA, a distinction was made between horizontal networks (mostly at the national level) and vertical networks (comprising a dominant funding body and one or more affiliated MFIs). Table 8.3 lists examples of both, all of which participated in the *Imp-Act* programme. A key issue, on the supply side, is the division of labour in provision of technical support between horizontal and vertical networks.

In the case of vertical networks the principal relationship is financial, with the sponsor agency raising seed funding (in the form of equity, loans and grants) to help selected MFIs establish themselves and grow as independent entities. Legal relationships vary: FINCA International and Promujer retain ownership of country programmes for a long period before floating them off as fully autonomous MFIs, whereas OPPORTUNITY International and PLAN International only fund MFIs that already have an independent ownership structure (CGAP, 2004b). In all four cases, the networks have exerted quite a strong influence over SPA, linking it to larger funding agreements and their

Table 8.3 Examples of MFI networks providing technical support

MFI network	Nature of network
Vertical	
FINCA International	US-based sponsor of 24 national programmes, three of them in the process of transformation into independent banks
OPPORTUNITY International	International NGO providing funding to more than 50 independent partner MFIs
PLAN International	International NGO, mainly supporting area-based development programmes, but also a growing number of independent MFIs
Promujer	US-based NGO, with MFIs in Bolivia (now largely independent), Peru, Mexico and El Salvador
Horizontal	
ASOMIF (Nicaragua)	National association of MFIs in Nicaragua, with more than 20 members
COVELO (Honduras)	Umbrella organization for 70 MFIs in Honduras
FINRURAL (Bolivia)	Umbrella organization for 15 MFIs in Bolivia, committed to promoting savings in rural areas
Microfinance Centre (Poland)	Specialist technical support agency for 66 member MFIs across 22 countries in Eastern Europe, the Balkans and Central Asia
PROMUC (Peru)	Consortium of seven NGOs operating a unified village banking service, extended to other NGOs through 'franchise' agreements

own feedback requirements. They also have a strong incentive to promote uniformity of SPA systems in order to facilitate consolidated reporting to donors across the entire network. For example, PLAN International has a particular need for feedback on how their investment in MFIs affects child welfare, given that this is the core of its own mission and fundraising strategy. However, in this case, the sponsored MFIs also have their own boards and are able to articulate a distinct interest in SPA for internal purposes.

Horizontal networks generally lack the financial leverage of the vertical networks, and so rely more on voluntary participation of members.[15] However, there is considerable variation with respect to the 'subsidiarity' issue and to the division of labour between member MFIs and the network's secretariat. Two distinct models can be identified within the *Imp-Act* programme. In the first, typified by the COVELO network in Honduras, a particularly strong member MFI took a lead within the network to promote its vision of SPA more widely among members. In the case of Honduras this leadership was provided by ODEF.[16] Technical support passed from ODEF to eight other member MFIs through a series of training workshops, also supported by independent consultants (Copestake, 2004b; Garber, 2004). Participants were then required to pilot the tools covered and to report findings back to the network secretariat so they could be analysed in aggregate as well as at MFI level.

The ASOMIF network in Nicaragua explicitly sought to replicate the Honduran experience, but with leadership coming mainly from an external consultant, rather than from leading network members. Table 8.4 shows how this weakened the model. While workshops were nevertheless useful, it was not possible to pool data in order to publish it across the sector. It is also likely that the workshops contributed less to long-term institutionalization of SPA within the country.

The second model of horizontal network SPA is typified by FINRURAL in Bolivia. In this case it was the network secretariat itself that secured *Imp-Act* funding in order to set up an 'impact evaluation service' in which it retained a more dominant technical role (Marconi and Mosley, 2004). After an extensive learning, planning and design phase, the secretariat persuaded eight members to participate in a first round of subsidized studies. These all used the same research methodology, comprising a quantitative 'with–without' impact survey, plus complementary qualitative interviews. A second round of studies is now taking place without the external subsidy and with participation of more MFIs.

Part of FINRURAL's success can be attributed to the strong shared interest in producing consolidated findings arising from the need of members to defend

Table 8.4 Technical support of SPA through networks: experiences of COVELO in Honduras and ASOMIF in Nicaragua contrasted

COVELO in Honduras	ASOMIF in Nicaragua
Leadership from one MFI (ODEF) based on its prior experience	Diverse experiences: no one MFI played a lead mentor role or was held up as a role model
One person responsible for managing the training workshops	Shared responsibility among staff
Technical assistance to members to do follow-up tool implementation	No technical assistance after the training workshops
Participating MFIs required to commit to post-workshop piloting of the tools	No such commitment required
Training restricted to a select group of network members	Training open to all network and non-network members
Training in an agreed set of five tools	Participants selected a wider range of tools
Network offered to assist with rapid data analysis where MFIs lacked staff capacity	Data analysis left to the participant MFIs
Senior management participated in both workshops and in pilot of internal use of the tools	Less senior staff participation and continuity

themselves from external criticisms, as already discussed earlier in this chapter. Another important factor was the technical competence and strong leadership of the secretariat itself. The PROMUC secretariat in Peru, in contrast, has been far less successful in establishing a clear role for itself in this way. This can be attributed in part to lack of demand, but also to the more limited technical capacity of the central secretariat.

An important contrast between the COVELO and FINRURAL models is the vision for achieving sustainability of social performance assessment activities. In the first model, the goal is to establish strong SPA within member MFIs, with the secretariat facilitating this through training. In the second model, the vision is for the secretariat itself to retain a centralized role in carrying out some impact assessment activities. The difference in approaches can be explained by many contextual factors. For example, the second approach requires that MFIs delegate more powers to the centre; something that may be easier to do within a smaller and more tightly bound network. An important payoff from this is greater uniformity of methods, which in turn facilitates dissemination of consolidated findings. Although COVELO also succeeded in doing this on a limited scale, FINRURAL is more likely to be able to continue to do so.

MFC in Poland represents an interesting intermediate model. Like FINRURAL, it has strong internal technical capability. But with a large and widely spread membership, it is primarily concerned, like COVELO, with institutionalization of SPA at the individual MFI level. In this sense it is closer to the technical service provision of vertical networks, but with the critical difference that, like an independent consultancy firm, its technical support is delinked from the provision of financial support. While this creates some financial uncertainty it has nevertheless been able to provide long-term and flexible technical support (to PRIZMA in Bosnia-Herzegovina, for example). The commitment of this support to the strengthening of internal social performance management is not compromised by MFC's own accountability and feedback requirements (Cohen, 2004).

MFC has been able to concentrate on building SPA to meet internal MFI needs, rather than having to bolt it on to externally driven project-funding cycles. Involving an independent organization, but at the same time delinking it from funding, can also help avoid biases and enhance the credibility of SPA. As a membership organization, MFC can also offer clients 'voice' as well as 'choice' in the way it is run. This has been one factor perhaps in encouraging it to be acutely aware of the need to ensure social performance management systems are not just cost-effective but can also contribute to better financial performance.[17]

This discussion of MFC leads to the issue of the division of labour between independent consultants, vertical networks and horizontal networks in providing external technical support. A first point is that they are potentially interchangeable, particularly where the biggest problem has been a lack of financial and technical support for SPA of any kind. Most MFIs draw on all of them.[18] The problem is to ensure that external technical support builds capacity to meet the needs of MFIs themselves, rather than being subordinated to the needs of wider networks.[19] This risk is particularly acute in vertical networks where such support is linked to a lack of finance, whereas participation in horizontal networks tends to be more voluntary.

External stakeholders have their own goals and systems. These can differ so strongly from the MFI that scope for collaboration in social performance assessment is very limited and potentially muddling. For example, a donor might fund a bank on the basis that it is successfully providing financial services to poor clients, even though the bank itself has not set out to do so explicitly. In this case, it is appropriate for poverty and impact assessment to be carried out as independent public policy research by the donor, and with a minimum of cost and disruption to the bank itself.

At the other extreme, MFIs and their sponsors often have very closely aligned goals so it should be possible to carry out social performance assessment in a way that satisfies internal and external needs at the same time. This can still be difficult in practice. Being closer to its clients, MFIs are generally in a better position than external sponsors to assess the reliability of impact data. Hence the amount each is willing to invest in improving the quality of impact assessment will vary, particularly as quality improvement comes at the cost of timeliness. Such differences should be resolvable though negotiations about 'who does what' and how costs are divided up. For sponsors concerned with social impact, there is also an important point to be made here about attribution: if the MFI itself is using impact data to make decisions, then this is an important signal of the reliability of the information, though internal politics may, or course, intrude and sponsors need to be sufficiently well informed to understand how.

The way forward is for external funding of SPA (including donor missions) to be subject to closer scrutiny on sustainability grounds. The key question should be: how is this visit (mission, evaluation or review) contributing to strengthening the MFI's own internal systems of social performance assessment and management? A more radical step would be to consolidate all such visits into a more standard periodic social performance review on the model of the standard external financial audit (Copestake, 2003b). For the MFI this would provide a routine check on the quality of its social performance systems. It could also strengthen the credibility of its social performance claims. A single social performance review is also likely to be more cost-effective than having to respond to the *ad hoc* and overlapping evaluation requirements of multiple stakeholders. From the point of view of sponsors, such reviews should help to strengthen the capacity of the MFIs, as well as serving an accountability function. Sponsors can benefit from greater consistency and comparability in the way social performance reviews are conducted.[20]

Towards cost-effective SPA

The emphasis in this chapter so far has been on demand and supply for social performance assessment. A critical additional question is whether benefits arising from it are sufficient to justify the costs. This is no abstract test. Such systems are self-defeating if they place the financial viability of the MFI in jeopardy or undermine its capacity to grow. Costs of hiring specialist researchers and diverting staff from other activities are generally readily apparent. Benefits, both to the institution itself and more widely, are more uncertain. Clear 'industry' norms and guidelines for what constitutes appropriate expenditure on SPA are also lacking.

MFIs need to ensure that the immediate financial and time costs of SPA are justified by the benefits arising from more informed financial and social performance management. In short it is not enough for SPA to be useful, it must also be cost-effective. *Imp-Act* experience indicates that this is possible, but that it can take time. Several of the participating MFIs planned two rounds of data collection and analysis within their three-year action-research projects: the first being more exploratory and the second being to pilot the use of more cost-effective 'stripped-down' tools. The problem with this model was that the first round studies often overran both their budgets and timetable. While they generated findings on impact for a wider audience and proved a useful learning experience for those involved, they distracted from the need to focus on cost-effectiveness from the outset. In contrast, some participants were clear about this from the start, and this section reports on additional studies carried out on four of them (Copestake, 2004a). These were SEF in South Africa (Baumann, 2004), PRIZMA in Bosnia-Herzogovina (Woller, 2004), COVELO in Honduras (Copestake, 2004b) and FINRURAL in Bolivia (Marconi and Mosley, 2004).

These studies did not aim to quantify ultimate benefits, but rather to examine the widely held assumption that investment in SPA adversely affects financial performance. To the extent that SPA actually pays for itself then it is clearly cost-effective. Two of the studies refer to MFIs (PRIZMA and SEF) that have invested in systems integrated into routine operations. SPA in both these cases also integrates client assessment with poverty assessment and both organizations do so in line with an explicit strategy of securing a competitive 'down-market' niche. The other two case studies (COVELO and FINRURAL) examined SPA undertaken through networks, as described in the last section.

Comparative discussion of costs is essential, but, given differences between these and other MFIs, simple cost comparisons need to be treated with considerable caution.[21] First, for internal cost control purposes it is useful to compare the cost per client interviewed. Table 8.5 shows that in the case of FINRURAL, this amounted to nearly US$90 for the first round of studies, though this figure included costs of developing as well as using the impact assessment tools. In the case of COVELO, the cost per respondent was just over half this. Although this figure was pushed up by the high opportunity cost of

Table 8.5 Comparative cost-effectiveness of SPA (averages for 2002 and 2003)

	SEF (TCP)	PRIZMA	COVELO	FINRURAL
Country	South Africa	Bosnia-Herzegovina	Honduras	Bolivia
Type of SPA	Integrated social performance management system	Poverty score card, plus exit monitoring and focus groups	Exit survey and client-satisfaction focus groups	Social and economic impact assessment
Total cost of studies (US$)	42,706	42,056	60,000	153,000
Clients consulted	n/a	n/a	1,250	1,700
Total clients served (mean)	8,900	(est.) 10,000	60,600	165,000
Clients consulted/served (%)	n/a	n/a	2.06	1.03
Cost per client consulted (US$)	n/a	n/a	48	90
Cost per client served (US$)	4.80	4.21	0.99	0.93
Av. Loan outstanding/client (US$)	800	n/a	330	556

involving senior staff in interviewing, it was pushed down by use of much shorter questionnaires (for leavers) and focus groups (for those loyal to the programme).

Second, for broader benchmarking purposes it is useful to compare cost relative to the total number of clients served. Because FINRURAL and COVELO both relied on relatively small sample sizes this unit cost is much lower – just below US$1 per client in each case. In the cases of PRIZMA and SEF, the poverty assessment components of their systems were applied to all clients, with other tools used on a sample basis. Hence it is not surprising that average costs are consequently higher: roughly US$4 per client over the two years.

Given that each MFI carried out different kinds of SPA for different purposes, average costs cannot meaningfully be compared without reference to the benefits arising from them, and no attempt was made to carry out a full cost-benefit analysis. However, in three of the four examples, an attempt was made at least to estimate financial returns to MFIs themselves arising from the SPA; if such work can be shown to pay for itself then it does not compromise financial performance goals.[22]

PRIZMA

This organization found itself competing hard for customers in a market place crowded with new MFI start ups. It responded by seeking to specialize at the low-end of the market, explicitly targeting poor business operators, especially women. Its client status monitoring system is based on a standard form used on entry and at the beginning of every loan cycle. This includes six indicators that enable it to construct and monitor a poverty score for all clients. Follow-up assessment into quality of services is based primarily on periodic focus group discussions with active clients and twice yearly sample exit surveys.

Woller (2004) investigated whether the US$42,000 investment (or US$4.21 per client) in setting up this system and running it for two years could be justified. He concluded that the investment can most readily and plausibly be justified by an induced reduction in client exit rates between loan cycles. More specifically, if the average exit rate was 2.2 per cent lower as a result of the system (42.2 per cent instead of the actual rate of 44.4 in March 2004, for example) then it would have paid for itself. He concludes that not only is this plausible, but that continuation of the system even at the same cost (that includes development cost) is likely to be cost-effective as a mechanism for avoiding higher exit rates in future. In short, the system should be regarded as 'a normal cost of doing business' and the issue is not whether to employ such system, but whether an MFI can afford not to do so.

SEF

SEF uses a participatory poverty assessment tool both to select potential clients and to establish their poverty status for its Tšhomišano Credit Programme. Information is then routinely collected from them in each loan cycle, including on satisfaction with the services they use and progress against a small number of social indicators. Baumann (2004) estimated that the annual costs of the system were US$21,353, including amortized share of set-up costs. This works out at just under US$5 per client. His analysis of the cost-effectiveness of the system is very similar to the case of PRIZMA. In 2001 the programme suffered knock-on effects from a sharp downturn in the local economy and client exit rates rose to more than 25 per cent. However, by the end of 2002 the rate had been reduced to 18 per cent. If this reduction had not taken place then Baumann estimates SEF would have lost revenue amounting to US$360,000. It is unlikely, he argues, that quite such a sharp reduction in the exit rate could have been achieved without the existence of the impact monitoring system. The final step of the argument is again that running such a system is a necessary cost of doing business in order to be able to anticipate and manage potential shocks.

The experience of SEF in South Africa illustrates a further point. This is that establishing a useful SPA system is only the first step; systems then need improving and rationalizing through use. During the crisis of 2001 all aspects of SEF's programmes had to be reviewed and costs cut wherever possible (Roper, 2003). In the case of its impact monitoring system, the amount of data collected was rationalized, but emphasis also shifted to using it more effectively to inform decision making at the branch level and below, particularly with respect to how exit rates could be kept down. The main priority during this period was to improve SEF's financial position and SEF was able to do this in a way that mitigated adverse effects on clients. Data reliability is obviously important, but Baumann (2004) is particularly insistent on the point that SEF's social performance management system does not set out to quantify social benefits for outsiders, but to generate information about social performance in a way that staff at all levels of the organization (and indeed clients themselves) find useful.

COVELO network

Unlike PRIZMA and SEF, COVELO in Honduras did not set out to build or strengthen client status monitoring. Instead, it sought to convince network members that flexible client-assessment studies, using AIMS-SEEP tools, could be very cost-effective. The mechanism for doing this was a series of national training workshops, followed by collaborative piloting of each tool. Copestake (2004b) reviewed the cost-effectiveness of the first two rounds of studies: a survey of reasons for client exit and focus-group discussions on client satisfaction. An innovative feature of these studies was that senior management staff were encouraged to participate directly in the research. This increased their cost but with the pay-off that resulting insights quickly led to changes in policy and practice. Induced changes within four of the participating MFIs are listed in Table 8.6. This work is referred to as 'client assessment', and not SPA, because the purpose of the studies was more narrowly linked to improving quality of services, rather than overall social returns.

The bottom part of Table 8.6 calculates the induced increases in income needed to cover the full costs to each MFI of carrying out their studies, and then compares them with quantifiable benefits to the organization estimated by Villalobos Barahona (2004).[23] In the case of the first three organizations, returns comfortably exceeded costs. The fourth organization experienced many of the same benefits but only quantified the savings in paper and printing that arose from shortening loan application procedures. Overall the study found a combination of cost reduction, faster expansion and improved retention generated benefits comfortably higher than the average investment per MFI over the two years of just under US$10,000.[24]

The Honduras studies were undertaken at a particular moment in Honduran history when the MFIs were switching, under the pressure of competition, from a more supply-led to a more client-led approach to microfinance. Hence the investment was particularly timely in accelerating a strategic and cultural shift (especially diversification away from village banking) that would probably have eventually happened anyway. From a wider social performance perspective this may also have represented something of a retreat from short-term depth of outreach to long-term growth of outreach, though it fell beyond the scope of the research to quantify this. The story was also still rapidly changing. For example, some of the MFIs have begun to invest in client-status

Table 8.6 Changes by COVELO members, attributable to client assessment studies

	ODEF	FAMA	FINCA	COVELO
New management practices				
Training, supervision or incentive structures of field staff			Yes	Yes
Relocation, and or improvement of branch premises	Yes	Yes	Yes	Yes
Simplification of approval procedures to reduce time lags	Yes	Yes	Yes	Yes
Decentralization of functions to branches e.g. for disbursement	Yes			Yes
Increase branch opening hours by appointing full-time administrator			Yes	Yes
Budget to use at least two AIMS tools annually	Yes	Yes	Yes	Yes
Product changes				
Changes in terms, loan ceilings and interest rates on existing products	Yes	Yes	Yes	Yes
New savings products or scheme linked to loan payments	Yes		Yes	Yes
Collateralize household goods as an additional guarantee		Yes		
Diversification into solidarity group and individual loans (from village banks)		Yes	Yes	Yes
Permit new loans to some clients even in groups with some arrears	Yes	Yes		Yes
Introduction of loans specifically for agriculture	Yes			
Introduction of loans to cover cost of school fees and related expenses		Yes		Yes
Introduction of loans for improvement of business premises	Yes	Yes		
Cost effectiveness over the first two years?				
Increase in net income needed to cover cost of the studies (%)	13	2	6	9
Increase in net income actually quantified (%)	24	21	26	1

monitoring, along the lines of PRIZMA, in order to be able to more effectively manage their strategic positioning in the market on both social and financial grounds.

FINRURAL

This organization in Bolivia provides another, stronger example of the role national networks can play in rationalizing SPA. Social and economic impact surveys were conducted for a combined sample of 2,856 clients and non-clients belonging to eight member organizations. To ensure impartiality, the interviews were conducted by an independent consultancy firm and overall coordination was conducted by FINRURAL, rather than each MFI. The total cost per MFI came to just under US$20,000 (on average about US$1 per active client served). However, these costs were inflated by planning and piloting activities that will not be required in a second round of studies, which are expected to cost less than US$12,500 per institution (Marconi and Mosley, 2004).

Unlike the other case studies discussed in this section, FINRURAL is making no claim that these studies can pay for themselves through improved financial performance. Instead it is claiming that by planning studies collectively, and in a way that can be replicated, they can prove to be cost-effective ways of informing policy and practice about the strategic trade-offs of different approaches to microfinance. All participants in the first round confirmed that the studies had 'assisted relations with sponsors, potential clients and the general public', while several also identified more specific management lessons (ibid.). The willingness of a larger number of MFIs to pay for a second round of studies at cost price backs up this claim.

These four case studies are not representative of the *Imp-Act* programme, still less of the microfinance industry. Nevertheless, they do suggest that by 'learning through doing', it is possible to do SPA that is not only useful but also far more cost-effective than has often been the case in the past. The main limitation of the case studies presented is that estimation of incremental returns of SPA were restricted to those accruing to the MFIs themselves. In other words, no attempt was made to assess full social rates of return. However, three of the four studies demonstrated that costs of SPA could be covered by quantifiable induced financial savings to MFIs themselves. A danger with this message is that it suggests (misleadingly) the financial pay-off to SPA only lasts for as long as reductions in exit rates and increases in outreach are possible. Several of the authors make the key point that SPA also helped the MFIs to anticipate and forestall crises in MFI performance. In other words, SPA played a protectional as well as a promotional role for the MFI. Returns are likely to be even higher when the counter-factual is crisis rather than slower growth.

These are pioneering studies and considerable scope remains for better analysis of this kind. For example, more could be said about variation in net returns to different tools used by the same MFI, and to the same tool used by different MFIs. There is also scope for more precise and realistic modelling of costs and returns.[25] Both market competition and the commitment of MFIs to their social mission will continue to encourage further refinement of SPA methods and evaluation of its cost-effectiveness. Finally, although these cost-effectiveness studies were concerned mainly with MFIs themselves, they are also relevant for public policy. Donors and governments have generally sought to satisfy their need for accountability about the welfare effects of MFIs through independent and often very costly impact assessment studies. While these set out to assess social benefits to clients more rigorously, they are occasional, expensive and face many methodological difficulties. More systematic auditing and review of the SPA systems used by MFIs themselves could be more cost-effective. Although these may not aspire to the same level of scholarly rigour, the fact that they are repeated, valued and used also adds to their reliability. The ultimate test of the benefits of institutionalizing SPA is that MFIs themselves find it to be useful and continue to invest in it. The 'proof of the pudding' comes not just from one eating, but from demand for more.

Conclusion

This chapter has so far suggested six critical ingredients for successful institutionalization of social performance assessment in microfinance. First, effective SPA requires commitment at the top of the organization to the systematic pursuit of social goals. External stakeholders can help MFIs make these goals clearer and more precise, but their role is subordinate to that of the organization itself. Second, a critical foundation for all SPA is routine monitoring of the status of an MFI's clients and how this is changing. In most cases collection and use of data can be integrated into wider management information systems and decision processes. Third, in addition to such routine monitoring, all MFIs should develop their own capacity to analyse the data thus generated, and to supplement it where appropriate with additional investigation. There is scope for variation in how far this work is subcontracted to specialist researchers or network organizations, but all organizations must at the very least develop capacity to initiate, manage and respond to such work. Fourth, these tasks need to be understood and valued throughout the MFI. This entails ensuring that staff at all levels understand SPA's relevance to their own work, even if it is not of direct use to their own decisions. Fifth, flexible external technical support, particularly through networks, is indispensable in helping MFIs to set up and, in some cases, to run such systems, and in moving towards greater consistency of methods and uniformity of indicators. Finally, costs of SPA should be and can be proportionate to benefits. Like any other core activity of an MFI, SPA needs to be subject to rigorous cost control. These points are explored further in the final chapter.

CHAPTER NINE
Conclusions

James Copestake and Anton Simanowitz

Overview

In Chapter 1 we noted three concerns about the microfinance industry during the 1990s: excessive donor control over impact assessment, social mission drift and a lack of clarity over how far microfinance was contributing to poverty reduction. The subsequent chapters sought to address these concerns, drawing on findings from action-research under the *Imp-Act* programme. Here we begin with a brief summary of the main findings and arguments of each chapter. The second section presents a framework for analysing the nature and extent of 'room for manoeuvre' for MFIs to pursue social goals more systematically alongside financial goals, taking into account possible trade-offs between them. This is followed by summary guidelines for MFIs wishing to improve their social performance assessment systems.[1]

The book closes with a discussion of the implications for public and private investors in microfinance and directions for further research. Overall, we argue that outreach and impact of MFIs on poverty is generally positive but highly variable, leaving scope for substantial improvement. Investment in more purposeful and cost-effective social performance assessment systems can help them to become more effective agents of poverty reduction. However, in many parts of the world MFIs remain small players in the business of finance; stronger social performance monitoring and management is also needed at the wider level of financial systems.

Chapter 2 reviewed methods used by 23 *Imp-Act* participants to define, measure and target poorer clients. It looked in more detail at the absolute poverty measures used by six of them: FINCA, BRAC, LAPO, PRIZMA, SEF and CARD. The author noted wide variation in choice of indicators: South Asian MFIs were generally more focused on absolute income poverty, whereas in Eastern Europe they were more concerned with unemployment, for example. Poverty outreach was also measured using a range of non-money-metric indicators, such as house quality. Differences in operating environments and definitions make it hard to generalize about poverty outreach and about how this varies according to different approaches to targeting. Growth in overall client numbers, geographical targeting, tailoring of products/services to specific market segments and direct poverty screening can all help.

What is indispensable for reaching poorer clients is that MFIs themselves: 1) think through the specific underlying causes of poverty and the reasons for financial exclusion in their own area of operation; and 2) systematically monitor the poverty status of new, loyal and exiting clients so as to be able to assess how effectively different poverty outreach strategies are working. When several MFIs with a strong poverty mission began to do this they were surprised to find what a low proportion of clients could be classified as poor. FINCA International, for example, found that in 2003 only 35 per cent of a sample of its clients across 11 countries fell below national poverty lines, and only 17 per cent below extreme poverty lines.[2] The good news is that these and many other MFIs have made considerable strides in developing robust poverty monitoring systems. The most promising approach is to identify, validate and then routinely monitor a small number of poverty proxy indicators.[3]

Chapter 3 considered evidence of impact on poverty reduction from eight *Imp-Act* participants: PROMUC, CARD, FINCA, CMF, CERUDEB, SHARE, SAT and LAPO. The evidence is consistent with the prevailing consensus that impact of microfinance on income and poverty is generally positive, but that this is hard to prove rigorously.[4] At one extreme, PROMUC and FINRURAL quite successfully embarked on relatively sophisticated impact assessment studies entailing econometric analysis of panel data for clients and non-client comparison groups, though neither succeeded in fully addressing the problem of bias that arises from the existence of unobservable differences between non-randomly selected samples of clients and non-clients.[5]

Others (for example, SHARE and CERUDEB) relied on more modest before and after impact studies. Findings from these were consistent with the hypothesis of significant positive impact and raised interesting questions about the reason for branch-level variation in trends. The findings left even more room for doubt about how far reported improvements could be exclusively attributed to use of financial services. In general those MFIs who embarked on impact surveys struggled to cope with the practical and methodological challenges they posed, but nevertheless learned a great deal from the effort. While 'mid-range' impact studies done in conjunction with other research can make a positive contribution to understanding, they should not be entered into lightly and results need to be interpreted very carefully, as discussed below.

Chapter 4 reviewed outreach and impact of microfinance on a wider range of dimensions of poverty, focusing on findings obtained by eight *Imp-Act* participants: CYSD, PRADAN, SHARE, CARD, SAT, LAPO, Promujer and PROMUC. These organizations found it useful to look beyond income poverty to their effect on food security, housing, learning, attitudinal changes, children's education, health, family planning and interpersonal relationships, using a mixture of qualitative and quantitative methods. Findings here were often more ambiguous, suggesting that the trade-offs between financial performance and social performance of MFIs are sharper when the latter is defined more broadly than impact on income poverty. Assessing impact on this wider array of indicators was again dogged by methodological problems, particularly of attribution and representativeness.

Chapter 5 looked beyond direct impacts of microfinance and problems of financial exclusion to their effect on the more profound problems of social exclusion and weak citizenship rights. Seven *Imp-Act* participants investigated these issues directly: CYSD, PRADAN, BRAC, SHARE, FORA, INTEGRA (Romania) and INTEGRA (Slovakia). These dimensions of impact may be 'wider' but they are not necessarily 'indirect' and certainly not peripheral. For CYSD and PRADAN, for example, group-based microfinance is the means to tackling the deeper problems of social exclusion experienced by members of scheduled castes and tribes. The chapter adopted a 'concentric circle' approach: looking first at the quality of relationships within microfinance groups, before exploring how far these help to strengthen members' wider associational life. Such positive association is found in sharply contrasting contexts, though causation operates in both directions. For example, SHARE groups often build on government-sponsored groups, so improved access to government services is not necessarily a benefit of the former. Improved social capital also often accrues to better-off group members, so impacts can be polarizing. As in previous chapters, it emerges that strong wider social impacts are much more likely to take place when they are part of an MFI's explicit mission. This was the case for the INTEGRA foundations in Eastern Europe, for example.

Chapter 6 drew on *Imp-Act* research in India, Uganda and Kenya into wider impact in a different sense. It explored the extent to which the arrival of new generation MFIs has affected the overall financial landscape. It serves as a salutary reminder that many other organizations are often still more important than MFIs as providers of financial services to poorer people. For example, in East Africa people are likely to belong to informal rotating and accumulating savings and credit groups, and also to formal savings and credit cooperatives, while in India doorstep daily savings services provided by non-banking financial companies are important. Formal financial institutions also have a capacity to move down-market on a scale outstripping specialist MFIs, and stronger competition in more lucrative core markets can give them the incentive to do so.

Chapter 7 shifted from outreach and impact of microfinance to the question of how to improve these through positive organizational change, drawing particularly on a SWOT analysis of lessons learnt by 17 *Imp-Act* participants. Key determinants of social performance were reviewed under four headings: organizational mission and vision, operating environment, internal operational capability and external relationships. Organizational tensions are unavoidable and the review identified 14 particular dilemmas that have to be balanced: mission, growth strategy, board composition, choice of operating environment, targeting methods, product diversification, internal/ external recruitment, centralization, contract culture, investment in R&D, change management, financial relationships and investment in public relations. The chapter reinforced the argument running through earlier chapters that successful social performance hinges critically on strong leadership commitment and striking the right balance to suit diverse contexts. This serves as a warning against universal prescriptions of what constitutes good practice in microfinance. The chapter also serves as a reminder that while monitoring and assessing progress towards social goals are important, many other factors also affect social performance.

Chapter 8 reviewed factors behind successful institutionalization of social performance assessment in microfinance, drawing on evidence from 25 *Imp-Act* participants, but particularly a SWOT analysis of 17 of them. The analysis began with internal demand for social performance data and then reviewed how this is affected by external demand. The chapter then discusses internal capacity to generate the data and the role of external consultants, networks and funders in enhancing this. It argued that six factors are critical: 1) commitment at the top of the organization to the systematic pursuit of social goals; 2) systematic monitoring of the changing status of an MFI's clients; 3) a capacity to supplement these data where appropriate with additional investigation, whether by using internal staff or by contracting in; 4) an appreciation of the value of this work throughout the MFI; 5) flexible external technical support, particularly through networks, in helping to set up such systems – and in some cases to help run them; and 6) rigorous review and cost control. Four case studies were summarized (SEF, PRIZMA, FINRURAL and COVELO) to illustrate how systems developed along theses lines can be cost-effective to the point of enhancing financial as well as social performance.

A recurring argument through the book has been that it is not enough for SPA to be linked to broad goals and strategy; to be cost-effective and sustainable it must be used and seen to be used. Users differ. Some participants in *Imp-Act*, such as PRIZMA, were motivated by the desire to provide middle and senior management with timely information for day-to-day decision making. Others, such as SAT, focused on strategic planning at board and international network level, while FINRURAL's work concentrated on public and industry-wide need. At the other extreme, PRADAN focused on building the capacity of clients to analyse their own situation. Entry points for investing in SPA also matter. Some, such as CARD, linked it to long-term processes of organizational development, revisiting their mission, determining their information needs and designing a comprehensive system to meet them. Others, such as FOC-CAS, started with the more urgent need to understand why client exit rates were so high. Crises create an impetus to build more proactive systems to reduce risks of similar problems in the future – a point emphasized in the cost-effectiveness studies of SEF, COVELO and PRIZMA.

Trade-offs and the scope for improving social performance

In this section we draw on evidence presented in all chapters to explore further the argument that MFIs have significant potential to improve social as well as financial performance, and that better social performance data are needed to inform the choices (over prices, products, operational practices and strategies) that determine this balance. The issue of MFI room for manoeuvre can be addressed from both an 'aid industry' and a 'financial markets' perspective. From an aid perspective, MFIs have enjoyed more flexibility because of access to donor funding. The most widely accepted rationale for such aid, a version of the infant industry argument, is that private finance is likely to be in short supply for innovative but uncertain extension of financial services to serve new and poorer clients (Copestake, 1998; Hulme and Mosley, 1996). Strictly, this argument only justifies temporary subsidy, but it has been interpreted and enforced loosely. MFIs have had considerable discretion over how, how far and how quickly they should move towards full cost recovery for new services from relatively poor clients.

Viewed not from a development industry perspective, but from a financial markets perspective, MFIs have enjoyed room for manoeuvre to the extent that they have been operating in relatively immature markets with unmet demand for services that can be supplied at a cost that clients are willing to pay for. Market potential has grown with increasing population, urbanization, personal incomes and technical change (particularly cost-saving and risk-reducing innovations in financial technology). It is the combination of aid funding and untapped market potential that has enabled MFIs to pursue diverse strategies, to acquire distinct organizational styles and to develop a diverse range of group-based and individualized financial services.

This diversity has been explored in each chapter of the book and was more systematically reviewed in Chapter 7. Here, in contrast, we focus on core strategic options. These can most precisely be described graphically – see Figure 9.1. We are interested in the total effect of an MFI's decisions in any period on its overall financial and social performance. This is often presented as a stark trade-off: either improve financial performance or improve current social performance. For example, raising interest rates on loans is likely to improve financial performance but at an immediate cost to clients (reducing impact). However, in many situations an MFI is able to improve both its current social and financial performance simultaneously. Moreover, improved financial performance increases room for manoeuvre in the future. The challenge for managers is how to strike the best balance between the two sets of performance objectives over time.

MFIs face daily trade-offs, which together amount to major strategic choices over the balance between growth and quality of services provided. In making these choices, the underlying dilemma for those with an explicit social mission is *not* between financial and social performance, but between social performance *now* and social performance capacity for the *future*. Breadth,

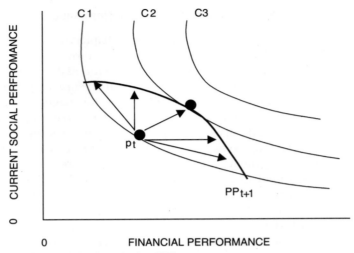

Figure 9.1 Strategic options facing MFIs

depth and quality of outreach are the key underlying indicators of social performance in all periods and financial performance is an important proxy indicator for future social performance capacity.

As shown in Figure 9.1, the most important dilemma is between: 1) strategies to enhance future social performance capacity, as measured by financial/operational self-sustainability and growth potential; and 2) strategies to enhance current social performance, as measured by depth and quality of outreach. From any given initial level of performance (p_t) an MFI is constrained in how it can change its strategic position within a given period by a performance possibility curve PP_{t+1}. This reflects its room for manoeuvre, the scope for investment, innovation and growth to enhance both social and financial performance. The MFI's mission is represented by a set of 'indifference' curves (C_1, C_2, C_3); each line represents a set of combinations of social and financial performance that are equally attractive (or hard to choose between). They may also be thought of as contours around a mountain, with the summit (maximum social and financial performance) in the top right hand corner.

Figure 9.1 illustrates changing possibilities over only one period, illustrated by five arrows. The horizontal arrow represents a *growth-first* strategy, subject to the constraint that current social performance should not get any worse. The arrow moving vertically upward represents a *current clients-first* strategy, subject to the constraint that financial performance should not get any worse. The arrow pointing up and right represents an *intermediate* strategy. As shown, and assuming the MFI is successful in reaching the PP_{t+1} line, then one intermediate strategy is optimal because it moves the MFI onto the highest possible indifference curve. The arrow moving up and to the left represents a *trade-off* strategy of improved current period social performance at the expense of financial performance. To be sustained this would require an increased rate of subsidy, but this could possibly be justified by the improved social performance. Finally, the downward sloping arrow represents another *trade-off* strategy, but this time to enhance financial performance by reducing current social performance. This might take the form, for example, of deliberately targeting richer and more profitable clients.

Performance in the current period will determine possibilities in the next period. These are not shown but could be drawn on the diagram as a new performance possibility curve (PP_{t+2}), hopefully to the right and above PP_{t+1}. The shape of the new curve depends on what strategy was chosen in the first period and how successful the MFI was in implementing it. Multi-period performance can also be plotted on the diagram. A virtuous cycle would take the organization up and to the right. Of course a vicious cycle of declining social and financial performance taking the MFI closer and closer to the origin is also possible.

The case of SEF in South Africa illustrates the point: within a few years it first introduced a more carefully targeted programme aimed at reaching poorer clients, then took steps to rationalize it in order to improve financial performance. FINCA, to give another example, started out with a strong poverty mission. It concentrated on strengthening financial performance through growth but has more recently begun to take strategic steps to strengthen its poverty focus. Similar stories can be told for many other MFIs. Faced with strong competition, PRIZMA judged that a strong poverty or 'down-market' focus made good commercial sense. BRAC, CARD and LAPO all retained a strong poverty mission but subject to achieving and then maintaining operational self-sufficiency in order to facilitate client expansion.

From the point of view of donors and social investors, such strategic trade-offs also arise in choosing how to allocate their funds between MFIs. We have seen that SHARE applied a minimalist solidarity-group methodology to combine excellent financial performance, growth and efficiency with significant depth of outreach and impact. It is well adapted to relatively high-potential areas of Andhra Pradesh with scope for growth in client livelihoods and rapid client growth. CYSD in Orissa, in contrast, sees microfinance (provided through self-help groups) as one component of an intensive strategy for strengthening the livelihoods of the poorest. It deliberately targets some of the most remote and inaccessible tribal communities in the state and people who have relatively weak links to markets. The intensive nature of CYSD's work, high operating costs and low economic potential of many of its self-help group members means that CYSD is not able to operate in a financially sustainable way and is dependent on ongoing donor support. A potential social investor choosing between CYSD and SHARE has to weigh up short- and long-term benefits of their contrasting strategies. At the same time, both organizations face similar dynamic trade-offs themselves, albeit from very different starting points.[6]

It is the diversity of such strategies and the way these reflect differences in underlying goals, resources, external relationships and market opportunities that is perhaps most striking. The picture is also a highly dynamic one. Market opportunities are affected by changes in client incomes, the stability of operating environments and technical change. While the market for micro-finance can hardly be described as mature, many areas have also been affected by greater competition (see Chapter 6). At the same time, donors are becoming more demanding in their specification of performance targets, while many MFIs are themselves more committed to reducing their donor dependence. The scissors-like combination of these market and aid industry changes should be a spur to further product innovation, cost saving, a search for new clients and better ways of retaining existing ones.

Guidelines for more cost-effective social performance assessment

The challenge

The more specific subject matter of the book is innovation in social per-formance assessment, not least for the purpose of ensuring that the manage-ment of the kinds of trade-offs discussed above can be more strongly evidence based. This is not a new topic. Many donors have been sympathetic to the view that the social returns of microfinance can be increased through concessionary funding and blending with other services, so long as such claims are backed up by reasonable evidence. Indeed they have in large measure taken responsi-bility for collecting it. However, in so doing they have tended to direct efforts towards long-term strategic questions, reinforcing a tendency for social per-formance to be separated from more routine operational decisions of the MFIs themselves. They have also weakened internal control of such work and thinking about what constitutes sufficient evidence. The cost, complexity and difficulty of meeting these standards has reinforced a division of labour in which MFIs have generally been happy to take a back seat, relying on the informal influence of daily contact with clients to inform their own decisions (and motivation).

Disquiet with this arrangement was a widely held motivation for partici-pation in *Imp-Act* and a factor behind the attempt to enable participating MFIs to address the issue of social performance assessment in a way that was at least partially uncoupled from external funding.[7] Key to this was the strong emphasis on allowing participating MFIs to frame their own research. The resulting diversity of activities created initial confusion, but over time an alternative vision of social performance assessment (as a systematic, con-tinuous and internally managed activity) did become clear. For example, pre-vious norms tended to put the 'cart' of impact assessment before the 'horse' of continuous monitoring of client (poverty) status – a habit that can be attributed in part to the role of impact assessment as a discrete event (easily packaged into a consultancy/research contract) within donor project/funding cycles. Likewise, it has taken time to understand that routine use of findings to inform operational decisions is itself an important mechanism for validating data quality.[8]

Rethinking the 'why', 'who for' and 'when' of social performance assessment took place at the same time as *Imp-Act* participants were grappling with practical questions of 'what', 'by whom', 'how' and 'how much'. These issues were highlighted particularly in Chapters 3 and 8, and are also vividly described by SEEP (2005). Costs, whether of hiring specialist researchers, or diverting staff from other activities, were generally readily apparent; benefits more uncertain. It is no surprise that some MFIs were too ambitious, and made limited progress in the time available towards the development of self-sustaining social performance assessment systems. For example, some collected more data than could possibly have been analysed effectively, while others suffered unexpected losses of key staff.

Practical questions also raised deeper methodological problems. For example, we have seen that the ripple effects of MFIs are so diverse that it is almost impossible to agree on one set of indicators (covering all levels of impact – individual, business, household, area, sector) to suit their diverse goals and operating environments. This 'fungibility' or scoping problem in turn raises the issue of attribution. The larger the unit at which an indicator is measured, the more complex are the influences upon it, hence the harder to isolate those changes that arise only from access to microfinance services. To address this problem, practitioners faced a difficult choice between combinations of quantitative and qualitative data collection, statistical and interpretive analysis. These had to be revisited afresh to reflect the reorientation towards multiple internal goals and uses.

The availability of more 'practitioner-oriented' tools, chiefly from the USAID AIMS project and MicroSave Africa, helped a great deal. But becoming familiar with such tools is one thing, effectively using them to inform management processes is another. The examples of CAME and the COVELO network illustrate. Both started with the goal of trying out the AIMS-SEEP client assessment tools, but they ended up doing so in equally valid, but radically different ways. CAME applied the tools in a rigorous way to inform major strategic decisions about their village banking model, while COVELO members sought in a more rough and ready way to inform a range of product and service delivery changes. An acceptance of diversity in the way MFIs carry out social performance assessment is itself important. Nevertheless, it is important to recognize commonalities and *Imp-Act* partners also came to considerable agreement over how social performance assessment should be conducted, as presented below.

The way forward – six questions

This section sets out a common framework for carrying out social performance assessment in order to improve the management of MFIs with a social mission.[9] Its starting point is the lesson that having a mission and turning it into a workable strategy is not enough. It is also necessary to build systems for routinely monitoring who intended clients are, their needs, how effectively they are being reached, whether services provided bring the expected benefits, and at what cost. In the absence of routine monitoring systems, social performance will not improve as fast as it could and mission drift is more likely. SPA must be viewed within the wider framework of social performance management: information should be 'pulled-in' by institutionalized demand rather than 'pushed-out' by a research and development department or by independent researchers. This vision is illustrated by Figure 9.2. The mission must be transformed into practical actions, based on a clear strategy and appropriate operational practices that take into account the prevailing operating environment. It should be continuously informed by feedback on the status of clients and the impact services are having on them.

Another way of summarizing this perspective is in the form of a checklist of the six questions, each of which is discussed in more depth below. Any MFI with a social mission (such as to reduce poverty) should have clear answers to all these questions or be committed to developing such answers:

- What are your social goals and how do you seek to achieve them?
- How do you monitor who uses and who is excluded from using your services?
- How do you monitor and assess why some clients leave or become inactive?
- How do you assess the effect of your services on loyal and active clients?
- How do you use/expect to use the information you collect?

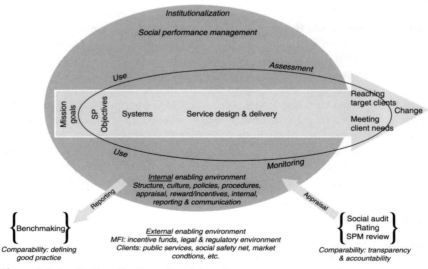

Figure 9.2 Institutionalization of social performance management

- How do you maintain and improve the quality of the systems and processes through which you answer these questions, including making them more cost-effective?

Goals, strategy and ownership

SPA should be linked to specific organizational goals and a clear strategy for how to achieve them. The strategy may minimalist (for example, to provide a safe and sustainable savings facility to as many people as possible) or it may be broader (for example, to empower women through group-based savings, credit and adult education). It may yield unexpected side effects and it may need revision, but that is no excuse for lack of clarity of intent. More specifically, a key argument of this book is that poverty reduction and other impacts through provision of microfinance services do not happen by accident; they require clear goals and careful planning. Statements of intent are meaningful only if the most powerful actors within an MFI – its board and senior management – are fully committed to them.

Client-status monitoring

Before assessing impact on clients it is logical to know who clients are and how this is changing over time. This may seem obvious, but much investment in impact assessment has nevertheless failed for lack of a sound monitoring foundation. The literature on this aspect of SPA has mostly been concerned with choice of indicators. However, whatever indicators are selected, the critical point is that the data are routinely and effectively summarized and reported in order that differences (for example, between branches and different categories of client) and trends over time can be systematically reviewed. It is better to have routine, disaggregated and reliable information on a few indicators than to drown in a sea of indicators. A particular challenge for many MFIs has also been to ensure that such monitoring systems clearly explain the extent to which the status of clients is changing due to new entry, exit and changed status of loyal clients (SEEP, 2004a; Copestake, 2001b). It is also important to ensure that routine status monitoring (for example, of poverty) and explicit targeting are not conflated in a way that creates incentives for data distortion.

Exit monitoring and assessment

Knowing how many clients are leaving is an integral part of any client-status monitoring system, as discussed above. However, exit data have additional significance because the act of leaving (or of allowing a savings account to become dormant) reveals clients' assessment of the quality of the services they receive through actions and not just words. One caveat to this is that it is necessary to find a simple and routine way of checking how far incidental factors, such as variation in mobility and morbidity, also explain variation in exit rates. Useful additional feedback on why clients are unsatisfied can be collected at the same time (*Imp-Act*, 2004c; Copestake, 2003c).

Impact assessment

The very act of remaining an active user of an MFI's services generally suggests their impact is positive. However, clients are not equally well informed and their experience of 'value added' is very variable; both an MFI's social and financial performance goals can benefit from better understanding why. There are three broad approaches to doing so.

The first favours statistical analysis of predetermined quantitative survey data about a representative sample of clients and non-clients. This approach is important for public policy analysis, but is generally too complex, time consuming and expensive for MFIs to use routinely – even to inform long-term strategic planning. More modest 'mid-range' impact surveys can be useful in conjunction with other methods, particularly to monitor change in a small number of key indicators. However, close and experienced supervision is needed to avoid time and cost over-runs, and to avoid biased interpretation of findings.

A second approach is to rely on expert collection, analysis and interpretation of more open-ended (qualitative) data from a range of sources, including key informants, in-depth interviews and focus groups. Insights can be rich and unexpected, but this can also be expensive and time consuming.[10] Experience with the QUIP suggests that in-depth interviews can be conducted more cost-effectively than has often been the case in the past (*Imp-Act*, 2004a; Wright-Revolledo and Copestake, 2004; Wright-Revolledo and Benique, 2003).[11]

This leads to the third approach, to rely on more applied methods of market research and participatory appraisal, including the use of satisfaction surveys and focus groups. On their own these tools may be less rigorous, but reliability can be enhanced both by repeated use and through cross-checking results from a variety of different sources including feedback from staff and routine reports on trends in client-level indicators. The metaphor of triangulation applies: it is better to take bearings from several points and to see where they cross, rather than to concentrate on trying to get a very precise bearing from one point. It is also better to do this as frequently as possible so as to be able to monitor how impact is changing over time. While each source will be imperfect, a complementary mix can be adequate. In contrast, large quantitative impact surveys are 'methodologically indivisible': reliable results can be obtained only from analysis of data from one or more rounds of hundreds of interviews.

Use of social performance data

The key test of SPA, emphasized by the idea of the feedback loop, is whether or not it is used (Cohen and Wright-Revolledo, 2003; *Imp-Act*, 2003; McCord, 2002). Decisions may be strategic, relate to product development, quality of service enhancement or routine operations. In each case, we start by considering what we already know and what gaps remain. For some MFIs this requires a significant investment in needs assessment; others start off with immediate priority questions and seek to augment their systems gradually. In many cases the most urgent question of the *Imp-Act* participants was *not* impact (Question 5), but either knowing more about who clients were (Question 3), or why they were leaving in such large numbers (Question 4). By directing often scarce resources at the most pressing questions, those responsible for SPA were able to develop credibility and trust within their organization, thereby generating internal support for more ambitious and longer term investment in SPA.

System improvement

Overall, we favour thinking about SPA in a flexible and adaptable way, rather than as a fixed blue-print. The balance between monitoring and assessment can be compared to the relationship between 'alarm bells' and 'emergency services' in fire prevention. The client-status monitoring system should be routine, comprehensive and generate simple, standardized data. Where statistics diverge or change unexpectedly, this should trigger further investigation. The 'emergency service' in the case of MFIs is the capacity to respond to alarm bells, by finding out in more detail what is happening to particular groups of clients and why, then acting on these findings. The system should be capable of handling big fires and small. It should also be capable of growing and changing in line with the MFI itself. Its existence should also raise general awareness of factors behind good social performance and encourage proactive action to avoid problems. Finally, there should be strong mechanisms for periodically checking the quality of the systems for generating data and responding to it, as well as reviewing the systems' appropriateness to changing organizational needs and priorities.

Wider interests and implications

External interests in improved SPA

The previous section has argued strongly that SPA systems should be developed first and foremost to meet the internal needs of MFIs themselves. But other agencies of course also have a legitimate interest in their social performance. These include bank regulatory and supervisory authorities, governments, commercial lenders, social investors, as well as private bilateral and multilateral donors. How can their demands for information be better met in ways that complement and support internal systems as well as complement systems for financial performance reporting? There is currently a lively debate over these issues, and it is useful to think of the concept of performance as a logical chain that starts with organizational processes (mobilizing and managing resources), leading to organizational outcomes (delivery of services), and then to impacts on clients and beyond. This is summarized in Table 9.1, which further distinguishes between assessment activities according to whether they primarily inform financial or social goals. Debate on what should be reported to external agencies hinges on how much attention should be given to each of these six boxes.

It is useful to start by considering how far *for-profit* investors in MFIs might be interested in their social as well as their financial performance.[12] With the rise of corporate social responsibility, many potential commercial investors in MFIs now share some interest in their social performance. For some this is 'two-faced capitalism'. *The Economist* (24 January 2004) argues that 'the problem with conscientious (as opposed to fake) corporate social responsibility is obvious: it is philanthropy at other people's expense'. But the same article also acknowledges two ripostes.[13] First, SPA can also make good business sense: building client loyalty, polishing brand reputation, motivating staff, pre-empting political risks and stimulating innovation. Second, the owners of financial institutions may themselves have a preference for managing the 'double bottom-line' (social as well as financial) of their business. Indeed, some are motivated to invest in MFIs in part by a desire to demonstrate social responsibility. Commercial investors can also (ironically) be particularly wary of association with MFIs whose interest rates appear to them to verge on usury. On both grounds, MFIs with systems in the right-hand column of Table 9.1 should be more attractive, so long as those systems are cost-effective and, of course, particularly if they also help to enhance long-term financial performance.

These same arguments largely apply when we turn to consider the interests

Table 9.1 Forms of performance assessment

Level of assessment	Goal served	
	Financial	Social
Organization (processes)	Financial audits; credit rating	Quality assurance; social performance reviews and audits
Organization (outcomes)	Audited financial accounts	Change in number and type of clients (including numbers joining and leaving in a period)
Client level and beyond (outcomes)	Market research	Client satisfaction studies; impact assessment and research

of *non-profit* sponsors of MFIs. Strong social performance management systems should again make MFIs more attractive to them. The 'pink book' of best practice guidelines for donors in microfinance (CGAP, 2004a) strongly endorses performance-based funding. It argues in favour of identifying a few core indicators to track performance (including general outreach and outreach to the poor) and warns against overburdening financial institutions with too many indicators. But it describes social performance measurement and monitoring as a 'frontier issue' in need of further clarification and innovation.

A range of initiatives are currently underway to address these issues.[14] Perhaps most important is the USAID initiative being undertaken by IRIS at the University of Maryland to identity a small number of reliable but practical proxy indicators of poverty.[15] Slightly broader in scope is a CGAP initiative, in collaboration with several international microfinance networks, to agree on a list of social development indicators with which to track the contribution of microfinance to the Millennium Development Goals: eradicating extreme poverty and hunger, achieving universal primary education, empowering women, reducing child mortality and improving maternal health. Both these initiatives can be classified as being concerned mainly with the second level of Table 9.1 and the second of the six questions listed in the previous section.

A distinct approach is to concentrate less on outcome indicators than on process indicators; the CERISE-led Social Performance Indicators Initiative (SPII) being an example (Zeller *et al*, 2003). Its proponents argue that measurable indicators of the *intent* of MFIs to achieve social performance are more easily collected than client-level impact data, but should be positively correlated with it. They used a consultative process to develop an initial list of 49 indicators that are divided into four groups: 1) outreach to the poor and excluded; 2) adaptation of products and services to target clients' needs and wants; 3) giving voice to clients within the organization; and 4) social responsibility, comprising good human resources policies, consumer protection and community liaison.[16] Woller (2005) criticizes this and similar lists on the grounds that 'neither offers an integrated conceptual framework specifying how the indicators relate to each other'. He argues that Schreiner's 'six dimensions of outreach' fills this gap, and identifies an initial list of 40 proxy indicators for the dimensions.[17] As with the SPII, a criterion for indicator selection is that they should be readily obtainable for most MFIs without requiring additional survey work.

Reports on pilot use of these lists are not yet available. Nor has it yet become clear precisely how MFIs and their sponsors will be expected to use them. The expectation is that a mixture of peer pressure and financial incentives (including access to donor funding) will encourage MFIs to publish such information, ideally alongside financial performance data on the micro-finance exchange or 'MiX market' website.[18] Such lists are also likely to form the basis of standardized scoring and social rating to inform the decisions of potential investors who are concerned about social performance but lack time and expertise to assess it themselves.

The six questions set out the last section can be viewed in this context as an alternative 'bid' to develop a benchmark or standard. As such it asserts that all MFIs should have both organizational and client-level outcome systems in place that are oriented to social goals, but stops short of prescribing precisely what they should be or which indicators should be used. Rather the questions emphasize organizational processes, leading towards development of a system that addresses all three levels. The questions could themselves form the basis of a simple self-rating system based on whether an MFI has improved or failed to improve on systems for answering each question over the previous year. Answers would of course be subjective, but they would still focus attention on real social performance (at the client level) rather than process indicators. Avoiding more complicated standards should also help to reduce the risk of creating incentives to *appear* to perform rather than *actually* to perform.[19] In short, what is more important than any scoring system, is the extent to which clearer social performance standards stimulate organizational learning and hence improved performance. By focusing on six broad but simple questions there is a better chance of 'stimulating innovation above an agreed quality floor, rather than encouraging development of a more rigid compliance-oriented culture' (Pay, 2005).[20]

The central argument of this book is that the key to improved social performance is for MFIs themselves to retain full control over their own destiny, which includes finding better ways to monitor and manage progress towards their stated goals. The development of stronger external social performance standards holds out prospects for better management practice, but is also a potential threat to MFI self-determination. The financial stake of external agencies already gives such agencies considerable influence over MFIs; they spend substantial resources in visiting, evaluating, reviewing and auditing them. The most practical way in which they can improve social performance is by ensuring that such spending helps to strengthen MFIs' own internal quality control and enhancement systems. The six questions outlined in this chapter provide a checklist for reviewing how far they are doing this.[21] This is not necessarily incompatible with a quest to develop, legitimize and encourage the use of more quantitative social performance benchmarks, but the emphasis is significantly more towards the internal needs of MFIs and less towards the bureaucratic needs of those who invest in them.

To sum up, we argue that there are five things donors can do effectively to promote social performance management of microfinance. First, they can continue to invest directly in helping MFIs to improve their own social performance assessment and management systems. Second, they can align their own reporting requirement to strengthen this process rather than distract from it, thereby reducing wasteful duplication of review and reporting requirements. Third, they can encourage industry-wide investment in harmonization of social performance systems and associated training. An effective way to do this is often to work with and through MFI networks. Fourth, they can encourage MFIs to be transparent in sharing social performance data, for example by posting reports on the MiX market website (CGAP, 2003). Finally, and perhaps most important of all, they should demonstrate the value of social performance management by using such evidence (and the evidence that MFIs are themselves using it) to influence their funding decisions. All of the above will help to promote a global 'quasi-market' in which different forms of finance are aligned more closely to the financial and wider social value-added that MFIs generate.

Research and policy beyond the MFI level

While broadening the discussion to include external agencies, the previous section addressed only performance of individual MFIs. In contrast, earlier chapters of the book have been at pains to emphasize that the social performance of microfinance ultimately has to be viewed in a wider context. Chapter 6 suggested, for example, that the effect of MFIs on overall supply of financial services to relatively poor people in some areas has not been as great as might be assumed from the attention that they have attracted. More controversially, it can be argued that MFIs have, in some instances, distracted attention from the responsibilities of 'mainstream' (large-scale and fully regulated) financial institutions to improve access to financial services (CGAP, 2004a; *Imp-Act*, 2005a).

To date, the main thrust of an attempt to broaden the microfinance agenda has been to emphasize the potential that other financial intermediaries – commercial banks, postal services, credit unions – have in reducing financial exclusion. Their incentives to do so vary; specialist MFIs grew up precisely because for-profit institutions were reluctant to move down-market, while the state-sponsored financial institutions that had such a mandate generally proved unsustainable (Adams and Von Pischke, 1992). However, these incentives change with time. For example, penetrating mass 'bottom of the pyramid' markets can give multi-national businesses a competitive advantage that enables them to compete more effectively at the top (Pralahad and Hammond, 2002). Large private banks, like other large businesses, are also aware of the need to protect their reputation and 'goodwill' by adapting to changing public expectations of corporate social responsibility. The inefficiency of state and cooperative financial institutions in the past was generally associated with poor governance, corruption, political co-option and patronage. Where governments and politicians grant them greater autonomy then they too can play a bigger role in reducing financial exclusion. If so, then they can also learn from the progress MFIs have made in institutionalizing social performance management, and international donors should be encouraging them to do so.[22]

The potential relevance of social performance can also be extended to the sector level. Ultimately, the argument for financial liberalization is not just that it should be more efficient in sponsoring economic growth, but that it should create incentives for extension of sustainable financial services to previously excluded groups. Yet liberalization has also enabled banks (often at the prompting of new foreign owners) to shore up rates of return on capital in ways that reduce access, for example through branch closures, increases in minimum deposit requirements for savers, and shifts in loan portfolios from small to large clients.[23] In this context, there are grounds for arguing that governments should monitor social performance at the financial sector level more closely, and if necessary find ways to 'encourage' private financial institutions to meet more ambitious targets.[24] A pertinent example of this is South Africa (Arora and Leach, 2004) where Finscope has served as a useful watchdog of the social performance of the whole financial sector.

A big part of the attraction of microfinance is that it seeks to build useful and sustainable links between the financial system and public policy, to accept the potency of market competition and self-interest, but not to be limited by them. Becoming more effective as agents of poverty reduction has forced MFIs to combine standard business skills with new skills to measure and manage outreach and impact. They have grown into something large and more significant than a scattered archipelago of innovative practice in a sea of indifference. They have even wider potential as role models for larger financial institutions (and ultimately the financial sector as a whole) of how trade-offs between social and financial performance can be effectively managed and often overcome. In this sense, MFIs stand in a long and continuing tradition of seeking both to harness and to humanize capitalism.

Notes

1 Introduction

1 This definition deliberately avoids the issue of whether the aspirations are wants, basic needs or indeed human rights. Different people will choose different language. The important thing is to tailor services to be of greatest possible benefit over time to relatively poor people. Neither does this definition imply microfinance services should be restricted only to relatively poor people; improving access of poor people to services that are open to all is often more sustainable, for example.

2 The word 'access' here refers not only to physical availability of services but also to costs, quality, reliability and social discrimination. Poverty can be defined in terms of absolute or relative income, or indeed using a wider range of indicators of well-being.

3 These points are based on the closing remarks of Frank de Giovanni, of the Ford Foundation, at the final *Imp-Act* workshop, held in Bath in September 2004.

4 This optimism helped to stimulate a negative academic backlash, highlighting 'the dark side' or negative impact of microfinance. While it would be an exaggeration to say that this has in turn polarized debate, it does explain a degree of 'disconnect' between some academic and more policy-oriented literature on microfinance. This was graphically illustrated to one of the authors by a Ford Foundation officer in a café in Lima, in which he had no difficulty in sorting a large collection of literature on microfinance that he had just collected into two distinct piles!

5 No attempt is made to comprehensively review the massive literature relevant to these themes beyond making a few illustrative references.

6 At about the same time, participants at the Microcredit Summit began to argue for systematic 'auditing' of impact in place of conventional impact assessment. Several MFI networks – notably Freedom from Hunger and Opportunity International – were also starting to think about ways in which MFIs could track progress towards their social goals, rather than use occasional and costly assessment methods (see Cheston and Reed, 1999; Hatch and Frederick, 1998).

7 See Chapter 7 for a systematic review of the organizational factors that influence social performance.

8 Many MFIs provide non-financial services either in parallel or jointly with their financial services. Health and education are important for some *Imp-Act* partners. These types of complementary financial and non-financial provision are covered in the Chapter 2.

9 The original concept papers were produced by Paul Mosley (then at Reading University, UK), John Gaventa and Martin Greeley (at IDS Sussex, UK), James Copestake, Allister McGregor and Susan Johnson (at University of Bath, UK).

10 Of these, 23 were funded directly and seven were included as partners of the Micro-Finance Centre in Poland.

11 Overall guidance to the programme was given by a steering committee that met twice a year and comprised representatives from each region, two external advisers (Monique Cohen and Syed Hashemi) and two members of the UK team. A UK team management committee met quarterly and supervised the operations of the *Imp-Act* Secretariat, which coordinated day-to-day programme operations and dissemination.

12 Perhaps the most definitive set of impact assessments remain those of SEWA in India, Zambuko in Zimbabwe and Mibanco in Peru, carried out under the AIMS programme. See Snodgrass and Sebstad (2002).

13 Which is not to say that there were not also significant weaknesses in the way the project was set up and operated – not least the central management role assigned to the UK team.

2 Sustainable poverty outreach

1 The 'better financial markets leads to poverty reduction' argument points to the employment generated through loans to the non-poor and argues that this employment gives indirect benefits to the poor and is a substantial source of poverty reduction. Mosley and Rock (2004) provide an argument based on African data suggesting that, by some poverty definitions, this is likely to be the most important poverty outreach achievement of MFIs. However, there is no clear evidence that the employment generated through loans to the non-poor by MFIs results in employment for the poor. At least one authority (Ledgerwood, 1999) argues that most of the employment generated is family employment.

2 It is often (though not always) easier to collect expenditure or consumption data rather than income data using survey methods. Here income is used as shorthand for all three or for any money-metric measure of poverty.

3 This is a constrained choice. First, some choices may not be available, for example, safe water may not be available even for rich households. Second, some aspects of well-being are not particularly responsive, or only partially responsive, to extra money; empowerment of women is one such example.

4 It has been recognized in other sectors (Blair, 2000) that sometimes poverty reduction is only effectively achieved through universal provision and not targeting.

5 Poverty targeting is sometimes distinguished from poverty screening, the latter term being used for review of client applications rather than MFIs themselves selecting clients with specific characteristics. Both involve an assessment of poverty status. We can also distinguish these two activities from 'assessment' when the latter is used to mean review of poverty status of *existing* clients. Screening can be seen as 'passive' targeting and assessment as *ex post* evaluation of targeting success. In all three cases, the objective includes making a determination of poverty status, though the tools used may vary, as may the use of the information.

6   The effectiveness of targeting can be evaluated in terms of *'vertical efficiency'*, that is the proportion of all clients/programme participants in the target group, and *'horizontal efficiency'*, that is proportion of the total target group reached by a programme. Microfinance approaches to measuring poverty outreach usually focus on vertical efficiencies (such as later sections in this chapter); there has been less emphasis on horizontal efficiency in the literature. The paper from BRAC in the accompanying volume on Managing Social Performance gives an illuminating account of how one MFI has addressed horizontal efficiency.

7   For example, as CARD reported in their final *Imp-Act* report: 1) heterogeneous groups perform better; 2) entrepreneurs stimulate linking supply chain-processing-distribution-sales within their own centres and among centres; 3) first-time loan takers learn from more experienced members; 4) centres developed their own legal means to manage arrears and loan recovery; and 5) groups devised creative ways to raise centre funds that can cover for missed payments and other uses. In FINRURAL, some microfinance groups grew into fields of activity other than finance. In particular, some members of microfinance groups had diversified from simply supporting each other's businesses into running a joint canteen, provision of coordinated volunteer help in a medical centre and campaigning together against the government's removal of import duties on second-hand clothes (that had badly hit the interviewees who sold clothes). The usefulness of including more powerful clients in MFI work has also been observed in many branches of the microfinance programme of IRDP in Bangladesh, especially their landless women's programme, and has been observed in solidarity group approaches of *Imp-Act* partners elsewhere, for example, CRECER in Bolivia.

8   Inequality is a quite distinct aspect of well-being from poverty. Poverty is most sensibly defined in absolute terms of deprivation, or what Amartya Sen calls absence of capabilities. Economic or social inequality might be associated with this but even where absolute poverty is absent, these inequalities are a source of ill-being. It is no fun being relatively poor even if you can afford to eat.

9   According to Van de Ruit and May (2003), studies drawn from a number of Demographic and Health Surveys (DHS) and Living Standards Measurement Studies (LSMS) throughout the developing world have tested the validity of proxy measures in assessing latent expressions of well-being (Montgomery *et al*, 2000; Morris *et al*, 2000; Filmer and Pritchett, 1998). These studies have found that proxy measures have significant explanatory power over specific demographic outcomes. Filmer and Pritchett (1998) argue that proxy measures are more stable than consumption measures, while Sahn and Stifel (2000) found proxy measures to be powerful in panel series data. This evidence suggests that proxy indicators are reliable indicators of well-being.

10   Another popular approach to proxy indicators is participatory wealth ranking; popular because it is relatively cheap and, when well executed, is a 'quick and clean' method of targeting. It is also consistent with a participatory learning and action approach in which the realities of poor borrowers and their aspirations are at centre stage in designing service delivery and impact assessment. However, it is easy to do badly and so it has problems of credibility with external audiences.

11   The Living Standards Measurement Survey is a household expenditure survey used in many estimates of national poverty across the developing world. It is promoted by the World Bank, which has supported such surveys. It is essentially similar to most expenditure surveys but there has been some standardization of instruments

to facilitate comparison and the approach also allows the addition of specific modules on topical areas.

12   In fact the legislation specifies that 50 per cent of USAID support to microenterprise should be received by households below the dollar-a-day poverty line *or* below 50 per cent of the national poverty line. Whilst these overlap partially, generally these two definitions will not identify the same number of households. In almost all countries, the dollar-a-day line identifies fewer poor households than the national poverty line so it is not clear how much difference there would be. In a very few cases the dollar-a-day line is higher than the national poverty line and so identifies more poor households than even 100 per cent of those poor by the local measure. This is the case in India and a cause for concern since, on either measure, India has more poor people than any other country. In the Indian case a dollar-a-day is above the national poverty line so an MFI could meet the dollar-a-day criterion by lending to households just below the dollar-a-day line, in which case they may not have any households below 50 per cent of the national poverty line.

13   This section is partially based on detailed reporting of results from *Imp-Act* partners. When reporting specific results from individual partners some descriptive text on purposes, methods or results is taken *verbatim*, with minor adjustments, from the final reports of partners or related documents. This is especially the case for CARD, SEF, PRIZMA and SEF. We have not used speech marks to indicate specific quotations but have referenced each table or figure used and given references to source material used for each organization.

14   The identification of the poverty index is based on data for the sample of non-clients only in order to avoid bias. In the default mode this would be a sample of 300 randomly selected households.

15   This is akin to the problem with dollar-a-day measures as an absolute arbiter of poverty outreach. There are dimensions of poverty that may not correlate with income; poor access to health and education services might be one such or, in another dimension, insecurity of individuals, particularly women, and the threat of violence.

16   The PWR replaced an earlier method of targeting (the 'visual poverty indicator') based primarily on housing quality. This was found to be inaccurate in South African conditions.

17   In January 2003 CARD decided to add 'food security' as a fourth means test indicator. Professor Chua of the Asian Institute of Management assisted CARD in developing a research programme to test these indicators.

3   Direct material impacts

1   Our empirical focus is mainly on the welfare gains from income generated by loans specifically, but it is important to recognize that both savings and insurance products are other forms of 'consumption-smoothing' that are capable of significant welfare affects. For the very poorest, there is evidence that safe and flexible savings opportunities are the most important service MFIs can offer. See Rutherford (2004).

2   SHARE use relatively simple but effective targeting instruments – occupation and land holding – and have relatively dense populations of their target group. Both

these factors have facilitated their achievement of strong social and financial performance.

3   See, for example, SEEP (2000); Hulme (2000a); Ledgerwood (1999).

4   A related design problem is that of non-random placement of programmes. If an MFI works in a particularly poor area and impact assessment is based on a comparison group from a less poor area it is likely that impact on poverty will be underestimated. These design problems, as well as the attribution issue, are common to impact assessment activities in most contexts, not just microfinance. Ravallion (2001) uses a story format to provide an authoritative, though technical, account of design and analysis needs to address these problems.

5   For statistical interpretation, a further requirement in drawing conclusions about a population (of clients) from a sample study is that the sample, and the comparison group, are selected randomly. Most often, some attention is given to this, but not always with the degree of care appropriate to each level of sampling from programme-level to client-level that would satisfy conditions for genuine randomness. Commonly, geographic programme areas are selected for study, and then within the area a random sample selection of clients is drawn. The results are then often generalized across all geographic areas, perhaps with a caveat or two, but not usually with a statistical assessment of reliability of results at programme level. It is a matter for conjecture rather than rigorous analysis to assess the actual inaccuracies and biases introduced by failure to randomize. The study of SHARE by the National Institute of Rural Development (Rangarchayula, 2003) from the *Imp-Act* studies is a good example of where there is a sufficiently high degree of confidence in the approach adopted to randomness of selection so that the results are reliable at a programme level, subject of course to confidence limits. Whilst larger sample sizes can allow *ex-post* matching of member and non- or new member samples, the problems of randomness will remain. Use of new members as a control group may anyway constrain sample size.

6   With data from two or more points in time for both the comparison group and the client sample, it is possible to compare 'difference of differences'. For example, it might be established that proportionate changes in enterprise profits are greater for clients than non-clients. This is a considerable improvement on one-off studies, though it still potentially suffers from selection bias. See the PROMUC case study in this chapter.

7   For contrasting studies of failure, see Huq (2004) and Lont (2004).

8   Impact studies, even those focusing on the external agenda, generally have a lot of information on clients, such as: age, education, household status, household economic activities, client enterprises, business practices, control of income decisions, knowledge, skills and attitudes. They do not always use the data effectively, often focusing more on income and loan repayment issues. Few studies bring serious sociological insights into their assessment of household impacts.

9   The results are abstracted from a very substantial body of research findings. The evidence selected tries to provide a sense of the range of concerns addressed and the weight of evidence. This is particularly true for the evidence in tabular form; the tables selected provide a good representation of the analyses undertaken but there is no attempt to be comprehensive for any one organization. The individual reports obviously provide a much richer treatment of each case.

10   Copestake *et al* (2005) provide a comprehensive summary of PROMUC findings and

a systematic comparison of the two poverty assessment tools and two impact assessment tools that they used during the *Imp-Act* programme.

11 The significance of the computed coefficients was at the 1 per cent level after adjusting for likely heteroskedasticity.

12 See Wright-Revolledo (2003).

13 The MCPI has 22 regular members of which 10, including CARD, are financially sustainable.

14 Since 2002, the Grameen Bank has operated what, for some time, was called Grameen II, which is a modification of aspects of the Grameen system to improve service delivery. Addressing the problem of rising default, changes focused on better staff–client relations and modification of loan instruments.

15 Among these clients, 81 per cent were women, with an average age of 39 and 10 years of schooling. Average family size was five members and 86 per cent of the interviewed clients resided and worked in non-rural locations: urban (59 per cent) and peri-urban (26 per cent).

16 On the assumption, as the report makes clear, that no other interventions occurred that would undermine attribution of income gains to use of loans.

17 The fourth indicator, the dependency ratio (the ratio of children and old people to working adults), was used as an 'independent' variable; presumably this was meant as a check on the comparability of the mature clients and new entrants though this was anyway established through comparison of essential demographic characteristics in the entry-level data. It is not clear why it was included in the comparative poverty measures.

18 Working with Opportunity International, SAT helped in the development of the CIMS approach as a part of a global Opportunity International programme to strengthen the capacity of partner MFIs to monitor outreach and impact.

19 The 2002 SEEP survey of practitioners also identified data analysis as the biggest stumbling block (SEEP, 2004b).

4 Direct social impacts and the Millennium Development Goals

1 In addition to references cited in the text this chapter draws extensively on unpublished partner reports and reviews listed in the references section at the back of this volume, in particular: Dash (2004), Kabeer and Dash (2004), Cortijo and Kabeer (2004), Garuba (2004), PRADAN (2004), PROMUC (2004), Promujer (2004) and Opoku (2004).

2 As distinct from various indirect impacts that are discussed in Chapter 5.

3 Although Chen and Mahmud include both 'cognitive' and 'perceptual' change as elements of their typology, we would argue that 'perceptual change' is subsumed within cognitive change that relates to changes in the mental faculty of 'knowing' through perceiving, recognizing, conceiving, judging, reasoning and imagining.

4 My thanks to Jennifer Sebstad for drawing attention to this point.

5 Wider impacts: social exclusion and citizenship

1 In addition to cited references, this chapter draws extensively on unpublished

partner reports listed in the references section, in particular: Dash (2004), Cortijo and Kabeer (2004), Kabeer and Dash (2004) and PRADAN (2004).

2   Self-help group members set up a collective savings fund from which they provide loans to each other.

3   See Wood and Sharif (1997).

6   Impact in local financial markets

1   In addition to references cited in the text, this chapter draws extensively on unpublished partner reports listed at the back of this volume; in particular: Kulkarni (2003), Sabageni (2003), Sabageni *et al* (2002), and SHARE (2003). Also Johnson (2004).

2   During the 1990s, after a series of banking crises, the Central Bank of Kenya brought the regulatory requirements for NBFIs (non-bank financial institutions) into line with those of the commercial banks.

3   See Johnson (2004a).

4   Data for savings held by the Post Office were not available because accounts are held centrally and not on a branch basis.

5   The data in Table 6.1 do not take into account multiple membership of MFIs (or similarly multiple use of other services). There is some evidence to suggest that over the period 2001–02 clients had taken multiple loans and over-exposed themselves with a consequent rise in default. As a result, MFIs in the area started to share information more systematically on defaulters.

6   The New Kenya Overall Price index indicates that prices rose by 17.3 per cent between December 1999 and June 2002. See CBK Statistical Bulletin (2002).

7   See Rutherford (1999).

8   This may also suggest a predatory element to the deepening of the market to poorer clients.

9   This has also been found to be the case in Bangladesh. See Sinha and Matin (1998).

10   Although client and non-client groups participated in the research, these results are likely to be favourable to the position of SHARE in particular because: 1) the equal numbers in client and non-client groups over-represents them compared to a random sample; and 2) non-client groups were identified through snow-balling methods from client groups so that they were also more likely to be aware of SHARE's services than a random sample.

11   See Johnson (2004b); Chiteji (2002); Velez-Ibanez (1983).

12   Some commentators question the sustainability of this rapid expansion in terms of longer term credit discipline.

13   It is unlikely that this data captures all ROSCAs and ASCAs in existence in Uganda.

14   The Government programme *Entandikwa* is no longer operating but has been superceded by the Poverty Alleviation Programme and other support for rural microfinance development.

15   See Wright and Rippey (2003) for more detail.

16   Data from Mixx Market for December 2003.

17   See also Seibel (2003).

18   See Rhyne (2001).

19   Finscope in South Africa has developed a survey of this type. See www.finscope.co.za

7 Organizational determinants of social performance

1 This definition of social performance emphasizes outcomes at the MFI-level. Conceptually it builds on Schreiner's six dimensions of outreach (Copestake, 2003b; Schreiner, 2002). Others use the term more broadly to refer also to organizational processes as well as outcomes (see Chapter 9).

2 The companion volume (Brody et al, 2005) and a special edition of the IDS Bulletin (Brody et al, 2003) provide more in-depth case studies of some of the MFIs' experiences.

3 To do this more effectively, selection of organizations would have had to be tailored to specific hypotheses and more standardization would have been needed in research activities. In this respect, the review of village banking by Westley (2004) makes for interesting comparison. First, it focuses more narrowly on one type of MFI in one continent. Second, he deliberately selected better performing MFIs.

4 Strengths, Weaknesses, Opportunities and Threats. A second SWOT focused more narrowly on progress in institutionalizing social performance assessment during the three years. This is reported in Chapter 8.

5 Where possible, points are also supported with illustrative footnotes that refer to specific MFIs.

6 Fowler (1997) lucidly explores the same theme for NGOs in development more generally, while Edwards (1997) looks more specifically at organizational learning within NGOs. Both authors have also subsequently elaborated on these themes in other publications.

7 SAT in Ghana sets even more specific impact goals: to improve material, political, social and spiritual well-being. Promoters of self-help groups are among several whom state that the long-term benefits of helping people to manage money collectively and effectively are at least as important to them as individual material benefits of improved access to financial services.

8 One exception that to some extent proves the rule is FINCA International. It is committed to the transformation of its affiliates in Guatemala, Uganda and Kyrgyzstan from NGO programmes into independent regulated financial institutions. However, this commitment also generated concern in the board in the USA about whether these affiliates would then abandon their social missions.

9 PROMUC is an interesting example being an umbrella body formed to coordinate the microfinance activities of a network of NGOs. However, the arrangement has failed to provide sufficiently strong central leadership to transform several relatively small microfinance programmes into a single and more dynamic microfinance institution.

10 Honduras provides an interesting example where a new legal structure for MFIs (as 'private development finance institutions') allows them to mobilize and use deposits, while remaining under the control of a board of trustees, rather than shareholders. The price for this freedom is rigorous accountability to the banking supervisory authority.

11 CYSD and PRADAN in India differ from the others because since they aim to promote the financial services of autonomous self-help groups, rather than provide such services directly themselves on a self-sustaining basis.

12 CMF is an example of an organization that has recently made a strong shift towards the former, firing its female director (with an activist background) in the process.

13   CYSD and PRADAN provide contrasting examples. Another example is FINCA
International. This was dominated for some time by a core of highly experienced
staff with a strong sustainability mission, but the board has also become active in
reasserting the need to avoid mission drift by strengthening social performance
goals too.

14   Other MFI board issues that could affect social mission were not raised. These
include the division of responsibilities between board and director, frequency of
meetings, rules of turnover and succession, and whether the board represents
shareholders or not. See Sa-Dhan (2003) for a comprehensive review of the literature on microfinance boards and governance.

15   BRAC in Bangladesh is perhaps the clearest example. It is big enough to operate not
only its own research unit but set up its own university.

16   Leading examples are PRIZMA in Bosnia and PROMUJER in Bolivia. Both operate in
environments where proliferation of MFIs led to market saturation, forcing hard
thinking about how to secure a market niche in order to survive.

17   Westley (2004) provides an interesting contrast. With a narrower focus on four
leading village banking MFIs in Latin America, he provides a detailed discussion
of the following: length and structure of meetings, arrears control, loan sizes and
scales, loan repayment frequency, loan terms, loan prepayment, tracking of individual payments, loan guarantees, forced savings, voluntary savings and internal
account loans. See also Churchill *et al* (2002) for further reflections on the village
banking model.

18   K-Rep in Kenya experienced some problems of this kind with its farmer service
associations. In a completely different setting CAME in Mexico suffered somewhat
during the three years of the *Imp-Act* programme from the introduction of too many
innovations too quickly, although in this case the problem concerned operational
change as much as product change.

19   See Westley (2004).

20   Even within each of these broad models there are dilemmas. For example, although
PRADAN works exclusively with the SHG model and has a strong social performance focus, it still faces internal dilemmas over how to balance livelihood and
social (including gender empowerment) goals.

21   In contrast, Honduran MFIs have shifted sharply from group to individual lending
in the last five years on financial grounds, without being able to monitor the social
effects of this in any detail (Copestake, 2004b).

22   Shared commitment to the social goals of microfinance is one aspect of this, but
there are many cultural variations: feminist, Gandhian and Christian, for example.
These are perhaps more important than official MFI literature suggests given MFIs'
sensitivity to criticism for being in any way sectarian. Opportunity International,
for example, cultivates an external image of enlightened capitalism, but internally
its Christian ethos is important.

23   This is less true for organizations such as CYSD and PRADAN that are promoting
SHGs, rather than providing financial services directly.

24   The comments on organizational culture emphasize communication, information
flows and 'learning culture' more than other aspects of organizational culture,
including values, incentive systems, norms of staff behaviour and of leadership.
This perhaps reflects a bias arising from the particular interest of *Imp-Act* in
information flows.

25   CAME in Mexico city is an example of an MFI that faced a potential financial crisis

when the regulated financial institution that held village bank accounts threatened prohibitive increases in bank charges for each transaction.

26 FINCA International was treated in the study as a single MFI although it had 24 separate country programmes. Opportunity International, in contrast works with autonomous MFIs, including SAT in Ghana. PROMUJER-Peru is one of four PROMUJER MFIs in Latin America, although its sister organization in Bolivia is now fully autonomous. CARD is a good example of an autonomous MFI that has successfully worked with a range of donors and international networks, as well as being an active member and supporter of the Microfinance Council of the Philippines (Joyas and Alip, 2004). One of its sponsors is PLAN International, which has moved gradually from running its own microfinance programmes to sponsoring independent MFIs.

27 This was particularly evident in East Africa.

28 Chapter 8 explores the case of interaction between vertical and horizontal networks in relation to social performance assessment.

29 All the dilemmas can be linked back to the boxes of quotations, but in some cases we have drawn more than one dilemma from a single box or collapsed several boxes into a single dilemma.

30 We are *not* suggesting establishing absolute scales and scores for each issue as this would go against the core argument that 'best practice' is not absolute but context specific. For example, an extreme position may well be justified for some MFIs for some periods, not least to correct for past excesses in the opposite direction.

8   Institutionalizing social performance assessment

1 In this case the reviewers were asked to identify factors internal and external to each organization that favoured or inhibited institutionalization of SPA.

2 An important example is that of FINRURAL in Bolivia. Members of this network saw a need for impact assessment in part to differentiate themselves more clearly from more aggressively commercial MFIs, which faced massive popular criticism for having contributed to growing over-indebtedness.

3 See *Imp-Act* (2004a); Wright-Revolledo and Copestake (2004).

4 Examples of MFI leadership within national networks are: ODEF and the COVELO Network in Honduras, SEF within the community microfinance network in South Africa, and CARD within the Microfinance Council of the Philippines. Elsewhere the network agency itself has been more proactive (for example, CMF in Nepal, MFC in Poland, FINRURAL in Bolivia, ASOMIF in Nicaragua). CGAP (2004b) provides a general survey of MFI networks globally and reviews their broader functions.

5 FINCA International in Honduras was in the unique position in the *Imp-Act* programme of participating both through the global FINCA International network and the national COVELO network. Senior staff reported that the two projects were complementary: the former emphasizing generation of comparable poverty outreach statistics, the latter emphasizing client assessment and generation of data to inform debates at the national level.

6 These criticisms do not fall only on donors. SAT in Ghana, for example, was perhaps held back in developing a sustainable SPA system for itself by being charged with a lead role in developing a system for the whole network.

7   Monitoring, in this case, refers to routine collection and reporting of statistics about number, turnover and social characteristics of clients. Evaluation refers to analysis of these data both on their own and through supplementary (often qualitative) data collection in order that inferences can be drawn about the causal chains linking changes in client-level indicators to the financial services they are using.

8   See Noponen (2003) for a detailed description of the ILS.

9   A partial exception to this is the case of NGOs, such as CYSD and PRADAN, that exist to support more informal user-controlled microfinance organizations, such as self-help groups. See the final chapter of Fisher and Sriram (2002) for a discussion that also includes reflections on 'the art of capacity building' in microfinance.

10   Participating organizations received financial support (often combined with funds from internal and other sources) solely to cover an agreed three-year plan of action research to strengthen SPA.

11   Most opted to recruit local rather than international consultants. Several (CARD, MFC, COVELO, ASOMIF, FINRURAL) also used the project to work within national networks. *Imp-Act* also facilitated (separately) regional meetings of partners. Participants particularly valued the opportunity for exchange beyond regional networks, for example, thematic groups explored how to reach very poor clients, how to measure wider impacts and how to strengthen the role of local networks.

12   Alternatively, where the MFI has been created out of a larger 'holding' NGO then the latter may retain such research capacity.

13   Examples here include FINRURAL, PROMUJER, PROMUC, SHARE and FINCA International.

14   This table draws on discussion with many *Imp-Act* participants, as well as my own experience as a consultant, particularly in Southern Africa. Germane examples include PRADAN and CYSD in India, PROMUJER in Peru and CAME in Mexico.

15   The argument is a summary and update of earlier *Imp-Act* work on horizontal networks, reported in Copestake (2003a).

16   CARD played a similar role in the Philippines (see Joyas and Alip, 2003).

17   MFC's approach is documented in a series of ten 'spotlight notes' produced between June 2003 and March 2004. These review its approach to SPA, as well as providing case-study material from its partners' experiences. See www.mfc.org.pl/research

18   For example, FINCA in Honduras participated in the COVELO initiative within the country to promote the use of AIMS-SEEP tools, as well as the FINCA International initiative to promote poverty assessment, both sponsored by *Imp-Act*.

19   A possible example of the latter under the *Imp-Act* programme is technical assistance from OPPORTUNITY International to SAT in Ghana. Arguably, promotion of the Internal Learning System within Indian MFIs has also been too strongly driven by external interests (Noponen, 2003).

20   The final review process carried out of *Imp-Act*-funded projects provides experience on how to conduct social performance reviews and is summarized in practice note No. 5 (*Imp-Act*, 2005c).

21   For more detailed elaboration of how costs were calculated, see the original papers that are published together in a special edition of the *Small Enterprise Development Journal* (Copestake, 2004a).

22   Strictly this is better described as a form of financial analysis, rather cost-effectiveness analysis (that explores the relative costs of different ways of achieving

the same benefit) or cost-benefit analysis (that attempts to quantify all the most important costs and benefits to all stakeholders).

23 This includes costs to the MFIs of participating in the training networks, but not the costs to the COVELO network of running the workshops.

24 See Copestake (2004b) and Villalobos Barahona (2004). for a more comprehensive discussion. Note that sampling of clients ensured that cost per client of the studies was significantly lower than in the case of PRIZMA and SEF.

25 None of the studies take into account the fact that while client exit generally represents a loss to MFIs, it may also be a benefit if less reliable clients are screened out before they become over-indebted (Copestake, 2003b).

9 Conclusions

1 More detailed guidelines are set out in *Imp-Act* (2005a).

2 Likewise members of the PROMUC network were shocked by survey findings on depth of poverty outreach where there was more explicit geographical targeting. Copestake *et al* (2005) provide more details and argue strongly from PROMUC experience in favour of a poverty correlate approach to monitoring poverty outreach over use of the CGAP poverty assessment tool. PROMUC is not alone. A more recent USAID study of nine other Peruvian financial institutions found that only 10 per cent out of 1,551 interviewed clients were below a US$2 a day benchmark (Zeller *et al*, 2005).

3 Work subsequently commissioned by USAID and being carried out by the IRIS Centre at the University of Maryland promises to add substantially to knowledge on how to do this in a way that strikes the best possible balance between practicality and reliability in design of such systems. See www.povertytools.org

4 Defining rigorous as drawing inferences logically (from stated evidence and assumptions) in a way that can be peer reviewed.

5 Subsequent multiple regression analysis of the PROMUC data found that the change in household income over a year was higher for both richer and poorer halves of the sample, but significantly greater for the richer half (Copestake *et al*, 2005). For another case study that concluded that poorer clients benefit much less than richer clients see Shaw (2004).

6 Mosley and Rock (2004) use SEF and CERUDEB to pose a similar strategic dilemma, albeit subject to considerable uncertainty about underlying figures. This is between choosing to subsidize SEF, whose poverty reduction impact is based on directly targeting very poor clients, and CERUDEB, whose poverty reduction impact depends more on indirect employment creation for poor people.

7 Not that this was easy. Such is the resilience of established ways of thinking that many participants (academics and practitioners) frequently slipped back into thinking of the work as primarily addressing external accountability needs.

8 The basis of this view is twofold. First, internal staff are in a strong position to cross check findings against their own experience. Second, frequent generation and use of data constitute stronger feedback, increasing opportunities for organizational learning.

9 More detailed guidelines are available in the companion publication (*Imp-Act*, 2005b).

10   The key problem with specialist social science models of impact assessment is that they are designed for a different purpose: to generate once-and-for-all self-sufficient objective truth to often quite narrow questions, rather than to inform multi-level and continuous decision making. Such models also undervalue the opportunity for validation available to MFI managers through day-to-day encounters with clients, staff and other key informants.

11   The QUIP studies of PROMUC found 38 out of 60 randomly selected clients were unambiguously better-off as a result of joining village banks, whereas 9 found it difficult to make an overall judgement and 13 were unambiguously worse-off.

12   For MFIs themselves, the main motive for securing private funding is to scale-up. But to the extent that such funding affects their governance, there is a risk that room for manoeuvre could be reduced in other ways; the concept of mission drift has a political/structural, as well as a psychological/cognitive dimension (Copestake, 1998). Strong SPA systems should help MFIs to identify such risks and dilemmas.

13   This argument is also expanded in a later article (*The Economist*, 22 January 2005).

14   These draw heavily on models with wider applications than microfinance. For general surveys see Woller (2005); Clark *et al* (2003); Tulchin (2003).

15   See www.povertytools.org and Zeller (2005).

16   On the importance of consumer protection in microfinance, see McAllister (2003).

17   Schreiner's six dimensions of outreach are: worth, cost, scope, depth and breadth (Schreiner, 2002).

18   See www.mixmarket.org

19   For general discussion of the dangers of standards, benchmarks and 'audit culture', see Copestake (2003b); Strathern (2000); Power (1997).

20   This quotation was actually made with reference to AA1000, a 'foundation process standard' developed by the Institute for Social and Ethical Accountability.

21   See *Imp-Act* (2005c) for further discussion of how a social performance review based on the six questions can be bolted onto other auditing, rating and review activities.

22   *Imp-Act* (2005a) explores such relationships further.

23   In Kenya and many other countries, liberalization was also associated with open-market financing of public deficits prompting banks to shift from private lending to investment in safer and more lucrative treasury bills. With time, stability and new entry there are grounds for hope that competitive pressures will force the financial system to look outwards and 'downwards'; but this cannot be taken for granted.

24   More technically put, the core argument here is that the negative externalities of financial exclusion and positive externalities of financial inclusion are too big to maintain a hermetic seal between social policy and financial policy.

References

Adams, D.W., Graham, D.H. and Von Pischke, J.D. (1984) *Undermining Rural Development with Cheap Credit*, Westview Press, Boulder, Colorado.

Adams, D.W. and Von Pischke, J.D. (1992) Microenterprise credit programs: déjà vu, *World Development*, **20**, pp 1463–70.

Appadurai, A. (1989) Small-scale technologies and large-scale objectives, in *Conversations between Economists and Anthropologists: Methodological Issues in Measuring Change in Rural India*, ed P. Bardhan, Oxford University Press, New Delhi.

Arora, S.S. and Leach, J. (2004) *Towards an inclusive financial sector in India: do recent developments in South Africa hold any lessons*? DFID unpublished memo, London.

Bansal, H. (2003) SHG-Bank linkage program in India: an overview, *Journal of Microfinance* **5** (1), pp 21–50.

Barnes, C., Gaile, G. and Kibombo, R. (2001) *The impact of three microfinance programs in Uganda*, USAID-AIMS, Washington DC.

Bauman, T. (2004) Cost-effectiveness study of the Small Enterprise Foundation, South Africa, *Small Enterprise Development*, **15** (3), pp 28–40.

Bell, R., Harper, A. and Mandivenga, D. (2002) Can commercial banks do microfinance? Lessons from the Commercial Bank of Zimbabwe and the Co-operative Bank of Kenya, *Small Enterprise Development*, **13** (4), pp 35–46.

Blair, H. (2000) Participation and accountability at the periphery: democratic local governance in six countries, *World Development*, **28** (1), pp 21–39.

Brody, A., Copestake, J.G., Greeley, M., Kabeer, N. and Simanowitz, A. (eds) (2003) Microfinance, poverty and social performance, *IDS Bulletin*, **34** (4), pp 1–156.

Brody, A., Greeley, M., Wright-Revolledo, K. (eds) (2005) *Managing Social Performance in Microfinance*, ITDG Publishing, London.

Buckley, G. (1997) Microfinance in Africa: is it either the problem or the solution?, *World Development* **25**, pp 1081–93.

CAME (2004) *Vôces desde CAME: El Impacto de los Microcréditos*, Plaza y Valdes, Mexico.

Central Bank of Kenya (2002) *Statistical Bulletin*, Central Bank of Kenya, Nairobi.

CGAP (2003) *Building Financial Systems that Work for the Poor: CGAP Phase III Strategy for 2003 to 2008*, CGAP, Washington DC.

CGAP (2004a) *Building Inclusive Financial Systems: Donor Guidelines on Good Practice in Microfinance*, CGAP, Washington DC.

CGAP (2004b) What is a network? The diversity of networks in microfinance today, *Focus Note*, **26**, CGAP, Washington DC.

Chambers, R. (1992) Poverty in India: concepts, research and reality, in *Poverty in India, Research and Policy*, eds B. Harriss, S. Guhan and R.H. Cassen, Oxford University Press, New Delhi.

Chambers, R. (1993) *Challenging the Professions: Frontiers for Rural Development*, ITDG Publishing, London.

Chambers, R. (1997) *Whose Reality Counts?* ITDG Publishing, London.

Chen, M.A. and Mahmud, S. (1995) Assessing change in women's lives: a conceptual framework, *BRAC-ICDDRB Joint Research Project Working Paper*, **2**, Dhaka, Bangladesh.

Cheston, S., and Reed, L. (1999) Measuring transformation: assessing and improving the impact of microcredit, *Journal of Microfinance*, **1** (1), pp 22–43.

Chiteji, N.S. (2002) Promises kept: enforcement and the role of rotating savings and credit associations in the economy, *Journal of International Development*, **14**, pp 393–411.

Churchill, C., Hirschland, M. and Painter, J. (2002) *New Directions in Poverty Finance: Village Banking Revisited*, SEEP, Washington DC.

Clark, C., Rosenzweig, W., Long, D. and Olsen, S. (2003) *Assessing Social Impact in Double Bottom Line Ventures, a Methods Catalogue*, Report to the Rockefeller Foundation, [online] www.rockefeller.org

Coady, D., Grosh, M. and Hoddinott, J. (2004) Targeting outcomes redux, *World Bank Research Observer*, **19** (1), pp 61–85.

Cohen, M. (2002) Making microfinance more client led, *Journal of International Development*, **14**, 335–50.

Cohen, M. and Wright-Revolledo, K. (2003) How do microfinance organizations become more client-led? Lessons from Latin America, *IDS bulletin*, **34**, 94–105.

Copestake, J.G. (1998) NGO-donor collaboration and the new policy agenda – the case of subsidised credit', *Public Administration and Development*, **16**, pp 855–66.

Copestake, J.G. (2000) Impact assessment of microfinance and organizational learning: who will survive?, *Journal of microfinance*, **2** (2), pp 119–134.

Copestake, J.G. (2001a) Inequality and the polarizing impact of microcredit: evidence from Zambia's copperbelt, *Journal of International Development*, **14**, pp 743–55.

Copestake, J.G. (2001b) Towards a general framework for client monitoring within microfinance organizations, *Imp-Act research note*, **5**, [online] www.*Imp-Act*.org

Copestake, J.G. (2003a) Horizontal networks and microfinance impact assessment, *Journal of Development Practice*, **13** (5), pp 537–41.

Copestake, J.G. (2003b) Simple standards or burgeoning benchmarks? Institutionalising social performance monitoring, assessment and auditing in microfinance, *IDS bulletin*, **34**, 54–65.

Copestake, J.G. (2003c) Unfinished business: the need for more effective microfinance exit monitoring, *Journal of Microfinance*, **4**, pp 1–30.

Copestake, J.G. (2004a) Social performance assessment of microfinance: cost-effective or costly indulgence? *Small Enterprise Development*, **15** (3), pp 11–17.

Copestake, J.G. (2004b) Cost-effectiveness of microfinance client assessment in Honduras, *Small Enterprise Development*, **15** (3), pp 52–61.

Copestake, J.G. (2005) Flexible standards for controlled empowerment? Microfinance as a case-study of aid management, in *Aid Impact and Poverty Reduction*, eds S. Folke and H. Nielson, Palgrave/Macmillan, Basingstoke.

Copestake, J.G., Dawson, P., Fanning, J.P., Mckay, A. and Wright-Revolledo, K. (2005) *Monitoring Diversity of Poverty Outreach and Impact of Microfinance: A Comparison of Methods Using Data from Peru, Development Policy Review*, September.

Daley-Harris, S. (ed) (2002) *Pathways Out of Poverty, Innovations in Microfinance for the Poorest Families*, Kumarian Press, Bloomfield.

Dollar, D. and Kraay, A. (2000) *Growth is Good for the Poor*, mimeo, World Bank, Washington DC.

Dunford, C. (2002) *What's Wrong with Loan Size?*, Freedom from Hunger, California.

Dunn, E. (1999) *Microfinance Clients in Lima, Peru: Baseline Report for AIMS Core Impact Assessment*, AIMS, Washington DC.

Edwards, M. (1997) Organizational learning in non-government organizations: what have we learned?, *Public Administration and Development*, **17**, pp 235–50.

Evans, P.A.L. (2000) The dualistic leader: thriving on paradox, in *Management 21C*, ed S Chowdhury, Financial Times/Prentice Hall, London.

Filmer, D. and Pritchett, L. (1998) Estimating wealth effects without income or expenditure data – or tears: educational enrolment in India, *World Bank Policy Research Working Paper*, 1994, Development Economics Research Group, World Bank, Washington DC.

Fowler, A. (1997) *Striking a Balance: A Guide to Enhancing the Effectiveness of Non-Government Organizations in International Development*, Earthscan Publications, London.

Fowler, A. and Kinyanjui, K. (2004) *Indigenous Foreign Seed on African soil: The Story of K-Rep*, Acacia Publishers, Nairobi.

Government of Kenya (1998) *First Report on Poverty in Kenya*, Ministry of Planning and National Development, Nairobi.

Greeley, M. (2003) Poverty reduction and microfinance – assessing performance, *IDS Bulletin*, **34** (4), pp 10–20.

Handy, C. (1994) *The Empty Raincoat: Making Sense of the Future*, Hutchinson, London.

Hatch, J.K. and Crompton, P. (2003) *FINCA Client Assessment, 2003: A Report on the Poverty and Impact of 11 Country Programs*, FINCA International, Washington DC.

Hatch, J.K. and Frederick, L. (1998) *Poverty Assessment by Microfinance Institutions: A Review of Current Practice*, USAID: Microenterprise Development Office, Microenterprise Best Practice Project, Washington DC.

Hospes, O. and Prosé, M. (2004) Secrets of institutional transformation: the low politics of financial self-help organizations in post-colonial Africa, in *Livelihood and Microfinance, Anthropological and Sociological Perspectives on Savings and Debt*, eds H. Lont and O. Hospes, Eburon Academic Publishers, Delft.

Hudson, R. (2003) *In-Depth Quantitative Assessment of the Uganda Microfinance Environment*, unpublished report by TMS Financial, South Africa for MicroSave, Nairobi.

Hulme, D. (1999) *Client Drop-outs from East African MicroFinance Institutions*, MicroSave, Nairobi.

Hulme, D. (2000a) Impact assessment methodologies for microfinance: theory, experience and better practice, *World Development*, **28** (1), pp 79–98.

Hulme, D. (2000b) Is microdebt good for poor people? A note on the dark side of microfinance, *Small Enterprise Development*, **11** (1), pp 26–29.

Hulme, D. and Mosley, P. (1996) *Finance Against Poverty: Effective Institutions for Lending to Small Farmers and Micro-Enterprises in Developing Countries*, Routledge, London.

Huq, H. (2004) Surviving in the world of microcredit: a case from rural Bangladesh, in *Livelihood and Microfinance, Anthropological and Sociological Perspectives on Savings and Debt*, eds H. Lont and O. Hospes, Eburon Academic Publishers, Delft.

Imp-Act (2003) The feedback loop: responding to client needs, *Imp-Act practice note*, **1**, [online] www.*Imp-Act*.org

Imp-Act (2004a) QUIP: the qualitative individual in-depth interview protocol, *Imp-Act practice note*, **2**, [online] www.*Imp-Act*.org

Imp-Act (2004b) QUIP: understanding clients through in-depth interviews, *Imp-Act practice note*, **2**, [online] http://www.ids.ac.uk/impact/Publications/PracticeNotes/PracticeNotes2QUIPFinal.pdf

Imp-Act (2004c) Learning from client exit, *Imp-Act practice note*, **3**, [online] www.*Imp-Act*.org

Imp-Act (2005a) *Guidelines for Social Performance Management of Microfinance*, IDS: Brighton.

Imp-Act (2005b) Working with formal financial institutions to expand and deepen access – ensuring performance and accountability, *Imp-Act policy note*, **2**, [online] www.*Imp-Act*.org

Imp-Act (2005c) Reviewing the social performance of microfinance institutions, *Imp-Act practice note*, **5**, [online] www.*Imp-Act*.org

Johnson, S. (1998) Programme impact assessment in micro-finance: the need for an analysis of real markets, *IDS Bulletin*, **29** (4), pp 21–31.

Johnson, S. (2004a) Gender norms in financial markets: evidence from Kenya, *World Development*, **32** (8), pp 1355–74.

Johnson, S (2004b) 'Milking the elephant': financial markets as real markets in Kenya, *Development and Change*, **35** (2), pp 249–75.

Johnson, S. (2004c) The impact of microfinance institutions in local financial markets: a case study from Kenya, *Journal of International Development*, **16** (3), pp 501–17.

Johnson, S. (2005) Gender relations, empowerment and microcredit: moving forward from a lost decade, *European Journal of Development Research*, **17** (2), pp 224–48.

Johnson, S., Mule, N., Hickson, R. and Mwangi, W. (2002) The managed ASCA model: innovation in Kenya's microfinance industry, *Small Enterprise Development*, **13** (2), pp 56–66.

Joyas, L.M. and Alip, A.R. (2004) Institutionalizing impact monitoring and assessment of microfinance: experiences from the Philippines, *IDS Bulletin*, **34** (4), pp 85–93.

Kabeer, N. (2002) Citizenship and the boundaries of the acknowledged community: identity, affiliation and exclusion, *IDS Working Paper*, **171**, Institute of Development Studies, Brighton.

Kabeer, N. (2003a) Assessing the wider social impacts of microfinance services: concepts, methods, findings, *IDS bulletin*, **34** (4), pp 106–114.

Kabeer, N. (2003b) *Mainstreaming Gender Equality in Poverty Eradication and the Millennium Development Goals: A Handbook for Policymakers and Concerned Stakeholders*, Commonwealth Secretariat/International Development Research Centre, Canada.

Kabeer, N. (2004) Imagining the 'social': towards a citizen-centred social policy for the poor in poor countries, *IDS Working Paper*, **191**, Institute of Development Studies, Brighton.

Kaffu, E. and Mutesasira, L.K. (2003) *The Evolution of the Uganda Microfinance Sector: A Longitudinal Study from December 2001 to March 2003*, MicroSave, Nairobi.

Khandker, S.R. (2003) Microfinance and poverty: evidence using panel data from Bangladesh, *Policy Research Working Paper*, **2945**, World Bank, Washington DC.

Khandker, S.R. and Pitt, M. (2002) *The Impact of Group-Based Credit on Poor Households: An Analysis of Panel Data from Bangladesh*, World Bank, Washington DC.

Kline, S. (2003) Sustaining social performance: institutionalizing organizational learning and poverty outreach at PRIZMA, Bosnia-Herzegovina, *IDS Bulletin*, **34** (4), pp 34–43.

Ledgerwood, J. (1999) *Sustainable Banking with the Poor, Microfinance Handbook: An Institutional and Financial Perspective*, The International Bank for Reconstruction/The World Bank, Washington DC.

Lister, R. (1997) *Citizenship: Feminist Perspectives*, Macmillan, Basingstoke.

Littlefield, E., Morduch, J. and Hashemi, S. (2003) Is microfinance an effective strategy to reach the Millennium Development Goals?, *CGAP Focus Note*, **24**, CGAP, Washington DC.

Long, N. (1992) From paradigm lost to paradigm regained? The case for an actor-oriented sociology of development, in *Battlefields of Knowledge*, eds N Long and A Long, Routledge, London and New York.

Lont, H. (2004) The goose with the golden eggs: an unsuccessful linkage group in urban Indonesia, in *Livelihood and Microfinance, Anthropological and Sociological Perspectives on Savings and Debt*, eds H Lont and O Hospes, Eburon Academic Publishers, Delft.

Lont, H. and Hospes, O. (eds) (2004) *Livelihood and Microfinance, Anthropological and Sociological Perspectives on Savings and Debt*, Eburon Academic Publishers, Delft.

Marconi, R. and Mosley, P. (2004) The FINRURAL impact evaluation service: a cost-effectiveness analysis, *Small Enterprise Development Journal*, **15** (3), pp 28–40.

Mathie, A. (2001) *Including the Excluded: Lessons Learned from the Poverty Targeting Strategies used by Microfinance Providers*, occasional paper, The Coady International Institute, St. Francis Xavier University, Antigonish, Nova Scotia.

Mayoux, L. (2001) Tackling the downside: social capital, women's empowerment and micro-finance in Cameroon, *Development and Change*, **32**, pp 421–50.

McAllister, P. (2003) *Trust through Transparency: Applicability of Consumer Protection Self-Regulation to Microfinance*, SEEP, Washington DC.

McCord, M. (2002) *The Feedback Loop: A Process for Enhancing Responsiveness to Clients – Or, What do we do with All this Client Data?*, MicroSave, Nairobi.

McGregor, J.A., Alila, P., Copestake, J.G., Johnson, S., McCormick, D. and Njoka, J. (1999) *The Impact of Interventions in the Small and Micro-Enterprise Sector in Kenya*, Centre for Development Studies, University of Bath, Bath.

Microfinance Gateway (2003) *CGAP Poverty Assessment Tool: Assessment of Client Poverty Levels*, KWFT, Brighton, [online] http://www.microfinancegateway.org/poverty/pat/kwft.html

Ministry of Finance and Economic Planning (2001) Poverty indicators in Uganda, *Discussion Paper*, **4**, Ministry of Finance and Economic Planning, Kampala.

MiX (2002) Focus on standardization, *The Microbanking Bulletin*, **8**, [online] www.mixmarket.org

Montgomery, M.R., Gragnolati, M., Burke K.A. and Paredes, E. (2000) Measuring living standards with proxy variables, *Demography*, **37** (2), pp 155–74.

Morduch, J. (1999) The microfinance promise, *Journal of Economic Literature*, **37** (4), pp 1569–1614.

Morduch, J. (2000) The microfinance schism, *World Development*, **28** (4), pp 617–29.

Morduch, J. and Haley, B. (2002) Analysis of the effects of microfinance on poverty reduction, *NYU Wagner Working Paper*, **1014**.

Morris, S.S., Carletto, C., Hoddinott, J. and Christiaensen, L.J.M. (2000) Validity of rapid estimates of household wealth and income for health surveys in rural Africa, *Journal of Epidemiol Health*, **54**, pp 38–87.

Mosley, P. and Hulme, D. (1998) Microenterprise finance: is there a conflict between growth and poverty alleviation, *World Development*, **26** (5), pp 783–90.

Mosley, P. and Rock, J. (2004) Microfinance, labour markets and poverty in Africa: a study of six institutions, *Journal of International Development*, **16** (3), pp 429–66.

Nalela, R. (2003) *Case Study: Centenary Rural Development Bank, Paving the Way Forward for Rural Finance*, an International Conference on Best Practices, Washington DC.

Nannyonjo, J. and Nsubuga, J. (2004) Recognising the role of microfinance institutions in Uganda, *Bank of Uganda Working Paper*, **WP/04/01**, Kampala.

Noponen, H. (2003) Assessing the impact of PRADAN's microfinance and livelihoods interventions: the internal learning system, *IDS Bulletin*, **34** (4), pp 66–75.

North, D. (1990) *Institutions, Institutional Change and Economic Performance*, Cambridge University Press, Cambridge.

Otero, M. (1999) Bringing development back into microfinance, *Journal of Microfinance*, **1** (1), pp 8–19.

Otero, M. and Rhyne, E. (eds) (1994) *The New World of Microenterprise Finance*, ITDG Publications, London.

Pay, C. (2005) *Social Accounting: A Method for Assessing the Impact of Enterprise Development Activities?*, unpublished paper from Traidcraft Exchange, Gateshead.

Power, M. (1997) *The Audit Society: Rituals of Verification*, Oxford University Press, Oxford.

Prahalad, C.K. and Hammond, A. (2002) Serving the world's poor profitably, *Harvard Business Review*, **80**, pp 48–57.

Rangacharyulu, S.V. (2004) *Targeting of and Droputs Among SML Clients*, a report for Centre for Quantitative Techniques, National Institute of Rural Development, Hyderabad.

Ravallion, M.. (2001) The mystery of the vanishing benefits: an introduction to impact evaluation, *The World Bank Economic Review*, **15** (1), pp 115–40.

Rhyne, E. (1998) The yin and yang of microfinance: reaching the poor and sustainability, *MicroBanking Bulletin*, **2**, pp 6–8.

Rhyne, E. (2001) *Mainstreaming Microfinance: How Lending to the Poor Began, Grew and Came of Age in Bolivia*, Kumarian Press, Bloomfield.

Roper, K. (2003) Refining performance assessment systems to serve sustainability, poverty outreach and impact goals: the case of the Small Enterprise Foundation, South Africa, *IDS Bulletin*, **34** (4), pp 76–84.

Rutherford, S. (1999) *The Poor and Their Money*, Oxford University Press, Oxford.

Rutherford, S. (2004) The microfinance market: huge, diverse – and waiting for you, in *Livelihood and Microfinance, Anthropological and Sociological Perspectives on Savings and Debt*, eds H. Lont and O. Hospes, Eburon Academic Publishers, Delft.

Sa-Dhan (2003) *On the Road to Effective Governance of Microfinance Organizations: A Discussion Paper*, Sa-Dhan (the Association of Community Development Finance Institutions), New Delhi.

Sahn, D.E. and Stifel, D.C. (2000) Poverty comparisons over time and across countries in Africa, *World Development*, **28** (12), pp 2123–55.

Schreiner, M. (2002) Aspects of outreach: a framework for discussion of the social benefits of microfinance, *Journal of International Development*, **14** (5), pp 591–603.

Sebageni, G., Kaggwa, S. and Mutesasira, L. (2002) *Where There is No Banker: Financial Systems in Remote Rural Uganda*, MicroSave, Nairobi.

Sebstad, J. and Cohen, M. (2001) *Microfinance, Risk Management and Poverty*, AIMS project report, Management Systems International, Washington DC [online] www.mip.org

Sebstad, J., Neill, C., Barnes, C. with Chen, G. (1995) *Assessing the Impact of Microenterprise Interventions: a Framework for Analysis*, USAID, Washington DC.

SEEP (2001) *Learning from Clients: Assessment Tools for Microfinance Practitioners*, SEEP with USAID (AIMS project) and Management Systems International, Washington DC.

SEEP (2004a) Integrating poverty assessment into client assessment, *SEEP Network progress note*, **1**, [online] http://www.seepnetwork.org

SEEP (2004b) Obstacles to client assessment, *SEEP Network progress note*, **7**, a joint publication of The Client Assessment Working Group and *Imp-Act*, University of Bath, Bath.

SEEP (2005) *Building Successful Microfinance Institutions through Client Assessment*, SEEP, Washington DC.

Seibel, H.D. (2003) Centenary Rural Development Bank, Uganda: A Flagship of Rural Bank Reform in Africa, *Small Enterprise Development*, **14** (3), pp 35–46.

Sen, A. (1987) *The Standard of Living: The Tanner Lectures Clare Hall*, Cambridge University Press, Cambridge.

Sender, J. (2003) Rural poverty and gender: analytical frameworks and policy proposals, in *Rethinking Development Economics*, ed Ha-Joon Chang, Anthem Press, London.

Shaw, J. (2004) Microenterprise occupation and poverty reduction in microfinance programs: evidence from Sri Lanka, *World Development*, **32** (7), pp 1247–64.

Simanowitz, A. (2001) From event to process: current trends in microfinance impact assessment, *Small Enterprise Development*, **12** (4), pp 11–21.

Simanowitz, A. *et al* (2000) Overcoming the obstacles of identifying the poorest families: using participatory wealth ranking (PWR), the CASHPOR House Index (CHI), and other measurements to identify and encourage the participation of the poorest families, especially the women of those families, *Microcredit Summit 2000*, New York, [online] http://www.microfinancegateway.org/content/article/detail/1578/

Sinha, S. and Matin, I. (1998) Informal credit transactions of micro-credit borrowers in rural Bangladesh, *IDS Bulletin*, **29** (4), pp 66–80.

Smets, P. and Bähre, E. (2004) When coercion takes over, in *Livelihood and Microfinance, Anthropological and Sociological Perspectives on Savings and Debt*, eds H Lont and O Hospes, Eburon Academic Publishers, Delft.

Snodgrass, D.R. and Sebstad, J. (2002) *Clients in Context: The Impacts of Microfinance in Three Countries, Synthesis Report*, AIMS project report, Management Systems International, Washington DC, [online] www.mip.org

Srinivasan, G. (2002) Linking self-help groups with banks in India, *Small Enterprise Development*, **13** (4), pp 47–57.

Ssemogerere, G. (2003) Financial sector restructuring under the SAPs and economic development, with special reference to agriculture and rural development: a case study of Uganda, in *African Voices on Structural Adjustment*, eds T. Mkandawire and C.C. Soludo, Africa World Press, Trenton, New Jersey and Asmara, Eritrea.

Strathern, M. (2000) *Audit Cultures: Anthropological Studies in Accountability, Ethics and the Academy*, Routledge, London and New York.

Thorbecke, E. (2004) Conceptual and measurement issues in poverty analysis, *Wider Discussion Paper*, **04**.

Transparency International (1997) *Survey on Corruption in Bangladesh*, Transparency International Bangladesh, Dhaka.

Tulchin, D. (2003) *Microfinance's Double Bottom Line*, Social Enterprise Associates for the MicroCapital Institute, with funding from the Ford Foundation, Mexico.

Uganda Bureau of Statistics (2001) *Uganda National Household Survey 1999/00: Report on the Socio-Economic*, Uganda Bureau of Statistics, Entebbe.

Van de Ruit, C. and May, J. (2003) Triangulating qualitative and quantitative approaches to the measurement of poverty: a case study in Limpopo Province, South Africa, *IDS Bulletin*, **34** (4), pp 21–33.

Van de Ruit, C., May, J. and Roberts, B. (2001) A poverty assessment of the Small Enterprise Foundation on behalf of the Consultative Group to Assist the Poorest, *CSDS Research Report*, **39**, University of Natal, Durban.

Velez-Ibanez, C.G. (1983) *Bonds of Mutual Trust: The Cultural Systems of Rotating Credit Associations among Urban Mexicans and Chicanos*, Rutgers University Press, New Brunswick, New Jersey.

Von Pischke, J.D. (1991) *Finance at the Frontier: Debt Capacity and the Role of Credit in the Private Economy*, World Bank, Washington DC.

Von Pischke, J.D., Adams, D. and Donald, G. (eds) (1983) *Rural Financial Markets in Developing Countries: Their Use and Abuse*, John Hopkins University Press, Baltimore.

Westley, G.D. (2004) *A Tale of Four Village Banking Programs*, Sustainable Development Department, Best Practices in Latin America Series, Inter-American Development Bank, Washington DC.

Woller, G. (2002) From market failure to marketing failure: market orientation as the key to deep outreach in microfinance, *Journal of International Development*, **14**, pp 305–24.

Woller, G. (2004) The cost-effectiveness of social performance assessment – the case of PRIZMA in Bosnia-Herzegovina, *Small Enterprise Development Journal*, **15** (3), pp 41–51.

Woller, G. (2005) *Proposal for a Social Performance Measurement Framework in Microfinance: The Six Aspects of Outreach*, unpublished paper produced by the Chemonics Consortium for the USAID AMAP project, Washington DC.

Woller, G. and Schreiner, M. (2002) *Poverty, Lending, Financial Self-Sufficiency, and the Six Aspects of Outreach*, a study sponsored by the Poverty Lending Working Group of SEEP, Washington DC.

Wood, G.D. (2000) Prisoners and escapees: improving the institutional responsibility square in Bangladesh, *Public Administration*, **20**, pp 221–37.

World Bank (2000) *Corruption in Bangladesh: Costs and Cures*, World Bank, Dhaka.

Wright, G.A.N. (2000) *Microfinance Systems: Designing Quality Financial Services for the Poor*, University Press, Dhaka.

Wright, G.A.N. and Rippey, P. (2003) *The Competitive Environment in Uganda: Implications for Microfinance Institutions and their Clients*, MicroSave, Nairobi.

Wright-Revolledo, K. and Copestake, J.G. (2004) Impact assessment of microfinance using qualitative data: communicating between social scientists and practitioners using the QUIP, *Journal of International Development*, **16** (3), pp 355–67.

Zeller, M., Johannsen, J. and Alcaraz, G. (2005) *Developing and Testing Poverty Assessment Tools: Results from Accuracy Tests in Peru*, report to USAID: Accelerated Microenterprise Advancement Project, The IRIS Center, University of Maryland, [online] www.povertytools.org

Zeller, M., Lapenu, C. and Greeley, M. (2003) *Social Performance Indicators Initiative*, final report, Comite d'Echange, de Reflexion et d'Information sur les systemes d'Epargne-credit (CERISE), Paris, [online] www.cerise-microfinance.org

Imp-Act Reports

Alexeeva, E., Mosley, P. and Olejaravo, D. (2004) *Microfinance, Social Capital Formation and Political Development in Russia and Eastern Europe: A Pilot Study of Programmes in Russia, Slovakia and Romania*, unpublished *Imp-Act* report.

BRAC (1996) *Beacons of Hope*, BRAC Impact Assessment Findings, Dhaka.

CARD (2004) *The Impact Highway: CARD's Homecoming to Client-Centered Approaches*, CARD Final Report to *Imp-Act*, May 2004.

Centenary Rural Development Bank (2004) *Ford Foundation Loan Impact Assessment Programme Final Report*, Centenary Rural Development Bank, Uganda.

CMF (2003) *Impact Assessment Study of Four Savings and Credit Cooperatives in the Hill Regions of Nepal*, unpublished *Imp-Act* report.

Cohen, M. (2004) *Review of the Microfinance Centre: Adapting the Feedback Loop to the Assessment of a Network*, unpublished report for *Imp-Act*, Microfinance Opportunities, Washington DC.

Cortijo, M.J. and Kabeer, N. (2004) An assessment of SHARE's wider social impacts.

Cortijo, M.J .and Kabeer, N. (2004a) *The Wider Social Impacts of Microfinance in Andhra Pradesh: A Case Study of SHARE Microfin Ltd*, unpublished *Imp-Act* report.

Dash, A. (2004) Improving the impact of microfinance on poverty: The CYSD case study.

Dash, A. and Kabeer, N. (2004) *Livelihoods, Social Capital and Citizenship: The Challenge of Working in India's Poorest State*, unpublished *Imp-Act* report.

Dunn, E. and Tvrtkovic, J. (2003) *Microfinance Clients in Bosnia and Herzegovina: Report on Baseline Survey*, Foundation for Sustainable Development of the Federation of Bosnia and Herzegovina, unpublished *Imp-Act* report.

FINCA (2004) *Imp-Act Client Assessment Report*, unpublished *Imp-Act* report.

Garber, C. (2004) *Using Microfinance Networks to Promote Client Assessment: Case Study of ASOMIF in Nicaragua*, unpublished paper for *Imp-Act*, SEEP, Washington DC.

Garuba, S.A. (2004) *LAPO: Impact Assessment Systems – Social Performance Monitoring*, unpublished *Imp-Act* report.

Hishigsuren, G. (2004) *Impact Assessment Findings using the SEEP-AIMS Tools at the Sinapi Aba Trust, Ghana*, unpublished *Imp-Act* report.

Johnson, S. (2004) The dynamics of competition in Karatina's financial markets: assessing the impact of microfinance in Kenya, *Imp-Act Working Paper*, 9, *Imp-Act*, Brighton.

Kabeer, N. and Dash, A. (2004) A socio-economic analysis of CYSD's impacts: teaching the poor and excluded.

Kabeer, N. and Matin, I. (2005) *The Wider Social Impacts of BRAC's Group-Based Lending in Rural Bangladesh: Group Dynamics and Participation in Public Life*, unpublished *Imp-Act* report.

Kabeer, N. and Noponen, H. (2005) Social and economic impacts of PRADAN's Self-help Group Microfinance and Livelihoods Promotion Program: analysis of Jharkhand, India, *Imp-Act Working Paper*, 11, *Imp-Act*, Brighton.

Kulvarni, V. (2003) The dynamics of competition in Guntur's financial markets.

Opaku, L. (2004) Integrating holistic client transformation impact indicators with monitoring and accreditation systems.

PRADAN (2004) Final *Imp-Act* programme report.

PROMUC (2004) Final Report: Monitoring and impact assessment project for 'La Chanchita' Community Bank Programme.

Promujer (2004) Final Report: Promujer Peru Impact Assessment.

Sebageni, G. (2003) *Imp-Act Local Financial Markets Study: Uganda Supply Side Research*, unpublished *Imp-Act* report.

SHARE (2003) *Study on Local Financial Markets*, unpublished *Imp-Act* report.

Sinapi Aba Trust (2004) *Final Report, Impact Assessment Findings, Using the SEEP-AIMS Tools*, unpublished *Imp-Act* report.

Todd, H. (ed) (2001) *Paths Out of Poverty: The Impact of SHARE Microfin Ltd in Andhra Pradesh, India*, unpublished *Imp-Act* report.

Villalobos Barahona, I. (2004) *Estudos Imp-Act de Costo-Efectividad de Sistemas de Evaluación de Impacto en Microfinancieras de Hondura, CA*, unpublished *Imp-Act* report.

Vyasulu, V. (2003) *Relative Poverty Assessment of New Self-Help Group Members, Koraput District*, unpublished *Imp-Act* report.

Wright-Revolledo, K. (2003) *PROMUC: Aide Memoire*, Department of Economics and International Development, University of Bath, Bath.

Wright-Revolledo, K. (2004) *Researching Diverse Impacts of Microfinance: Findings from a Qualitative Study in Peru*, unpublished *Imp-Act* report.

Wright-Revolledo, K. (2004) Assessing the social performance of microfinance using the QUIP: findings from Huancayo, Chimbote and Cajamarca, Peru, *Imp-Act Working Paper*, 10, *Imp-Act*, Brighton.

Wright-Revolledo, K. and Benique, D. (2003) *Report on the First Implementation of QUIP with PROMUC, Peru*, unpublished *Imp-Act* report (in Spanish).

Index

More Books on Microfinance from

PUBLISHING

Practical Microfinance
A Training Manual

Malcolm Harper

- **Photocopiable training manual containing step-by-step descriptions for 22 sessions**

- **Extensively tested around the world**

This training manual is designed to meet the needs of those who train staff for banks, microfinance institutions and NGOs engaged in modern or new paradigm microfinance.

Practical Microfinance provides detailed step-by-step descriptions for 22 sessions which together offer a complete 5- to 10-day course on microfinance. The sessions may also be used individually, selected from to make up tailor-made courses, or integrated with other materials. The sessions cover a wide range of topics including: introduction to financial accounts; undertaking field visits; analysis of microfinance institutions; group and individual lending; micro-insurance and micro-savings; and measuring the impact of microfinance.

Paperback•ISBN 1-85339-563-3•192pp•£19.95•US$35.95•€28.95
Not available from ITDG Publishing in South Asia.

To order this and other leading books for development visit www.developmentbookshop.com or contact us:
☎ + 44 (0)1926 634501 or ✉ orders@itpubs.org.uk